Edited by G. Goos, J. Hartmanis and J. van Leeuwen

T0238091

pringer

rlin
idelberg
w York
rcelona
ng Kong
ndon
lan
ris
gapore
kyo

pen Hypermedia ystems and ructural Computing

nternational Workshop, OHS-6
International Workshop, SC-2
Antonio, Texas, USA, May 30 – June 3, 2000
eedings

 Springer

rhard Goos, Karlsruhe University, Germany
is Hartmanis, Cornell University, NY, USA
van Leeuwen, Utrecht University, The Netherlands

lume Editors

gfried Reich
iversität Linz, Abteilung für Informationssysteme
tenbergerstr. 69, 4040 Linz, Austria
mail: sre@ifs.uni-linz.at

nneth M. Anderson
iversity of Colorado, Boulder, Department of Computer Science
OT 717, Campus Box 430, Boulder, CO 80309-0430, USA
mail: kena@cs.colorado.edu

taloging-in-Publication Data applied for

e Deutsche Bibliothek - CIP-Einheitsaufnahme

en hypermedia systems and structural computing : 6th international
rkshop ; 2nd international workshop ; proceedings / OHS-6 ; SC-2,
n Antonio, Texas, USA; May 30 - June 3, 2000. Siegfried Reich ;
nneth M. Anderson (ed.). - Berlin ; Heidelberg ; New York ;
rcelona ; Hong Kong ; London ; Milan ; Paris ; Singapore ; Tokyo ;
ringer, 2000
Lecture notes in computer science ; Vol. 1903)
SBN 3-540-41084-8

 Subject Classification (1998): H.5.4, H.5.1, H.4, H.3, C.2, D.4

SN 0302-9743
BN 3-540-41084-8 Springer-Verlag Berlin Heidelberg New York

s work is subject to copyright. All rights are reserved, whether the whole or part of the material is
cerned, specifically the rights of translation, reprinting, re-use of illustrations, recitation, broadcasting,
roduction on microfilms or in any other way, and storage in data banks. Duplication of this publication
arts thereof is permitted only under the provisions of the German Copyright Law of September 9, 1965,
s current version, and permission for use must always be obtained from Springer-Verlag. Violations are
le for prosecution under the German Copyright Law.

inger-Verlag Berlin Heidelberg New York
ember of BertelsmannSpringer Science+Business Media GmbH
Springer-Verlag Berlin Heidelberg 2000
ated in Germany

esetting: Camera-ready by author, data conversion by PTP-Berlin, Stefan Sossna
ated on acid-free paper   SPIN: 10722646   06/3142   5 4 3 2 1 0

Preface

This volume contains the final proceedings for the Sixth Workshop on Open Hypermedia Systems (OHS6) and the Second Workshop on Structural Computing (SC2). Both workshops were held at the 11th ACM Conference on Hypertext and Hypermedia in San Antonio, Texas, USA from 30 May to 3 June 2000. These workshops are organized under the umbrella of the Open Hypermedia Systems Working Group (OHSWG, <http://www.ohswg.org/>). The OHSWG was formed at OHS2 in 1996 and its primary focus is enabling interoperability between open hypermedia systems. Each workshop addresses this goal from different perspectives (see the introductions to each workshop for more details). However, the topics presented in these proceedings are by no means limited to interoperability. Indeed, issues ranging from metadata and mobility to user-interface design are addressed.

This volume would not have been possible without the support of Springer-Verlag, Heidelberg. In particular, we would like to thank the executive editor of the LNCS series, Mr. Alfred Hofman.

July 2000

Siegfried Reich
Kenneth M. Anderson

Table of Contents

Papers from the 6th Workshop on Open Hypermedia Systems (OHS6)

Papers from the 2nd Workshop on Structural Computing (SC2)

Introduction to OHS6

Siegfried Reich

Department of Information Systems
University of Linz
Altenbergerstraße 69
4040 Linz, Austria
sre@ifs.uni-linz.ac.at

An Open Hypermedia System (OHS) is typically a middleware component which provides hypermedia functionality to applications on a user's desktop. Hence, existing tools and applications can be hypermedia-enabled using the functionality provided by an open hypermedia system.

Starting with OHS1 (held at ECHT '94 Edinburgh, Scotland [7]), a series of workshops on the overall theme of open hypermedia has been organized: OHS2 (held at Hypertext '96 Washington, D.C. [6]), OHS3 (held at Hypertext '97 in sunny Southampton, UK [3]), OHS4 (held at Hypertext '98 in Pittsburgh, PA [4]), and OHS5 (held at Hypertext '99 in Darmstadt, Germany [5]). Uffe Wiil has (co-)organized the previous OHS workshops and his excellent work has led to the overall quality and high reputation of this series in general.

The OHS community has established itself as a very active part of the hypermedia research community. In March 1996, members of the OHS community formed the Open Hypermedia Systems Working Group (OHSWG). Ever since, the OHSWG has been pursuing the difficult and rewarding task of addressing interoperability between open hypermedia systems. Proposals for reference architectures, OHS protocols, application scenarios, the distinction between different hypertext application domains, issues of OHS and Web integration, and many more contributions from both researchers and practitioners have built the repertoire of subjects that have been addressed at previous workshops (for an overview of these see <http://www.aue.auc.dk/~kock/HomePage/events.html>).

OHS6 took place on Tuesday, May 30, 2000, in San Antonio, TX, in connection with the 11th ACM Conference on Hypertext and Hypermedia. OHS6 carries on the tradition of the OHS workshops with exciting high quality research topics and talks around the subject of open hypermedia systems. Consequently, OHS6 had four sessions (see the Agenda for details) ranging from interoperability issues via the World Wide Web to metadata and mobility.

Session 1 entitled "'OHP—The Suite of Open Hypermedia Protocols" can be considered the core interoperability session. The idea of a standardized protocol for Open Hypermedia Systems—the Open Hypermedia Protocol (OHP)—has been around for several years [1,2] and the three papers of this session are grouped around that topic. *Millard et al.* ask the question what the future role of OHP should be; *Bouvin* reports on experiences using the protocol and also suggests issues to be considered for future development; and *Wiil* proposes a standardized storage interface for open hypermedia systems.

S. Reich and K.M. Anderson (Eds.): OHS/SC 2000, LNCS 1903, pp. 1–2, 2000.
© Springer-Verlag Berlin Heidelberg 2000

Sessions 2 and 3 then dealt with the World Wide Web. *Rhee et al.* discuss issues of connection management; *Feise* proposes a way-back machine for keeping a history of the Web; *Mahfouz* then examines factors that influence the user interface design of Web sites; *Neümuller* discusses the application of computer semiotics to hypertext theory and the World Wide Web.

Finally, Session 4 "Music, Metadata and Mobility" is mainly driven by the Intelligence, Agents and Multimedia research group at Southampton, UK. *Blackburn and DeRoure* discuss content based navigation in music; *Moore and Moreau* argue that typed links are a powerful means for dealing with metadata; *Thompson et al.* describe a prototype system that supports ad hoc linking scenarios.

Given the success of OHS6 which provided an excellent set of papers and discussions and raised important new issues, the 7th Workshop on Open Hypermedia Systems (OHS7) will be held at Hypertext 2001 in Århus, Denmark, August 14-18, 2001.

References

1. Hugh C. Davis, Antoine Rizk, and Andy J. Lewis. OHP: A draft proposal for a standard open hypermedia protocol. In Wiil and Demeyer [6], pages 27–53. UCI-ICS Technical Report 96-10, Department of Information and Computer Science, University of California, Irvine.
2. Siegfried Reich, Uffe K. Wiil, Peter J. Nürnberg, Hugh C. Davis, Kaj Grønbæk, Kenneth M. Anderson, David E. Millard, and Jörg M. Haake. Addressing interoperability in open hypermedia: The design of the open hypermedia protocol. *New Review of Hypermedia and Multimedia*, 5:207–248, 1999.
3. Uffe Kock Wiil, editor. *Proceedings of the 3rd Workshop on Open Hypermedia Systems, Hypertext '97, Southampton, England, April 6-11*, 1997. Scientific Report 97-01, The Danish Centre for IT Research.
4. Uffe Kock Wiil, editor. *Proceedings of the 4th Workshop on Open Hypermedia Systems, Hypertext '98, Pittsburgh, PA, June 20-24*, June 1998. Technical Report CS-98-01, Aalborg University Esbjerg.
5. Uffe Kock Wiil, editor. *Proceedings of the 5th Workshop on Open Hypermedia Systems, Hypertext '99, Darmstadt, Germany, February 21-25*, February 1999. Technical Report CS-99-01, Aalborg University Esbjerg.
6. Uffe Kock Wiil and Serge Demeyer, editors. *Proceedings of the 2nd Workshop on Open Hypermedia Systems, ACM Hypertext '96, Washington, D.C., March 16-20. Available as Report No. ICS-TR-96-10 from the Dept. of Information and Computer Science, University of California, Irvine*, March 1996. UCI-ICS Technical Report 96-10, Department of Information and Computer Science, University of California, Irvine.
7. Uffe Kock Wiil and Kaspar Østerbye, editors. *Proceedings of the ECHT '94 Workshop on Open Hypermedia Systems*, September 1994. Tech. Report R-94-2038, Dept. of Computer Science, Aalborg Univ.

Standardizing Hypertext: Where Next for OHP?

David Millard, Hugh Davis, and Luc Moreau

Intelligence, Agents, Multimedia,
University of Southampton, Dept. of Electronics and Computer Science,
Southampton, UK
dem97r@ecs.soton.ac.uk

Abstract. Over the last six years the Open Hypermedia Systems Working Group (OHSWG) has been working in a coordinated effort to produce a protocol which will allow components of an Open Hypermedia System to talk to one another in a standardised manner. In this paper we reflect on this work and the knowledge that has come out of it, evaluating the different approaches to standardisation in the light of our experiences. We discuss the problems we encountered and redefine the goals of the effort to be more realistic, presenting the Fundamental Open Hypermedia Model (FOHM) as an example of this more realistic approach. Finally we describe a possible future path that encompasses the research interests of the OHSWG while still leading ultimately to interoperability.

1 History of the OHP Effort

1.1 Original Proposal

The First Workshop on Open Hypermedia [25] was held at Edinburgh in conjunction with ECHT'94. This workshop was concerned with the growing class of hypermedia systems such as Chimera [2], DHM [9], HyperForm [24], Microcosm [5], Multicard [20] and the HB/SP series [21], which clearly separated hypertext structure (links) from the content (documents). The participants in this workshop were keen to provide hypertext link services which could provide hypertext structure for documents which were displayed using existing desktop applications such as Word for Windows and Emacs. This workshop lead to the formation of the Open Hypermedia Systems Working Group (OHSWG), the full history and rationale behind the work of this group can be viewed on their web pages [1].

An interesting finding of this first workshop was that although the major area of interest for the participating research groups was the design and implementation of link servers, most of their time was being spent on the implementation of clients; the researchers were spending significant effort producing text and graphics clients for the link services, either by writing them from scratch or writing macros to adapt existing desktop applications. A proposal from Antoine

S. Reich and K.M. Anderson (Eds.): OHS/SC 2000, LNCS 1903, pp. 3–12, 2000.
© Springer-Verlag Berlin Heidelberg 2000

Rizk was that the group could contribute by producing a lightweight message based protocol that could be used to communicate about simple link service functions. The rationale was that all link services had an approximately similar data model and that the operations that the link services could perform were also similar; all that would be required was a simple "shim" (protocol converter) that could convert between the client protocol and the server protocol, and then it would be possible for groups to share client implementations. The idea was simple and lead to the production of the first draft of the Open Hypermedia Protocol (OHP) [6] which was presented at the next workshop in 1996.

What happened next to OHP may well be a familiar story to other groups who have attempted to produce an application level protocol. The committee effect started to take hold and the protocol grew; there were discussions about whether we were going to use a message passing interface or an API; there were arguments about the on-the-wire protocol to be used, and the group became confused about aspects of resource location and naming instead of concentrating on hypertext. Furthermore, the increasing influence of the World Wide Web throughout this period tended to change original assumptions by producing a system that was open in very different ways from the OHSWG systems.

However, there were some good outcomes from this stage of the work. The scope of the project changed from attempting to provide a lightweight communication mechanism for shared clients and heterogeneous link servers, to attempting to create a reference model and implementation for open hypertext systems. A standardized data model and basic set of operations was agreed and the groups concerned produced native OHP link servers, and agreed a temporary on the wire protocol that made possible a significant demonstration at Hypertext '98, and a paper on the experiences to that stage [18].

1.2   The Hypertext 98 Demonstration

Two systems were developed for a demonstration of interoperability at Hypertext '98 (held in Pittsburgh, USA).

One from the University of Arhus, Denmark, and the other developed at the Multimedia Research Group (MMRG) at the University of Southampton.

During the development of these systems several problems became evident. Both with the protocol itself and also, more importantly, with the scope of the original draft proposal. The original draft was meant as a standard interface between clients and servers, to allow software reuse. This has increased in scope dramatically and become an all-encompassing effort to understand the nature of hypermedia and thus produce standards to provide for it. However it was soon understood that such a large goal was impossible to realise within a single protocol and as a result the protocol was split into several domains, each domain dealing with a particular type of hypermedia.

The original OHP protocol was therefore renamed OHP-Navigational (OHP-Nav) and reduced in scope to deal exclusively with navigational (node/link) hypermedia. Other domains were envisaged such as Spatial Hypermedia [12] (OHP-Space) and Taxonomic Hypermedia [22] (OHP-Tax).

The protocol itself had been originally based on the Microcosm message format [8], a sequence of tag/value pairs. However this proved difficult to parse so the OHSWG adopted XML as a suitable format [3] and the OHP-Nav message set and hypermedia objects were all defined as XML elements in a Document Type Definition (DTD).

1.3   The Hypertext 99 Demonstration

At the OHSWG's meeting at Southampton (OHS 4.5) it was decided that as the Hypertext '98 demonstration had formed such a positive focus point for the group a similar demonstration should be attempted for Hypertext '99 in Darmstadt, Germany. It was also decided that since we had demonstrated interoperability at Hypertext '98 we should now concentrate on showing some of the features of the protocol, ironically removing the need to interoperate.

Some of the more successful parts of the Hypertext '98 demonstration were the collaboration aspects. So the Danish contribution to the Hypertext '99 demonstration was an extension of this simple support into a more advanced system called 'Construct'. The Southampton contribution was to investigate a definition of computational links, where opaque computation objects are included in the hypertext model and can be referenced similarly to other objects. This resulted in a component based system known as 'Solent'.

Another system demonstrated at Hypertext '99 was CAOS [19], a spatial hypermedia collaborative system. Discussions within the working group turned to the definition of OHP-Space, starting us thinking about whether the different domains were actually that different after all.

2   What Were the Problems with OHP?

2.1   What Were We Trying to Standardize?

It has already been mentioned that the purpose of OHP has changed a great deal since the protocol first appeared. Initially a basic client-server communication protocol it has grown to reflect the concerns of a large community of researchers. Even given that we understood what functionality we were going to standardize there is still the question of what actually will become standard in the system. I.e. how will components actually talk to one another? There are two approaches:

1. *A programming API* : By using a standardised API client source code compatibility is preserved, whatever the servers involved, and server source code remains valid whatever the clients. This requires specifying:

   a) the system calls,
   b) the callbacks to be used,
   c) the data to be exchanged.

Examples would be to use CORBA and its interface definition language IDL, Microsoft DCOM or a Java component system using Java Beans.

One should note that in this approach the data representation is dependent on the binding (i.e. the IDL compiler for the chosen language and the chosen implementation of the communication module).

2. *An on-the-wire communication model* : This involves defining:

   a) the syntax of the messages (e.g. an XML hierarchy),
   b) a set of requests, associated responses and their syntax,
   c) the data and its syntax,
   d) how to setup the transport medium (e.g. opening socket on a port, etc.).

At one time or another both approaches have been argued for. However the need to produce communicating systems that actually worked resulted in the group returning to the on-the-wire approach, even though the API approach seems cleaner and allows us to concentrate on the hypertext issues rather than the networking ones. The API approach also preserves source code compatibility. The implementers just need to implement two APIs, one for the client and another for the server. If they then find that a new on-the-wire protocol should be used, they can change their implementation without altering the source code of the components involved.

However it is still not a perfect solution as it may require recompiling applications when a different medium is required. This is indeed the case with CORBA where binary applications are ORB dependent. This does not give a lot of freedom to the final user as a binary is typically compiled for a fixed communication medium.

Recently, Southampton researchers have been experimenting with implementing hypertext functionality on top of agent frameworks; in particular, the Java-based SoFAR [15], the Southampton Framework for Agent Research, was the focus of this experiment. SoFAR adopts an abstract communication model, where agents communicate using "virtual channels", identified by a startpoint and an endpoint; the latter is a client-side proxy used to initiate communications and the former is a server-side entity, extracting messages from the communication channel and passing them on to agents. Startpoints are specified by an interface, and agents communicate by activating methods of this interface. Every communication module provides its own implementation of the startpoint and endpoint interfaces, relying on a specific communication mechanism (rmi, encrypted communications, ...).

This modular organisation of the system preserves binary code compatibility of applications. Indeed, applications do not have to be recompiled when new communication modules are introduced. When an application starts a communication with a startpoint, for which the code is not loaded in memory, SoFAR and the JVM are able to load the required implementation dynamically. This property requires the language and/or the operating system to be able to load binary code dynamically. In the absence of such a facility, SoFAR would revert to a source code compatibility: it would require applications to be recompiled for every new communication module, in a similar fashion to the CORBA/IDL model.

As the on-the-wire communication model is typically adopted for Internet protocols (normally ASCII and socket based), there is a simple argument that says that since it works for the World Wide Web and the Internet it can work for OHP to! Unfortunately this approach has several disadvantages:

1. Writing efficient socket communications is a very difficult task, involving threads, polling, etc. It is very easy to produce inefficient communication systems.
2. Such libraries have to be rewritten for every application. This results in the risk of a bad implementation, where data is not properly formatted or parsed. The CORBA approach with a stub compiler avoids this problem by generating code automatically.
3. It becomes extremely difficult to deal with non-protocol data and requests, such as routing information for mobile agents, garbage collection or session management.

The DLS approach [4] is an instance of the on-the-wire protocol standardisation, except that the DLS does not specify but reuses off-the-shelve protocols or communications medium, such as sockets, http, XML, LDAP, SoFAR or tuple space.

Both approaches to interoperability have their advantages and disadvantages. On the wire protocol has the "taste" of the Internet community and a simplicity that is very appealing, while the programming API allows further techniques to be transparently added (mobility, etc.). In both cases, a data model has to be adopted. The data model specifies the type of data and its associated meaning (in terms of protocol primitives) exchanged during communications. The data model does not specify the syntax of data (this depends on the approach: ontologies in SoFar, or XML over sockets).

Remark 1. The data model does not force components to adopt such a representation internally: it simply requires them to *exchange* such data. Once defined the data primitives can serve as a guide to specify requests.

Without precluding any approach, API or on-the-wire, is the need to specify a powerful data model that supports all of the hypertext features that need to be standardised.

2.2 A Communications Infrastructure

Even given a data model and some communication medium, there remains the need for some type of infrastructure over which that model can be discussed by a variety of components. This infrastructure is different from the network and itself may run independently over different lower network protocols (sockets, rmi, etc.). In effect it is a framework in which components can discover each other and exchange data.

In OHP this is represented by the message headers and bodies (although not the requests themselves). Using this basic framework, OHP allows a component to send multiple requests in a single message and track messages around the system. It was also reasoned that in any complex system total semantic understanding by all components was unobtainable. To avoid the problems this would cause it was at one time argued that performatives [7] [11] should be added to the OHP header. Performatives describe the overall intention of message in concise clear terms that all components of the system can understand (e.g. this is an information message or this is a request). In this way if the component does not understand the content of the message it can still reason about the intention and make decisions about the message as a result (even if that is just to forward the message somewhere else).

In an effort to keep the OHP definitions as simple as possible performatives were never formally added. However we have never lost the belief that they are useful. In fact we now believe that disagreements within the group regarding performatives were a symptom of a much larger and fundamental problem. In the OHP specification no clean separation was made between the communication infrastructure and the definition of the hypermedia model and its operations. As a result we failed to notice that many of the problems we faced were not ours to solve in the first place!

2.3   Is OHP too Large in Scope?

One of the noticeable things about the whole OHP effort is the way that the scope of the original proposal has increased out of all proportion compared to its original intent. The OHP has grown from a simple protocol that would allow standardized clients to talk to any OHS into a mammoth undertaking that involves all of the components of a system and which includes multiple domains of hypertext and many levels of functionality (e.g. computations and collaboration). Much effort has since been directed into breaking this huge problem domain into manageable chunks, creating OHP-Nav, OHP-Space, OHP-Tax and a whole host of associated protocols. The problems we have faced would seem to indicate that the scope of the protocol should be dramatically reduced.

2.4   Is OHP too Small in Scope?

Considering the size of the task now before us this may seem like a ridiculous question. However the goals of the protocol have been moving since its inception and perhaps it is time we re-examined exactly what they are. When OHP was conceived the OHS architecture considered was a client/server one, ideal for intra-LAN systems. As technology has moved on, and we move into an age of distributed information and intelligent agents, it is possible that by increasing that scope we actually 'offload' some of the bigger difficulties to the places where they belong. It is not the job of the OHSWG to create distributed computing environments, any more than it is to create a language for exchanging knowledge.

In other words, by accepting that the scope of OHP is actually the massively distributed management and navigation of knowledge we no longer have to deal with any of the communication infrastructure issues mentioned above. Instead we have to build OHP on top of existing networks and prototype frameworks that support the dynamic exchange of knowledge between distributed components.

In effect OHP would become a semantic language that could be implemented via a variety of syntactical languages over existing communication infrastructures.

3 Where Does FOHM Fit in?

The Fundamental Open Hypermedia Model (FOHM) [13] is an abstract data model that supports arbitrary associational information and can be used to represent Spatial, Navigational and potentially Taxonomic structure. The relationship between these domains is defined formally and interoperability is achieved by mapping from one domain to FOHM and then back to a different domain.

3.1 Where Does FOHM Come from?

One of the components in the Solent system used for the second demonstration at Hypertext '99 was one that allowed the storage of arbitrary XML [16]. This component was very versatile and totally reusable as it understands nothing of the data structures it stored, only the structure of the XML itself, effectively an element tree. The problem with this approach was that the storage component was extremely slow as a result, taking a much longer time to retrieve a structure via pattern matching than a database would with structures it really understood (and had presumably indexed).

As a result of this experience, when we noticed that there was a great deal of overlap between the various domains of hypertext we decided to find the highest level of structure that worked across them all. Each domain could then be represented in that structure and cross-domain interoperability would be achieved.

3.2 What Is FOHM in Relation to OHP?

FOHM is an attempt to concentrate firmly on hypertext data structures and is based on the OHP-Nav data model, although it inherits none of the OHP protocol definition itself (headers, application requests, etc.). It is at this data model level that we believe the efforts of the OHSWG should be focused in the future.

Although we do not suggest that FOHM replaces the OHP model we do think that OHP could benefit from the lessons that FOHM teaches. That a powerful generic structure that models all the major domains is not only possible, but it results in a versatile hypertext environment that is greater than any single domain.

4   Where Next for OHP?

Before we can move forward with OHP we have to acknowledge the success we have already had with the protocol. It has managed to get a wide group of researchers to discuss the technology of hypertext on a common level and forms a basis for discussion only rivaled by the Dexter model [10]. We now have a well defined model for Navigational hypertext and are beginning to understand how this relates to other domains, such as Spatial and Taxonomic Hypertext. We also have a much greater understanding of the way our different systems are built and crucially can begin to understand the infrastructure that we require before true interoperability is possible.

As a result of these efforts the OHSWG is now in the position to finalise the existing OHP draft. This would provide a milestone by which other efforts could be judged, but we believe that it would still be a mistake. One which risks knocking OHP into obsolescence. Instead the question is how can we begin to incrementally move the effort forward again using the data model as a base?

In this paper we have argued that the most successful part of OHP has been the definition of an abstract data model and have explained how FOHM extends this model formally, providing a core data model and set of operations. Although this core can already be implemented by binding it to an appropriate infrastructure, it still needs to be extended to include the notion of perspective from Taxonomic hypertext as well as investigating other concerns, such as the interaction of the model with existing multi-user and security systems

It would be useful to produce several example bindings for different infrastructures. At a basic level the core data model makes this a trivial task, but that doesn't mean that all implementations are trivial! There is still room for interesting work on the distribution and architecture of implementations and the consequences that they might have for the model. Also there are other implementation concerns that remain beyond the scope of the model, for example the problems associated with naming [17].

Finally it is entirely appropriate to build other structures based on the core to deal with other hypertext issues, such as the provision for collaboration [23] and computation [14] within the system.

We may be building hypermedia systems but the navigation of hyperspace is much more then point and click, it involves a true understanding of how information spaces work, how they can be represented in different ways and how individual hyperwebs can be manipulated in a global information network. Above all else the goal of the OHP effort should be to increase that understanding.

References

1. Open Hypermedia Systems Working Group (OHSWG) home page. http://www.ohswg.org/.

2. Kenneth M. Anderson, Richard N. Taylor, and E. James Whitehead. Chimera: Hypertext for heterogeneous software environments. In *ECHT '94. Proceedings of the ACM European conference on Hypermedia technology, Sept. 18-23, 1994, Edinburgh, Scotland, UK*, pages 94–197, 1994.

3. Tim Bray, Jean Paoli, and C. M. Sperberg-McQueen. Extensible markup language (XML) 1.0. Technical report, World Wide Web Consortium (W3C) Recommendation 10-February-1998, February 1998.

4. Leslie A. Carr, David C. DeRoure, Wendy Hall, and Gary J. Hill. The distributed link service: A tool for publishers, authors and readers. *World Wide Web Journal*, 1(1):647–656, 1995.

5. Hugh C. Davis, Simon Knight, and Wendy Hall. Light hypermedia link services: A study of third party application integration. In *ECHT '94. Proceedings of the ACM European conference on Hypermedia technology, Sept. 18-23, 1994, Edinburgh, Scotland, UK*, pages 41–50, 1994.

6. Hugh C. Davis, Antoine Rizk, and Andy J. Lewis. OHP: A draft proposal for a standard open hypermedia protocol. In Uffe Kock Wiil and Serge Demeyer, editors, *Proceedings of the 2nd Workshop on Open Hypermedia Systems, ACM Hypertext '96, Washington, D.C., March 16-20. Available as Report No. ICS-TR-96-10 from the Dept. of Information and Computer Science, University of California, Irvine*, pages 27–53, March 1996. UCI-ICS Technical Report 96-10, Department of Information and Computer Science, University of California, Irvine.

7. FIPA. Fipa 97 specification, part 2: Agent communication language. Technical report, Foundation for Intelligent Physical Agents, Geneva, Switzerland, November 1997.

8. A.M. Fountain, Wendy Hall, Ian Heath, and Hugh C. Davis. Microcosm: An open model for hypermedia with dynamic linking" - hypertext: Concepts, systems and applications. In *European Conference on Hypertext (ECHT'90), INRIA, Versailles, France*, pages 298–311, November 1990.

9. Kaj Grønbæk and Randall H. Trigg. Design issues for a Dexter-based hypermedia system. *Communications of the ACM*, 37(3):40–49, February 1994.

10. Frank Halasz and Mayer Schwartz. The dexter hypertext reference model. *Communications of the ACM*, 37(2):30–39, 1994.

11. Yannis Labrou and Tim Finin. A proposal for a new KQML specification. Technical Report TR CS-97-03, Computer Science and Electrical Engineering Department, University of Maryland Baltimore County, Baltimore, MD 21250, February 1997.

12. Catherine C. Marshall and Frank M. Shipman. Spatial hypertext: Designing for change. *Communications of the ACM*, 38:88–97, 1995.

13. David E. Millard, Luc Moreau, Hugh C. Davis, and Siegfried Reich. FOHM: A fundamental open hypertext model for investigating interoperability between hypertext domains. In *Proceedings of the '00 ACM Conference on Hypertext, May 30 - June 3, San Antonio, TX*, pages 93–102, 2000.

14. David E. Millard, Siegfried Reich, and Hugh C. Davis. Dynamic service discovery and invocation in OHP. In Uffe Kock Wiil, editor, *Proceedings of the 5th Workshop on Open Hypermedia Systems, ACM Hypertext '99 Conference, Darmstadt, Germany, February 21-25. Available as Report No. CS-99-01 from the Dept. of Computer Science, 6700 Aalborg University Esbjerg, Denmark*, pages 38–42, 1999.

15. Luc Moreau, Nick Gibbins, David DeRoure, Samhaa El-Beltagy, Wendy Hall, Gareth Hughes, Dan Joyce, Sanghee Kim, Danius Michaelides, Dave Millard, Sigi Reich, Robert Tansley, and Mark Weal. SoFAR with DIM agents. An agent framework for distributed information management. In *PAAM 2000. The Fifth International Conference and Exhibition on The Practical Application of Intelligent Agents and Multi-Agents. April 10 - 12, 2000, Manchester, UK*, pages 369–388, April 2000.

16. Siegfried Reich, Jon P. Griffiths, David E. Millard, and Hugh C. Davis. Solent — a platform for distributed open hypermedia applications. In Trevor Bench-Capon, Giovanni Soda, and A Min Tjoa, editors, *Database and Expert Systems Applications. 10th Intl. Conference, DEXA 99, Florence, Italy*, volume 1677 of *LNCS*, pages 802–811, Berlin/Heidelberg/New York, August 1999. Springer.

17. Siegfried Reich, David E. Millard, and Hugh C. Davis. Naming in OHP. In Uffe Kock Wiil, editor, *Proceedings of the 5th Workshop on Open Hypermedia Systems, ACM Hypertext '99 Conference, Darmstadt, Germany, February 21-25. Available as Report No. CS-99-01 from the Dept. of Computer Science, 6700 Aalborg University Esbjerg, Denmark*, pages 43–47, 1999.

18. Siegfried Reich, Uffe K. Wiil, Peter J. Nürnberg, Hugh C. Davis, Kaj Grønbæk, Kenneth M. Anderson, David E. Millard, and Jörg M. Haake. Addressing interoperability in open hypermedia: The design of the open hypermedia protocol. *New Review of Hypermedia and Multimedia*, 5:207–248, 1999.

19. Olav Reinert, Dirk Bucka-Lassen, Claus A. Pedersen, and Peter J. Nürnberg. CAOS: A collaborative and open spatial structure service component with incremental spatial parsing. In *Proceedings of the '99 ACM Conference on Hypertext, February 21-25, 1999, Darmstadt, Germany*, pages 49–50, February 1999.

20. Antoine Rizk and Louis Sauter. Multicard: An open hypermedia system. In *ECHT '92. Proceedings of the ACM conference on Hypertext, November 30-December 4, 1992, Milan, Italy*, pages 4–10, 1992.

21. John L. Schnase, John L. Leggett, David L. Hicks, Peter J. Nürnberg, and J. Alfredo Sánchez. Open architectures for integrated, hypermedia-based information systems. In *HICSS 94 — 37th Annual Hawaii International Conference on System Science.*, 1994.

22. H. van Dyke Parunak. Don't link me in: Set-based hypermedia for taxonomic reasoning. In *Proceedings of the '91 ACM Conference on Hypertext, Dec. 15-18, 1991, San Antonio, TX*, pages 233–242, 1991.

23. Weigang Wang and Jörg M. Haake. Implementation issues on ohs-based workflow services. In *Proceedings of the 5th Workshop on Open Hypermedia Systems, ACM Hypertext '99 Conference, Darmstadt, Germany, February 21-25. Available as Report No. CS-99-01 from the Dept. of Computer Science, 6700 Aalborg University Esbjerg, Denmark*, pages 52–56, 1999.

24. Uffe Kock Wiil and John J. Leggett. HyperForm: using extensibility to develop dynamic, open and distributed hypertext systems. In *ECHT' '92. Proceedings of the ACM conference on Hypertext, November 30-December 4, 1992, Milan, Italy*, pages 251–261, 1992.

25. Uffe Kock Wiil and Kaspar Østerbye, editors. *Proceedings of the ECHT '94 Workshop on Open Hypermedia Systems*, September 1994. Tech. Report R-94-2038, Dept. of Computer Science, Aalborg Univ.

Experiences with OHP and Issues for the Future

Niels Olof Bouvin

Department of Computer Science, University of Aarhus,
Aabogade 34, 8200 Århus N, Denmark
`n.o. ouvin@daimi.aau.dk`

Abstract. The OHSWG has by now moved from specifications to running code. This is an important step, not only because this is the only way of maturing the specifications, but also because it strengthens the credibility of the OHSWG. Showing that the ideas expressed by the OHSWG can be implemented is however not enough, at least not if we desire a wider audience than ourselves. Concomitantly the XLink standard has begun to take shape, metadata on the Web seems to be on the rise, and interconnectedness is sharply rising with various small devices (such as WAP phones and PDAs) gaining access to the Internet. We are living in interesting times. Based on the experiences of developing the Arakne Environment, the author attempts to point out some worthwhile directions for future work within the OHSWG.

1 Introduction

The original goal of the Open Hypermedia Systems Working Group was to identify what constituted open hypermedia and to devise a common standard, so that open hypermedia systems could interoperate, and possibly share access to integrated third-party applications. Some of these goals have now been met. There is a common standard, and the Group has now several times at Hypertext conferences demonstrated heterogeneous hypermedia systems working together through the Open Hypermedia Protocol (OHP).

Existence has thus been established, and yet we do not find the world breaking our door down in order to get hold of this amazing technology. The author has over the last few years designed and developed an open component-based hypermedia system, the Arakne Environment, which is now based on the OHSWG compliant Construct servers. The experiences with converting to OHP are related in this position paper with some pointers for future concern are raised, especially with regards to future standardization work.

2 The Arakne Environment

The Arakne Environment has been described in ([2], [4], [3]), and for the purposes of this paper there is no need to go into great detail. Arakne is a framework for open hypermedia programs, and currently supports navigational, temporal, guided tour, and spatial hypermedia on the Web. The system has gone through

S. Reich and K.M. Anderson (Eds.): OHS/SC 2000, LNCS 1903, pp. 13–22, 2000.
© Springer-Verlag Berlin Heidelberg 2000

several iterations and now uses the OHSWG compliant Construct servers as structure servers. The original design idea was to create a system where functionality could be easily added without affecting the rest of the system — a hypermedia plug and play system. Over the design and development iterations this ideal has come closer.

3   Experiences with the Development of the Arakne Environment

This section will describe the process of converting the Arakne Environment to a native OHP application. As Arakne started out as a Ph.D. project there was never existing legacy applications, allowing for radical redesigns (such as replacing the hypermedia protocol used in the original version with OHP).

3.1   The Transition to OHP

The Arakne Environment did not start out using OHP. The original version relied on the Devise Hypermedia servers, but as the Construct servers were completed within the same project as Arakne, the transition to OHP began. One advantage in the context of this conversion was the code sharing between server and client, as both are written in Java. As OHP is language independent, the transition would under all circumstances have been possible albeit admittedly more time consuming. The open source nature of Construct does not limit the advantage of code reuse to the developers associated with Construct.

The first version of Arakne to utilize OHP was version 2.0. This was not a complete transition, as only the components that communicated with the structure servers were changed — the rest were (virtually) unchanged. This was a relatively simple operation as the original data model was based on DHM [12] (and thus Dexter [13]), and the gap to the OHSWG data model was relatively minor. The components communicating with the Construct servers would then transparently convert between the Arakne and the OHSWG data models, e.g. folding OHSWG anchors and endpoints into Arakne endpoints and vice versa. This 'hack' allowed us to get up to speed relatively rapidly, so that we could commence testing of the structure servers forthwith.

Given the nature of hypermedia conversion [15], this first step did not use the full functionality of the Construct servers. The features not supported by the hypermedia applications (known as 'NavLets' or 'views') could naturally not be utilized on the structure servers. The most important missing feature was the support for sessions, which is a key component in the OHSWG support for collaborative work.

This, and extensibility concerns, led to a complete redesign of the Arakne architecture and a full adoption of the OHSWG data model, resulting in the current version 2.1. This was a considerably more involved task as all existing components in the framework were either modified or completely rewritten and new components handling sessions and collaboration had to be added.

The current architecture allows users to be engaged in an arbitrary number of sessions using any number of hypermedia views. Each session has its own data model, coupling mode, and views, independently of other sessions. This has been accomplished without major changes in the views, while still allowing them room to extend support for collaboration between users as the view developers see fit.

The author would like to see more hypermedia systems support OHP, and there are some lessons that can be learned from the experience of converting Arakne to OHP.

The first lesson is that the system actually works! OHP can be used for more than once a year Hypertext Conference demonstrations. Arakne along with the Construct servers are thus among the growing number of validations of the basic design of the OHP. One of the original goals of OHP was to allow dissimilar hypermedia systems to interoperate and to share third party application integrations. In this context the Arakne Environment is probably special, as it does no longer have a hypermedia protocol of its own — it has fully embraced OHP.

The second lesson is it is not necessary to natively[1] support OHP. Using an extra component to convert from one data model to another is close in principle to the shim of [6], though the conversion is from a protocol to an API rather than from protocol to protocol. It should be noted that the task of converting Arakne to OHP was considerably smaller than e.g. establishing interoperability between Chimera and HyperDisco [19], where the target was true interoperability (we just wished to move Arakne from DHM to OHP), and where there were significant dissimilarities between the systems, including features, programming language, and protocol format. DHM and OHP are fairly close — both utilize XML (or at least tagged ASCII) for transport, the data model are similar, and the transition to OHP was made easier by the existence of available Construct Java libraries. The method used to integrate Chimera and OHP (under development as this is written) is in principle similar to the one used by the version 2.0 Arakne. Existing Construct libraries are plugged into Chimera with additional code to handle the conversion back and forth. This is a more ambitious and exciting integration, as Chimera (as opposed to Arakne 2.0) natively supports sessions.

3.2   Adding New Functionality — "Embrace and Extend"

One of the original design goals of the Arakne framework was to provide a general framework for all Web augmentation hypermedia tools. In practice the first version integrated Navette (a navigational hypermedia tool and a successor to DHM/WWW [9]) and Ariadne [14] (a guided tour tool not originally developed for Arakne). The latest hypermedia tool to be integrated with Arakne is CAOS [17] (a spatial hypermedia tool), which also originally was not developed for Arakne. By having an open architecture, Arakne has thus been able to "embrace and extend" already existing hypermedia tools. As support for collaborative work is now an integrated part of Arakne, this functionality is made available for the new views.

---

[1] i.e. abandon the existing data model etc. in lieu of OHP

3.3   New Protocols

New structural domains (such as spatial hypermedia [16]) are emerging and are swiftly becoming one of the most dynamic and interesting areas in hypermedia (as witnessed by popularity of the Structural Computing workshops). Hypermedia is no longer "just" navigational links and anchors.

OHP handles navigation and collaboration through sessions. The Construct servers have been extended to provide additional services through the OHP-Comp (composites) and OHP-Space (spatial hypermedia). New services can be added to the Construct servers and Arakne, as they become available. Indeed, with the development of the Esbjerg CSC tools [18], adding new services has become even easier.

The new structural domains are areas where the OHSWG can contribute tremendously to the hypermedia community at large by providing solid protocols and structure servers. We have the knowhow and the robust servers, and should be able to help other workers in the hypermedia community. The active discussions following the presentation of CSC by Wiil and Nürnberg at HT2000 were witness to that this is an idea whose time has come.

3.4   The Evolution of OHP

It should be noted that the OHP of the Construct servers does not fully follow the Darmstadt DTD. This is not so much of a problem as it might first seem, for standards must necessarily be validated through implementation. Some changes and clarifications became necessary and were subsequently implemented. It should however be clear that the changes made to OHP must be documented and published, in order to support further discussion and development of the OHP. The issue of proper protocol documentation will be dealt with in section 4.

4   The Need for Further Standardization

A basic requirement of any standard is a precise and unambiguous definition. Unfortunately, the current OHSWG OHP specification is lacking in this respect. This leads to problems with interoperability between different implementations, exactly what OHSWG was supposed to solve! This section will describe the problem and propose possible solutions.

4.1   The Problem with XML

One result of the OHSWG 4.5 meeting was creation of the On the Wire group, who was given the task to determine what transport layer the Open Hypermedia Protocol should utilize. The author was a member of this group, and the eventual recommendation was to use XML documents over sockets as the basic entry point, with CORBA support left for more advanced servers.

The rationale behind choosing XML was fairly solid: XML is easy to parse with free XML parsers available for most programming languages; it is human readable which eases debugging considerably; and using validating XML parser guarantees adherence to a given grammar. All this combines to make the entry into OHP relative easy and painless. Furthermore one should not be blind to necessity of being "buzzword-compliant" in this wired world, and XML certainly fulfills that purpose.

One problem that has emerged over time with XML is the level of detail expressible with the DTD grammar. DTD is well suited for general syntactic declarations, but cannot express semantics nor more fine-grained syntactic aspects such as data types or ranges. This is witnessed by the proliferation of #CDATA (i.e. unspecified character data) in most DTDs. Thus the specification is not enough by itself. It must be accompanied by either exhaustive documentation or code implementing the standard, if not the implementation will be left to guesswork by the developer. Data and code are closely integrated in this setting, and this has several disadvantages. XML was originally set out (though admittedly like much Internet technology, it was over hyped at the time of its introduction) to ease data interchange by creating solid specifications to separate code and data. The reality is that while this goal has been partly accomplished, the devil (as always) is in the details and this is where XML is still lacking.

The lack of detailed specification has also hurt OHP. The Darmstadt DTD that forms the (excellent) basis for OHP contains many instances of #CDATA where the details are left to the implementation. While this is just a set of decisions to be made when dealing with one implementation of OHP (such as Construct), it becomes a problem when interoperability — one of the purposes of OHSWG — is the goal. As mentioned in section 3.4, the development of Construct led to a number of choices with regards to what OHP is. Another implementor of OHP can however not be relied on making the same choices — the hectic work leading up to last year's OHSWG demonstration showed the problems with this approach, as there were several areas where the different implementations had to be modified to accommodate the differences. One solution to this is to adopt an existing implementation; this is the case of the current OHP/Chimera integration (mentioned in section 3.1), but this requires a certain compatibility between the systems with regards to e.g. programming languages.

It was suggested by Peter J. Nürnberg at OHSWG 5.5 that the time has come for OHSWG to adopt a reference OHP implementation. The author agrees with this notion, but would like to see it extended. One of the requirements of a proposed standard submitted to the W3C is that there should be a clear specification and at least two independent and compatible implementations of the specification. This is a very important point, as it lessens the probability of idiosyncrasies in one implementation determining the specification and for tacit, unspecified details to make it into the final standard. If we are to move forward to make OHP a "proper" standard (at standard bodies such as IETF or W3C), as discussed in 5, we *must* address this issue. As long as we maintain compatibility OHSWG can only benefit from such a move. One benefit would be that is unlikely that "one size fits all" when it comes to server implementations, e.g. a structure server using a file-based storage suited for a small work group or an individual user, would not be applicable in the context of a large organization with more demanding performance and stringent backup requirements.

This still leaves the issue of clear and detailed specification. In the author's opinion XML continue to have much going for it — all the original advantages are still valid. OHSWG are however not the only party that has discovered that DTDs are insufficient for detailed specification. Currently several standards are under development to extend XML with a precise specification language. XML Schema [8] is an ambitious W3C standard currently in Draft state. XML Schema will allow the precise specification of data types and attributes as well as the definition of new data types. As such, it can form an excellent specification language for future versions of OHP.

It would better still, if we for future work could leave the highly detailed world of XML behind, and work with higher level specifications. The Esbjerg CSC tools [18] promises to be such a tool. Using IDL as a specification language, allows developers to work with a more natural level of detail, while developing new services or implementing existing ones. As CSC will have the ability to export DTDs (and conceivably this could be extended to XML Schemas), the low cost entry point of XML is maintained if a developer should desire to use XML on the wire. Furthermore by distinguishing between specification (IDL) and actual protocol, it is possible to support new protocols, such as CORBA, by implementing the changes in the CSC tools.

A modest proposal for future standards submitted to the OHSWG would be to accompany all specifications with open source code, so that other members rapidly could use the new standards, if they should so desire. Indeed, the open source nature of Construct, CSC, and to come, Arakne, are steps in such a direction.

4.2   The Existing Data Model

The OHP data model has been designed to be extensible. Through the use of key/value attributes, it is possible to customize the existing data types to most applications. Again this is something that works well within one implementation of OHP, but makes it difficult to export e.g. the LocSpecs of one OHP implementation to another, as the exact content of the LocSpec is left to the individual implementation. The OHSWG spans a wide field of hypermedia usage and media types and it is probably not realistic to expect a complete standardization on the content of e.g. LocSpecs. However, establishing shared standards for LocSpecs in common media types such as Web pages, XML documents, and bitmap images would facilitate one of the original goals of the OHSWG, namely the sharing of third-party application integrations. In this area we should also not hesitate to adopt standards such as XPointer [5] as we see fit.

4.3   An OHP Interchange Format

The author suspects that most of the hypermedia systems created by the members of OHSWG have an interchange format in one form or another — it is certainly the case for Webvise [11], Arakne, and Chimera [1]. There has previously been a call for an OHP interchange format [10], and at Aarhus we have developed and used an interchange format based on OHP (essential following Darmstadt minus the operations). This format has since been extended and is documented as the Open Hypermedia Interchange Format (OHIF) in [11]. A shared OHP interchange format would benefit us with regards to interchange, but it would also make an essential part of a future IETF/W3C OHP standard.

Interchange formats have also other uses. As a part of Coconut project of which the author is a member, a guided tour tool (Ariadne, which also is a part of Arakne) were changed into an applet and deployed on a Danish high-profile Internet portal http://www.opasia.dk/. The purpose was to give ordinary Web surfers access to guided tours authored by the editorial staff at the portal. One of the major concerns when designing this applet was scalability and a solution based on a structure server was ruled out partly because of scale, partly because of firewall concerns, and partly because of the Java applet sand box limitations. The generated guided tours were instead exported into a XML interchange format, which then could be easily downloaded from the portal. The system received wide use (at least 15.000 users had by January 2000 downloaded and used the applet). This is an illustration of a case where the interchange format is actually the main target and not some intermediary file.

5   The Way to Proper Standardization

It will avail us naught that we create an excellent open hypermedia standard if no one notices or uses it. At least not if we desire more than publication opportunities. Furthermore a standard based "only" on the collaboration of a bunch of academics is not likely to gather much steam in the IT industry.

As suggested by E. James Whitehead Jr. at the OHSWG 5.5 meeting the time has indeed come for us to disseminate OHP outside OHSWG by creating a "proper" standard.

That there is room for open hypermedia standard is supported by the emergence of XLink [7] — a standard for (largely) navigational hypermedia in (mainly) XML documents. The XLink community has in the context of XML been working with many problems familiar to the OHSWG. At this point the members of the OHSWG have an established infrastructure, we support more than navigational hypermedia, we have integrated numerous third-party applications, we have the know-how to integrate more, and we are not limited to the Web. If we can make our varied and sophisticated hypermedia applications interoperate through OHP, and provide others with the technology to do the same, we will have a strong demonstration of what OHP is capable of.

The first step to a proper standard will however be to establish something that we can present to the world, possibly using the tools described in section 4. Given that, it should be relatively painless to create a RFC. Such a standard should consist of at least an interchange format (see section 4.3), as well a specification of the operations that can performed on the hypermedia structures.

In other words, an extended version of Darmstadt. We are already close to this target, and it would be a pity not to go further. The worst-case scenario would be that our proposed standard is ignored by the rest of the world, but then at least we will ourselves have benefited from the clarification of pinning down the standard.

Beyond RFC, we must consider which standard body our standard belongs to — obvious choices are IETF or W3C, but the discussion of that should be deferred to the time we have created an actual RFC.

6   Conclusion

One of the purposes of this position paper has been to document the feasibility of adopting OHP, and the advantages that it gives. In order to stop OHP from becoming just yet another hypermedia protocol, it is important that the momentum is kept and that other hypermedia systems either convert or interface to the OHP. In that process we must further specify and standardize OHP. This will benefit us double: it will allow systems and users to interoperate and interact (and thus realizing the original goal of sharing third-party application integrations), and it is a showcase for the validity of the work of the Open Hypermedia Working Group. We must practice what we preach, if we are to be taken seriously.

7   Post Scriptum

As a result of OHSWG 6.0, the author has committed to lead in the creation of an OHP RFC. The creation and discussion of this important document can be expected to form a major part of the the OHSWG 6.5 meeting. As of this writing the contents of the RFC can be expected to contain at least the following:

- The navigational data model (preferably also composite and spatial)
- OHP-Nav (ditto OHP-Comp and OHP-Space)
- Session data model
- OHP-Session
- A mapping to protocols (XML, CORBA) based on the Esbjerg CSC work [18]
- An interchange format (presumably an extension and generalization of OHIF [11].

Acknowledgments. The author is a member of the Coconut project (http://www.cit.dk/coconut/), a joint research project consisting of Department of Computer Science, Aarhus University and Tele-Danmark Internet. The Danish National Center for IT-Research (http://www.cit.dk/) supports the Coconut project. The author wishes to thank René Thomsen, Michael Bang Nielsen, and Henning Jehøj Madsen for their work on Arakne, and Kenneth M. Anderson for valuable discussions.

References

1. K. M. Anderson. Integrating open hypermedia systems with the World Wide Web. In M. Bernstein, L. Carr, and K. Østerbye, editors, *Proc. of the 8th ACM Hypertext Conference*, pages 157–166, Southampton, UK, Apr. 1997.

2. N. O. Bouvin. Unifying strategies for Web augmentation. In *Proc. of the 10th ACM Hypertext Conference*, pages 91–100, Darmstadt, Germany, Feb. 1999.

3. N. O. Bouvin. Designing user interfaces for collaborative Web-based open hypermedia. In *Proc. of the 11th ACM Hypertext Conference*, San Antonio, USA, May 2000.

4. N. O. Bouvin and R. Schade. Integrating temporal media and open hypermedia on the World Wide Web. In *Proc. of the 8th International World Wide Web Conference*, pages 375–387, Toronto, Canada, May 1999. W3C.

5. R. Daniel, S. DeRose, and E. Maler. XML Pointer Language (XPointer). Technical Report W3C Working Draft 6 December 1999, W3C, Dec. 1999. http://www.w3.org/TR/xptr.

6. H. Davis, A. Lewis, and A. Rizk. OHP: A draft proposal for a standard open hypermedia protocol. In *Proc. of the 2nd Workshop on Open Hypermedia Systems*, number 96-10 in UCI-ICS Technical Report, pages 27–53, University of California, Irvine, USA, 1996.

7. S. DeRose, E. Maler, D. Orchard, and B. Trafford (editors). XML Linking Language (XLink). Technical Report W3C Working Draft 21-February-2000, W3C, Feb. 2000. http://www.w3.org/TR/xlink/.

8. D. C. Fallside (editor). XML Schema part 0: Primer. W3c working draft, W3C, Feb. 2000. http://www.w3.org/TR/xmlschema-0/.

9. K. Grønbæk, N. O. Bouvin, and L. Sloth. Designing Dexter-based hypermedia services for the World Wide Web. In M. Bernstein, L. Carr, and K. Østerbye, editors, *Proc. of the 8th ACM Hypertext Conference*, pages 146–156, Southampton, UK, Apr. 1997.

10. K. Grønbæk and L. Sloth. Supporting interchange of open hypermedia structures and contents. In U. K. Wiil, editor, *Proc. of the 5th Workshop on Open Hypermedia Systems*, number CS-99-01 in Technical Report, pages 34–37. Aalborg University Esbjerg, Denmark, Feb. 1999.

11. K. Grønbæk, L. Sloth, and N. O. Bouvin. Open hypermedia as user controlled meta data for the Web. In *Proceeding of the 9th World Wide Web Conference*, Amsterdam, Holland, May 2000. W3C.

12. K. Grønbæk and R. H. Trigg. Toward a Dexter-based model for open hypermedia: Unifying embedded references and link objects. In *Proc. of the 7th ACM Hypertext Conference*, pages 149–160, Washington DC, USA, 1996.

13. F. G. Halasz and M. Schwartz. The Dexter hypertext reference model. *Communications of the ACM*, 37(2):30–39, Feb. 1994.

14. J. Jühne, A. T. Jensen, and K. Grønbæk. Ariadne: A Java-based guided tour system for the World Wide Web. In *Proc. of the 7th International World Wide Web Conference*, Brisbane, Australia, 1998. W3C.

15. R. Killough and J. J. Leggett. Hypertext interchange with the Dexter model: Intermedia to KMS. Technical Report TAMU-HRL 90-002, Hypertext Research Lab, Texas A&M University, Aug. 1990.

16. C. C. Marshall and F. M. Shipman III. Spatial hypertext: Designing for change. *Communications of the ACM*, 38(8):88–97, 1995.

17. O. Reinert, D. Bucka-Lassen, C. A. Pedersen, and P. J. Nürnberg. CAOS: A collaborative and open spatial structure service component with incremental spatial parsing. In *Proc. of the 10th ACM Hypertext Conference*, pages 49–50, Darmstadt, Germany, 1999.
18. U. K. Wiil, P. J. Nürnberg, D. Hicks, and S. Reich. A development environment for building component-based open hypermedia systems. In F. M. Shipman, III, editor, *Proc. of the 11th ACM Hypertext Conference*, pages 266–267. ACM, May 2000.
19. U. K. Wiil and E. J. Whitehead Jr. Interoperability and open hypermedia systems. In U. K. Wiil, editor, *Proc. of the 3rd Workshop on Open Hypermedia Systems*, number SR-97-01 in CIT Scientific Reports, pages 137–145, Apr. 1997.

Towards a Proposal for a Standard Component-Based Open Hypermedia System Storage Interface

Uffe Kock Wiil

Department of Computer Science
Aalborg University Esbjerg
Niels Bohrs Vej 8, 6700 Esbjerg, Denmark
ukwiil@cs.aue.auc.dk

Abstract. This paper takes a first step towards defining a standard component-based open hypermedia system storage interface in the context of the Open Hypermedia System Working Group. The paper presents a proposal for the core set of services of such an interface. The existence of such an interface is one of the basic preconditions for interoperability at the middleware level in hypermedia systems. The proposed interface has been implemented both as a stand-alone hypermedia storage service and as a basic service in the Construct development environment. Both implementations are in Java and are based on underlying file system services.

1 Introduction

The Open Hypermedia System Working Group (OHSWG) [5] is the forum for definition of de facto standards for component-based open hypermedia systems (CB-OHS). Previous success stories of the OHSWG include the definition of a standard interface for navigational hypermedia called OHP-Nav [1,7]. The members of the OHSWG typically meet twice a year - at the Open Hypermedia System (OHS) Workshop at the annual ACM Hypertext Conference [20,15,10,11, 13] and at a working group meeting in between hosted by one of the participating institutions [2,8,6,12].

The common storage interface idea has been around for some time in the OHS community and has been discussed in various papers at past OHS workshops and working group meetings. The existence of such an interface is one of the basic preconditions for interoperability at the middleware level in hypermedia systems. At the latest working group meeting, OHS5.5 in September 1999 in Esbjerg, it was agreed that the author should come up with a proposal for a common storage interface.

This paper takes a first step towards defining a standard CB-OHS storage interface in the context of the OHSWG. The proposal is based on the "1 + 4" idea, which splits up the interface into a core set of services and a set of extensions dealing with more advanced services in the areas of access control, concurrency

S. Reich and K.M. Anderson (Eds.): OHS/SC 2000, LNCS 1903, pp. 23–30, 2000.
© Springer-Verlag Berlin Heidelberg 2000

control, version control, and notification control [1]. This paper presents a proposal for the core set of services of such an interface. We envision that the core set of services and each extension is defined as a separate interface. The proposed interface has been implemented both as a stand-alone hypermedia storage service and as a basic service in the Construct development environment [14]. Both implementations are made in Java and are based on the underlying file system services.

Section 2 provides a short overview of the previous work of the author to set the context for the present work. In Section 3, we present the storage interface proposal and, in Section 4, we describe the current status and plans for future work.

2   Previous Work

The previous work of the author is centered on a decade of hypermedia system development involving various systems including Hyperform (1990-1995) [16], HyperDisco (1993-1998) [17], and Construct (1997-) [18]. The author has also been involved in the OHSWG standards work since its beginning in 1996 [1,7,9].

Construct is a CB-OHS developed as the common code base successor of the DHM [3], HOSS [4], and HyperDisco systems. It is a major goal of the Construct project to be fully OHSWG standards compliant. For example, Construct provides a complete implementation of the OHSWG navigational interface standard (OHP-Nav).

The latest news in the Construct project is the addition of a set of development tools that assist the hypermedia system developer in building CB-OHS service components [19]. The development cycle has two steps (Figure 1):

1. The developer creates a UML diagram or an IDL specification for the interface of the service. Based on this input the UML to IDL tool (U2I) and the Construct Service Compiler (CSC) generates a skeleton service component.
2. The developer creates the semantic parts (methods bodies) of the operations defined in the interface. When the semantic parts are added to the skeleton service, the service component becomes fully operational in the Construct environment.

Experiences with the development of service components (e.g., development of a file-based implementation of the storage interface proposed in this paper [14]) have proven that the Construct development environment reduces both the time and complexity involved in development of CB-OHS service components.

---

[1] The term "1 + 4" was coined in 1997 in the early phases of the Construct project. It may turn out to be misleading as the development of the storage interface progresses. We may end up with more than 4 advanced service extensions. An example of an additional advanced service is search and query. Maybe the term "1 + n" would be more appropriate.

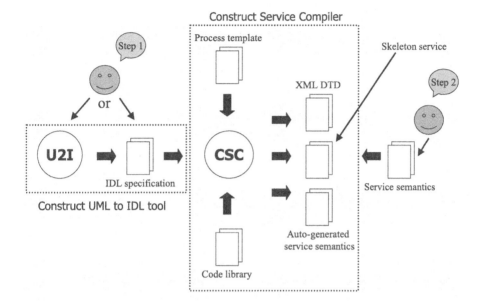

Fig. 1. The Construct Development Environment

3   Storage Interface Proposal

The presentation of the storage interface proposal is divided into two parts. Section 3.1 presents and explains some of the overall design decisions for the storage interface. Section 3.2 presents and explains a specification for the storage interface.

3.1   Storage Interface Design

A class diagram for the proposed core set of storage interface services is depicted in Figure 2. The basic storage entity in the proposed storage interface is the Unit. The StorageInterface is responsible for the persistent storage of Units. A Unit has a set of Characteristics, which contains Unit specific data. A Characteristic has one of four types:

- BinaryAttribute, which can contain binary data.
- Attribute, which can contain all types of attribute values.
- Relation, which can contain references to other Units.
- Behavior, which can contain computations.

A Characteristic has a name (type: string) and can contain several values. A Unit has three predefined Characteristics:

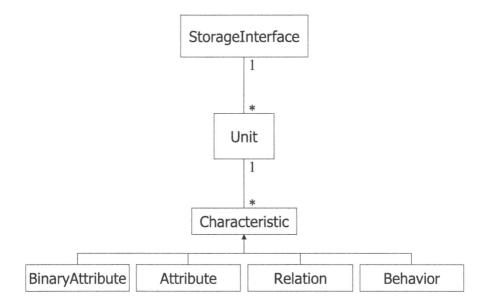

Fig. 2. Class diagram for the proposed storage interface

- Name (type: Attribute), which can contain a set of names. The name given when the Unit is created is the primary name. All other names are secondary.
- Type (type: Attribute), which can contain a set of types. The type given when the Unit is created is the primary type. All other types are secondary.
- ContentUrn (type: Relation), which can contain a reference to wrapped content located elsewhere (e.g., in the file system).

The argument for multiple names is simply that it may be useful to refer to a Unit using different names (e.g., in queries). The argument for multiple types is related to the issue of interoperability at the middleware level. Consider the following scenario: a navigational service and a spatial service share a store. In some cases, we may want the spatial service to be able to open navigational objects (e.g., nodes); and, likewise, we may want the navigational service to be able to open spatial objects (e.g., data). Having multiple types is a first step towards interoperability between the navigational and spatial services. An object created as a navigational node will have the primary type "nav.node" and additional attributes that only can be interpreted by the navigational service. A secondary type can then be added (say, "space.datum") together with attributes that only can be interpreted by the spatial service. This will allow applications of both types of services to open the Unit.

3.2   Storage Interface Specification

The navigational hypermedia interface, OHP-Nav, was specified using an XML DTD. At OHS 3.5 [8] it was agreed to use IDL to specify interfaces. This allows the work to take place at a much higher level of abstraction when defining interfaces. When the OHP-Nav XML DTD was defined, it turned out to be very time-consuming to decide and agree upon every single detail in the XML DTD. The CSC can generate an XML DTD from an IDL specification and, thus, save a considerable amount of time.

```
module store
{
    interface Characteristic
    {
        void addValue(in java::lang::Object value);
        void deleteValue(in java::lang::Object value);
        void getValues(out java::util::LinkedList values);
        void setValues(in java::util::LinkedList values);
        void deleteValues();
    };

    interface BinaryAttribute : Characteristic { };
    interface Attribute : Characteristic { };
    interface Relation : Characteristic { };
    interface Behavior : Characteristic { };

    interface Unit
    {
        void getPrimaryName(out string name);
        void setPrimaryName(in string name);
        void getPrimaryType(out string type);
        void setPrimaryType(in string type);
        void addSecondaryName(in string name);
        void deleteSecondaryName(in string name);
        void addSecondaryType(in string type);
        void deleteSecondaryType(in string type);
        typedef sequence<char> charArray;
        void getContent(out charArray content);
        void setContent(in charArray content);
        void addCharacteristic(in string characName, in Characteristic charac);
        void getCharacteristic(in string characName, out Characteristic charac);
        void deleteCharacteristic(in string characName);
    };

    interface StorageInterface
    {
        void createStorageUnit(in org::ohswg::construct::core::svc::Urn urn, in string name, in string type, out Unit unit);
        void readStorageUnit(in org::ohswg::construct::core::svc::Urn urn, out Unit unit);
        void writeStorageUnit(in org::ohswg::construct::core::svc::Urn urn, in Unit unit);
        void deleteStorageUnit(in org::ohswg::construct::core::svc::Urn urn, in boolean deleteContentUrn);
    };
};
```

Fig. 3. IDL specification of the proposed storage interface

Based on the above argumentation, the proposed storage interface has been specified using IDL (Figure 3). The IDL specification defines the elements of the class diagram in Figure 2 in more detail:

- StorageInterface defines operations to create, read, write and delete Units.
- Unit defines operations to handle names and types (primary as well as secondary), to manipulate the content, and to manipulate Characteristics. Units are referenced using a Urn type.
- Characteristic defines operations to manipulate the values.
- BinaryAttribute, Attribute, Relation, and Behavior inherit the properties of the Characteristic interface.

4   Current Status and Future Work

The Construct development environment is partially developed (late March 2000). The U2I tool is still under development. We expect to have the first running version of the U2I tool in the summer 2000. The CSC has been operational since January 2000. The CSC generates a code skeleton in Java based on an IDL specification like the one in Figure 3.

We have made two different "lightweight" implementations of the proposed storage interface: a stand-alone implementation and an implementation based on the CSC. Both implementations are made in Java and use the file-system to provide persistent storage of Units. Thus, these implementations will run on any machine that has Java's runtime environment (JRE) installed. The stand-alone implementation operates as an isolated hypermedia storage package that can be imported into other Java programs. The CSC implementation operates as a hypermedia storage component in the Construct environment and has become part of the "foundation" services in the Construct development environment.

We plan to continue the work on defining a storage interface to cover also the possible advanced extensions (at least the four mentioned in the Introduction). We also plan to continue to use the Construct development environment to develop different services and to integrate different applications to use these services. A demonstration of the Construct development environment and some of the generated services will be given at ACM Hypertext 2000 in June.

Acknowledgment. The Construct development environment is currently being developed at the Department of Computer Science, Aalborg University Esbjerg, Denmark and at the Department of Information Systems, University of Linz, Austria. The development team consists of Peter J. Nürnberg, David L. Hicks, Uffe K. Wiil, and Siegfried Reich.

References

1. Hugh C. Davis, David E. Millard, Siegfried Reich, Niels Olof Bouvin, Kaj Grønbæk, Peter J. Nürnberg, Lennert Sloth, Uffe Kock Wiil, and Kenneth M. Anderson. Interoperability between hypermedia systems: The standardisation work of the OHSWG (technical briefing). In *Proceedings of the '99 ACM Conference on Hypertext, February 21-25, 1999, Darmstadt, Germany*, pages 201–202, February 1999.
2. Hugh Charles Davis, editor. *2.5 Open Hypermedia Systems Working Group Meeting, Southampton, UK*, December 1996. http://www.ecs.soton.ac.uk/~hcd/.

3. Kaj Grønbæk and Randall H. Trigg. Design issues for a Dexter-based hypermedia system. *Communications of the ACM*, 37(3):40–49, February 1994.
4. Peter J. Nürnberg, John J. Leggett, Erich R. Schneider, and John L. Schnase. Hypermedia operating systems: A new paradigm for computing. In *Proceedings of the '96 ACM Conference on Hypertext, March 16-20, 1996, Washington, D.C.*, pages 194–202, 1996.
5. OHSWG. Technical report, The web site for the Open Hypermedia Systems Working Group (OHSWG), Available as http://www.ohswg.org/, 2000.
6. Siegfried Reich, editor. *4.5 Open Hypermedia Systems Working Group, Southampton, UK*, September 1998. http://www.ecs.soton.ac.uk/~sre/ohs/ohs45/.
7. Siegfried Reich, Uffe K. Wiil, Peter J. Nürnberg, Hugh C. Davis, Kaj Grønbæk, Kenneth M. Anderson, David E. Millard, and Jörg M. Haake. Addressing interoperability in open hypermedia: The design of the open hypermedia protocol. *New Review of Hypermedia and Multimedia*, 5:207–248, 1999.
8. Uffe Kock Wiil, editor. *3.5 Open Hypermedia Systems Working Group Meeting, Aarhus, Denmark*, September 1997. http://www.aue.auc.dk/~kock/OHS3.5/.
9. Uffe Kock Wiil. Open hypermedia: Systems, interoperability and standards. *Journal of Digital Information (JoDI). Special Issue on Open Hypermedia*, 1(2), 1997.
10. Uffe Kock Wiil, editor. *Proceedings of the 3rd Workshop on Open Hypermedia Systems, Hypertext '97, Southampton, England, April 6-11*, 1997. Scientific Report 97-01, The Danish Centre for IT Research.
11. Uffe Kock Wiil, editor. *Proceedings of the 4th Workshop on Open Hypermedia Systems, Hypertext '98, Pittsburgh, PA, June 20-24*, June 1998. Technical Report CS-98-01, Aalborg University Esbjerg.
12. Uffe Kock Wiil, editor. *Proceedings of the 5.5 Open Hypermedia Systems Working Group Meeting, Esbjerg, Denmark*, September 1999. http://www.aue.auc.dk/~kock/OHS5.5/.
13. Uffe Kock Wiil, editor. *Proceedings of the 5th Workshop on Open Hypermedia Systems, Hypertext '99, Darmstadt, Germany, February 21-25*, February 1999. Technical Report CS-99-01, Aalborg University Esbjerg.
14. Uffe Kock Wiil. Using the construct development environment to generate a file-based hypermedia storage service. In *Post Workshop Proceedings of the 6th Workshop on Open Hypermedia Systems (OHS6) and the 2nd Structural Computing (SC2) held in conjunction with ACM Hypertext 2000, San Antonio, TX*, Berlin/Heidelberg/New York, May 2000. Springer.
15. Uffe Kock Wiil and Serge Demeyer, editors. *Proceedings of the 2nd Workshop on Open Hypermedia Systems, ACM Hypertext '96, Washington, D.C., March 16-20. Available as Report No. ICS-TR-96-10 from the Dept. of Information and Computer Science, University of California, Irvine*, March 1996. UCI-ICS Technical Report 96-10, Department of Information and Computer Science, University of California, Irvine.
16. Uffe Kock Wiil and John J. Leggett. Hyperform: A hypermedia system development environment. *ACM Transactions on Office Information Systems*, 15(1):1–31, 1997.
17. Uffe Kock Wiil and John J. Leggett. Workspaces: the HyperDisco approach to Internet distribution. In *Proceedings of the '97 ACM Conference on Hypertext, April 6-11, 1997, Southampton, UK*, pages 13–23, 1997.
18. Uffe Kock Wiil and Peter J. Nürnberg. Evolving hypermedia middleware services: Lessons and observations. In *Proceedings of the 1999 ACM Symposium on Applied Computing (SAC '99), San Antonio, TX*, pages 427–436, February 1999.

19. Uffe Kock Wiil, Peter J. Nürnberg, David Hicks, and Siegfried Reich. A development environment for building component-based open hypermedia systems. In *Proceedings of the '00 ACM Conference on Hypertext, May 30 - June 3, San Antonio, TX*, pages 266–267, May 2000.
20. Uffe Kock Wiil and Kaspar Østerbye, editors. *Proceedings of the ECHT '94 Workshop on Open Hypermedia Systems*, September 1994. Tech. Report R-94-2038, Dept. of Computer Science, Aalborg Univ.

Heuristic Connection Management for Improving Server-Side Performance on the Web

Yoon-Jung Rhee, Nam-Sup Park, and Tai-Yun Kim

Dept. of Computer Science & Engineering
Korea University
1, 5-ga, Anam-dong, Seongbuk-ku, Seoul, 136-701, Korea
{genuine, nspark, tykim}@netla .korea.ac.kr

Abstract. HTTP/1.1 standard reduces latencies and overhead from closing and re-establishing connections by supporting persistent connections as a default, which encourage multiple transfers of objects over one
connection. HTTP/1.1, however, does not define explicitly connection-
closing time but specifies a certain fixed holding time model. This model may induce wasting server's resource when server maintains connection with the idle-state client that requests no data for a certain time.
This paper proposes the mechanism of a heuristic connection management supported by the client-side under persistent HTTP, in addition
to HTTP/1.1's fixed holding time model on server-side. The client exploits the tag information within transferred HTML page so that decides
connection-closing time. As a result, the mechanism allows server to use
server's resource more efficiently without server's efforts.

1 Introduction

HTTP was designed to be an extremely lightweight stateless protocol on TCP,
which is used in World Wide Web distributed hypermedia system to retrieve
distributed objects. HTTP messages are transported by TCP connections between clients and servers. Most implementations of HTTP/1.0[1] use a new TCP
connection for each HTTP request/response exchange. Therefore the transmission of a page with HTML content and embedded images involves many short-
lived TCP connections.

TCP connections are established with a 3-way handshake; and typically several additional round trip times (RTT) are needed for TCP to achieve appropriate transmission speed [17]. Each connection establishment induces user-
perceived latency and processing overhead. Opening a single connection per request through connection setup and slow-start costs causes problems of performance and latency. Thus, persistent connections were proposed [3,4] and are
new a default with the HTTP/1.1 standard [5]. HTTP/1.1 reduces latencies and
overhead from closing and re-establishing connections by supporting persistent
connections as a default, which encourage multiple transfers of objects over one
connection.

S. Reich and K.M. Anderson (Eds.): OHS/SC 2000, LNCS 1903, pp. 31–37, 2000.
© Springer-Verlag Berlin Heidelberg 2000

HTTP/1.1, however, must decide when to terminate inactive persistent connections. HTTP/1.1 specifies that connections should remain open until explicitly closed, by either party. That is to say HTTP/1.1 does not define explicitly when to terminate TCP connection. Current implementation of HTTP/1.1 uses a certain fixed holding-time model. This model may induce wasting server's resource. Current latency problems are caused by not only network's problem but also server's overloads having limited resource. This paper proposes the mechanism of a heuristic connection management on the client-side under persistent HTTP, in addition to HTTP/1.1's fixed holding time model on server-side. The client exploits the tag information in transferred HTML page so that decides connection-closing time.

This paper is structured as follows. In Section 2 we discuss the related works involved in implementation of persistent connection of HTTP/1.1. Section 3 contains our proposal of connection management. We finish with a conclusions and future works in Section 4.

2   Issues and Policies of Persistent Connection Management

In this section, we discuss persistent connection management issues involved in using resource. We also describe current implementation policies and it's problems of persistent connection management subsequently.

2.1   Issues of Persistent Connection

HTTP/1.1 does not specify explicit connection-closing time but provides only one example for a policy, suggesting using a timeout value beyond which an inactive connection should be closed [5]. A connection kept open until the next HTTP request reduces latency and TCP connection.

An open TCP connection with an idle-state client that requests no data consumes a server's resource, a socket and buffer space memory. The minimum size for a socket buffer must exceed the size of the largest TCP packet and many implementations pre-allocate buffers when establishing connections establishment overhead. The number of available sockets is also limited. Many BSD-based operational systems have small default or maximum values for the number of simultaneously-open connections (a typical value of 256) but newer systems are shipped with higher maximum values. Researches indicate that with current implementations, large numbers of (even idle) connections can have a detrimental impact on server's throughput [6,10].

The issues of connection management is to strike a good balance between benefit and cost of maintaining open connections and to enforce some quality of service and fairness issues [10].

2.2 Current Implementation Policies

The current version 1.3 of the Apache HTTP Server [7] uses a fixed holding-time for all connections (the default is set to 15 seconds), and a limit on the maximum allowed number of requests per connection (at most 100). The Apache implementation is a quick answer to the emerging need for connection management. The wide applicability and potential benefit of good connection-management makes it deserving further study.

Persistent connection management is performed at the HTTP-application layer. Current implementations of Web servers use a holding-time model rather than a typical caching model.

Using holding-times, a server sets a holding time for connection when it is established or when a request arrives. While the holding-time lasts, the connection is available for transporting and servicing incoming HTTP requests. The server resets the holding-time when a new request arrives and closes the connections when the holding-time expires.

In a caching model there is a fixed limit on the number of simultaneously-open connections. Connections remains open 'cached' until terminated by client or evicted to accommodate a new connection request.

A holding-time policy is more efficient to deploy due to architectural constraints whereas a cache-replacement policy more naturally adapts to varying server load.

Policies in the two models are closely related when server load is predictable [8]; a holding-time policy assigning the same value to all current connections is analogous to the cache-replacement policy LRU (evict the connection that was Least Recently Used). In fact, under reasonable assumptions the holding-time value can be adjusted through time as to emulate LRU under a fixed cache size (and hence adapt to varying server load) [8]. Heuristics to adjust the holding-time parameter were recently proposed and evaluated on server logs [2].

A problem in the effectiveness of connection-management policies in both models is the ability to distinguish connections that are more likely to be active sooner. LRU exploits the strong presence of reference locality but does not use further information to distinguish between connections [10].

3   Heuristic Connection Management

In this section, we propose the mechanism of a heuristic connection management supported by the client-side under persistent HTTP, in addition to HTTP/1.1's fixed holding time on server-side.

3.1 Proposal of Heuristic Connection Management

We define finishing time of transmission for HTML page and all embedded file in it as connection-closing time. For this definition to be implemented, we present a mechanism, which both client and server are able to close the TCP connection. Following are the mechanism of connection management supported by each client/server-side.

– Client-side : After first receiving a requested HTML file, client parse tag information in HTML involved in embedded files find out the number of files and file names and request pertinent files to the server subsequently. When Ending last embedded file's reception, client close connection with the server.
– Server-side : Server closes connection with client through the fixed holding time model that maintains connection for a certain time and close the connection with the client.

3.2   Implementation Algorithm

We present simple algorithm for implementing prototype for our proposal. Used methods are limited to "GET" message for file request and "CLOSE" message for closing connection.

The client starts to establish connection with pertinent server by user's ask, requesting "GET" message for first HTML file to the server. After receiving HTML file, client parse tag information in it about embedded files and request pertinent files to the server subsequently. When Ending last embedded file's reception, client requests "CLOSE" message for closing connection with the server and terminates connection. Connection is, also, closed when server finish the connection. Fig. 1 shows the client's algorithm presenting connection management.

```
egin
  get new URL from user
  open server.socket with new URL
  send "GET" method and URL.filename
  read stream from server
  display stream content
  search em edded file num er and filenames
      in received HTML file using tag information
  while (other em edded files remain)
     egin
       send "GET" method and filename
       read stream from server
     end while
  send "CLOSE" method to server
  close server.socket
end
```

Fig. 1. Client-side algorithm of prototype for connection management

Server establishes socket and watches incoming connection request. After Received connection request, server establishes connection with the client and send repeatedly the file correspond to requested file-name. Server send "CLOSE" message to current client for closing connection by the fixed holding time model that maintains connection for a certain time and close the connection with the client. After then, server releases resources, socket and socket buffer memory having been assigned to the client. Therefore, the next clients requesting connections to the server are able to receive faster and more fairness service. Fig 2 shows the server's algorithm presenting connection management

```
egin
  esta lish server.socket
  while (within a certain holding timeout)
     egin
      if accept "SYN" from client
         then open client.socket
      while (within a certain holding timeout)
         egin
          read stream
          if method in stream is "GET"
             egin
               get filename from stream
               if file exist then response
                 requested file
               else response "file not found"
             end if
          else if method in stream is "CLOSE"
               then close client socket and  reak
         end while
     end while
end
```

Fig. 2. Server-side algorithm of prototype for connection management

We expect that this mechanism supports balanced service reducing latencies and overhead by supporting persistent connections and server's overloading by connection management.

The initial prototype of this mechanism is presently under development with Java based. Current implementation focuses on compare three models, fixed holding time model, caching model and our heuristic model.

4   Conclusions and Future Works

We proposed the mechanism of a heuristic connection management supported by the client-side under persistent HTTP, in addition to HTTP/1.1's fixed holding time model on server-side. We defined finishing time of transmission for HTML page and all embedded file in it as connection-closing time. The client exploits the tag information in transferred HTML page so that decides connection-closing time. As the Processing for parsing of tag information in HTML file occurs on client-side, the mechanism allows server to use server's resource more efficiently without server's many efforts and supports a good balance between benefit and cost of maintaining open connections and to enforce some quality of service and fairness issues.

As future works, we plan for analysis and evaluation of performance of the mechanism. To progress, we apply this to Jigsaw server and Libwww client for better implementation results.

References

1. T. Berners-lee, R. Fielding and H. Frystyk: Hypertext Transfer Protocol - HTTP/1.0 RFC 1945, MIT/LCS, May 1996,
   `http://ds.internic.net/rfc1945.txt`
2. M. Elaud, C.J. Sreenan, P. Ramanathan and P. Agrawal: Use of server load to dynamically select connection-closing time for HTTP/1.1 servers, Submitted for publication, March 1999.
3. J.C. Mogul: The case for persistent-connection HTTP, Comp. Commun. Rev. 25 (4) (1995) 299-313,
   `http://www.research.digital.com/wrl/techreports/a stracts/95.4.html`
4. V.N. Padmanabhan and I.C. Mogul: improving HTTP latency, Comput. Networks ISDN Syst. 28(1/2) (1995) 25-35.
5. T. Berners-Lee, R. Fieding, J. Gettys, J.C. Mogul, H. Frystyk, L. Masinter, and P. Leach: Hypertext Transfer Protocol - HTTP/1.1 RFC2616 Jun 1999.
   `http://www.w3.org/Protocols/HTTP/1.1/rfc2616.pdf`
6. L.A. Belady: A study of replacement s for virtual storage computers, IBM Systems Journal 5 (1996) 78-101.
7. Apache HTTP server project, `http://www.apache.org`
8. E. Cohen and H. Kaplan: Exploiting regularities in Web traffic patterns for cache replacement, in: Proc. 31st Annu. ACM Symp. On Theory of Computing, ACM, 1999.
9. E. Cohen, H. Kaplan, J. Oldham: Managing TCP connections under persistent HTTP, Elsevier Scince B. V, 1999
10. G. Banga and J. Mogul, Scalable kernel performance for Internet servers under realistic loads, in: Rpoc. USENIX Annu. Technical Conf., USENIS Assoc., 1998,
    `http://www.cs.rice.edu/~gaurav/papers/usenix98.ps`
11. R.T. Braden: Requirements of internet hosts communication layers, FRC 1122, ISI, October 1989.
12. H.F. Nielsen, J. Gettys, A. Baird-smith, E. Prud'hommeaux, H.W. Lie, C. Lilley: Network Performance Effects of HTTP/1.1, CSS1, and PNG, in: Proc. ACM SIGCOMM '97 Conference, Cannes, France, August 1997.
13. V. Jacobson: Congestion avoidance and control, in: Proc. Of the ACM SIGCOMM '88 Conference, August 1988.
14. S. Spero: Analysis of HTTP Performance Problems,
    `http://sunsite.unc.edu/mdma-releas/http-pro .html`

15. B. Janssen, H. Frystyk and Spreitzer M: HTTP-NG architectural model, August 1998, `http://info.internet.isi.edu/in-drafts/files/draft-frystyk-httpng-arch-00.txt`

16. W.R. Stevens, TCP/IP Illustrated, Vol. 1, Addison-Wesley, Reading, MA, 1994

17. W.R. Stevens, TCP/IP Illustrated, Vol. 3, Addison-Wesley, Reading, MA, 1994

18. Z. Wang and P. Cao: Persistent connection behavior of popular browsers, `http://www.cs.wisc.edu/cao/papers/persistent-conection.html`.

Accessing the History of the Web: A Web Way-Back Machine

Joachim Feise

University of California, Irvine
Information and Computer Science
Irvine, CA 92627-3425, USA
jfeise@ics.uci.edu

Abstract. One of the deficiencies of the World Wide Web is that the Web does not have a memory. Web resources always display one revision only, namely the latest one. In addition, once a Web resource moves from one location (i.e., URL) to another, the resource at the original location ceases to exist.

Since the Web does not provide a mechanism to allow access to the revision history of resources, services like the Internet Archive have sprung into action to collect the history of important Web resources.

The Web way-back machine described here, currently under development by the author, utilizes collections of historical Web resources like the ones provided by the Internet Archive to allow online, read-only access to the revisioned resources.

1 Introduction

The World Wide Web is quickly becoming the standard way to present information in cyberspace. However, contents on the Web changes quickly, and there is currently no general way to access the history of Web-based resources. The resource authors may or may not use document management systems that provide a revision history of resources, but even if authors use such systems the resources as published on the Web still lack any historical metadata.

The process of collecting Web resources is well understood and is used on a daily basis by Web search sites, like Google [3] or AltaVista [1], as well as by the Internet Archive [4], an organization dedicated to creating an archive of Web resources over time. All these organizations use Web crawlers [12] to collect resources from the Web.

Web search sites and the Internet Archive differ in their processing and storage of the collected data, though. Web search sites only utilize the last resource revision collected. Access to previous revisions is not possible. The collected resources are processed in various ways to support efficient searches (for details, see, for example, the processing overview at Google [15]).

The Internet Archive stores its collected data in aggregate files with a size of up to 100 Megabyte [5]. This collection was started in October 1996 and has reached a size of approximately 14 terabytes. The size of this collection and the

S. Reich and K.M. Anderson (Eds.): OHS/SC 2000, LNCS 1903, pp. 38–45, 2000.
© Springer-Verlag Berlin Heidelberg 2000

aggregation of unrelated Web resources in large files facilitates offline access and analysis, but makes online, real-time access impractical. For example, it is unlikely that one organization alone can provide the facilities to allow online access to a collection of this size. In addition, the computational expense to extract resource metadata, like relationship information between resources, from the aggregate files precludes the fast access required by online use. To provide online access to this vast amount of data, a different approach is therefore necessary.

Each Web resource collected by a service like the Internet Archive is associated with a day and time stamp indicating the date the resource was collected. The history of a specific Web resource as stored by the Internet Archive is therefore comprised of the collection of documents from a specific location at discrete dates. Obviously, if the capturing frequency is low, this may not capture the full resource history. On the other hand, a high capturing frequency incurs a high bandwidth utilization, which may not be desirable for sites with bandwidth restrictions. In the case of static resources or resources with a low revision rate, a high capturing frequency would also result in redundant data, which, in the interest of minimizing storage requirements, would require an approach to detect duplicate entries.

This paper describes a Web way-back machine, currently under development by the author, which utilizes a proxy server and any standard Web browser with frame and JavaScript capabilities to allow online access to Web resources collected over time.

2   Resource Organization

As mentioned above, the organization of resources collected for the purpose of archiving is usually optimized for offline storage. An analysis of the storage format used by the Internet Archive, for example, reveals that this format is not suited for efficient online access. The data files aggregate the collected resources without any notion of relationships between the resources.

It is therefore likely that the histories of specific resources are scattered among several of these data files. For a proper representation of the changes of resources over time, the resource history needs to be available to the user. A real-time recovery of the history of any given resource from the Internet Archive data files would require an extraordinary amount of processing, which would be prohibitive for any Internet-scale use. It is also highly unlikely that the vast amount of data collected can be stored and presented by one organizational entity alone, nor is it desirable to put the responsibility for maintaining this amount of data into the hands of only one organization.

Distribution of the data storage across organizational boundaries therefore becomes a necessity. Ideally, the distributed nature of the data storage should be transparent to the user. Also desirable is the ability of dynamic reconfigurations of the data storage, for example to provide load balancing or to move parts of the data storage between organizations.

Organization and access of multiple versions of resources is generally the task of versioning and configuration management systems. These systems seem to be a natural fit for the task of providing fast online access to multiple versions of resources collected from the Web. However, configuration management systems are usually limited to an intra-organization scale. Conventional configuration management systems typically do not scale beyond these boundaries. There are numerous attempts to provide support for distributed operation in commercial configuration management systems, but these attempts are usually limited to simple client-server interfaces (for a detailed discussion see A. van der Hoek's Ph.D. dissertation [11].)

2.1   Data Storage

We chose to use the Network Unified Configuration Management System (NUCM) [11] for the storage and organization of the revisioned resources, since NUCM was designed to provide the transparent distributed storage capabilities required for the Web way-back machine. NUCM also allows dynamic reconfiguration of the data storage across machine boundaries.

Since configuration management systems like NUCM usually store each resource in a local filesystem, efficient filesystem access becomes important. In fact, the difficulty of accessing 100,000s of files efficiently led the Internet Archive to aggregate the collected resources in large files. Configuration management systems, however, usually use just one file for all of a resource's history, which decreases the burden on the filesystem. In addition, a clever organization of the resources can further alleviate this problem. A natural hierarchical organization of Web resources can be achieved by exploiting the organization of the URLs used to reference these resources. This organization mirrors the domain name structure of URLs.

At the top-level of the hierarchy, resources can be classified as belonging in one of the .com, .edu, .uk, .de, etc. domains. The second level would comprise organization names like uci, microsoft, etc. The hierarchical decomposition continues along the whole domain name, followed by an analogous decomposition of the actual directory path of the URL.

A resource referenced with the URL `http://www.ics.uci.edu/~jfeise/index.html` would therefore be referenced in the NUCM configuration management system as `//nucm_root/edu/uci/ics/www/~jfeise/index.html`. If necessary, a finer grained storage system can easily be devised. In fact, since the number of resources in the .com domain is likely to cause the same filesystem efficiency problems as outlined above, a more useful mapping between URLs and the filesystem storage may separate resources by the first two letters of the organization name. This scheme can easily be extended, so that the resource `http://www.microsoft.com/index.html` may be stored in NUCM under `//nucm_root/com/mi/cr/microsoft/www/index.html`.

The dynamic reconfigurability of NUCM allows to perform storage schema extensions when necessary. It is therefore possible to start out with the coarse grained mapping, and refine it as desired during the population of the system or even during the use of the Web way-back machine, if performance problem manifest themselves.

The transparent nature of resource distribution in NUCM allows for branches in resource tree being located on different machines and across organizational boundaries. For example, the branch `//nucm_root/com` could be located on one machine, while the the the branch `//nucm_root/com/mi/cr/microsoft` may be stored on a different machine located in a different organization. A move of the branch to yet another location would not affect the tree structure at all.

3   Resource Access

The use of a Web way-back machine should be as transparent to the user as possible. This implies that the user should be able to view current Web resources and archived versions of the same or other resources from the same browser with a minimum of required browser configuration changes. The easiest way to accomplish this goal is to configure the user's Web browser to use a proxy server. The proxy server then would have the task of distinguishing between requests for normal, current Web resources and requests for historical revisions of Web resources.

3.1   Client

Ideally, a modification to the browser would allow users to specify the kind of requests they issue. In the case of requests for historical versions of Web resources, the user also needs to be able to specify the date or revision of interest. This information would then be sent with the request to the proxy server, in the form of an additional line in the HTTP header of the request. Unfortunately, the existing Web browsers do not provide facilities for the addition of such browser extensions. In particular, none of the existing browser extension capabilities, like plugins or ActiveX controls, allow for the modification or addition of HTTP headers.

It is therefore necessary to use other data transfer mechanisms like cookies or scripting approaches. An analysis of the cookie specifications [7,6] shows that cookies are not suitable for the task at hand, since cookies are designed to be exchanged between the browser and the target Web site. Although interception and manipulation of cookies in the proxy server is possible, the requirement of a user-changeable date or revision of interest rules out the use of cookies, which can not be modified in the browser.

The approach we chose is therefore based on the use of frames and JavaScript in the Web browser. These features are available in the vast majority of browsers available in the marketplace. Text-only browsers like Lynx and very old graphical browsers like Mosaic and early versions of Netscape Navigator and Microsoft's Internet Explorer would be excluded from using the Web way-back machine, though.

The browser displays two frames, a navigation frame and a resource frame. The navigation frame contains several dialog elements to select a date of interest or a specific revision of the resource. The navigation frame also allows to easily navigate between revisions or between dates. In addition, the navigation frame can easily be extended to provide information like the date when the resource was collected, or the frequency of collection.

The navigation frame also needs to contain an off-switch, to indicate to the proxy server that the user no longer wishes to view historical revisions of Web resources.

3.2   Server

Once the user's Web browser is set up according to the discussion above, a proxy server is utilized to receive the user input and provide the user with the appropriate resource.

Like browsers, proxy servers do not support the functionality required for this task natively. Unlike browsers, however, a variety of proxy servers are distributed as Open Source. Even the leading Web server, the Apache server [2], can be used as proxy server. However, the Apache server is not optimized to serve as proxy server. We therefore settled for the Squid proxy server and Web cache [10], which, like Apache, is distributed as Open Source.

The availability of the source code for the proxy server allows us to implement the functionality required to support our Web way-back machine. Specifically, we require the proxy server to receive and process any action the user performs in the navigation frame in the Web browser.

As long as the user does not utilize the navigation frame, or the off-switch in the navigation frame is selected, the proxy server performs its standard processing, i.e., for each incoming request, it first checks if the requested Web resource is in the proxy's cache. If it is, the resource is delivered to the requestor. If the proxy determines that it does not hold the Web resource, it in turn requests it from the original Website or from another proxy server. The details of this process are described in RFCs 2186 [13] and 2187 [14], as well as in the Squid documentation [8,9].

A different processing path is chosen in the proxy server if the user selects a specific date or revision in the navigation frame in the browser.

First, if the user selects a specific date or revision in the navigation frame, the navigation frame in turn encodes this selection in a URL and sends this data as a request to the proxy server. A special URL handler (e.g., a CGI handler) decodes the request and stores the selection data in the proxy server for later use.

Second, when the user now requests a resource, the proxy server determines that a historic revision of the resource is required. At this point, the path of standard processing is left, and the proxy server utilizes the NUCM configuration management system to locate the appropriate revision of the requested resource.

4   Limitations

As is customary in configuration management systems, requests with specific dates are mapped to the last resource with a date equal or prior to the requested one. It is therefore possible that subsequent requests with different dates return the same resource. In order to indicate this possibility to the user, the proxy server, in addition to the requested resource, updates the navigation frame with the revision of the resource and the date the resource was collected.

Unfortunately, this mechanism can not be applied to a resource that changed locations during its history. In this case, the revision history of this resource would be treated as two independent revision histories, with the separation between them at the date of the location change. The resource at the original location does not change after this date anymore, and the revision history does not contain any indication that the location of the resource changed.

Resources that are deleted at a certain point in time present another special case. Unless the collection archive explicitly records that a resource no longer exists, no knowledge about deletions exists or can be inferred from the resource collection.

The Internet Archive, for example, allows Web administrators to opt out of the collection process. If the administrator of a Web site does so, no further resources from that Web site are collected. However, the previously collected resources are still accessible in the collection archive. In this case, the limited revision history therefore does not reflect the real revision history of the resources anymore.

Another factor limiting the accuracy of the projected revision history is the fact that the frequency of the resource collection is finite. It is therefore likely that some resource changes on highly dynamic Web sites will not be recorded.

The collection of resources is usually performed with the help of Web crawlers, which automatically visit Web sites, retrieve the resources, and follow any links contained in them. In order to limit the bandwidth impact of these crawlers, they generally do not collect all the resources of a Web site in one transaction. This can easily lead to link inconsistencies within supposedly identical revisions. A possible scenario for this problem is a reorganization of a Web site during the short time that a well-behaved Web crawler pauses between consecutive visits.

5   Early Results

As proof of concept, I implemented a first, limited prototype to show the feasibility of the approach and perform first scalability tests. This prototype does not use real Web resources, but instead relies on artificially generated resources, created by a small helper program and stored in a NUCM database. Tests with the prototype showed that first-time access to a versioned resource is reasonably fast, even if the NUCM database storing the resources is accessed over a LAN on a machine different from the proxy server. The access time in this setting is in the order of 2-3 seconds. Co-locating the proxy server and the NUCM database on the same computer increases the access time roughly by a factor of 3. Subsequent accesses to different revisions of the same resource remained in the under 1 second range, even with the NUCM archive located on a different computer on the LAN.

However, the tests showed that the population of a NUCM archive at a rate of even one second for the local filesystem case will require some thought as the amount of resources to be stored grows. At this rate, the population of a NUCM archive with just 1 million resources would take about half a month. The author is investigating the feasibility of bypassing the NUCM API in order to increase the speed of the population process, thereby avoiding the overhead of maintaining a temporary NUCM workspace on the local machine solely for the purpose of populating the database.

Arguably, the population time could be considered negligible, given that the population task is a one-time process. However, we feel that in the interest of scalability, the population process should be able to handle the current one billion resources collected by the Internet Archive in a reasonable amount of time.

6 Future Work

I intend to expand the existing prototype to a fully functional Web way-back machine. We have established contact with the Internet Archive in the expectation to get access to parts of the Web resources the Archive has collected. Use of resources from this collection will allow the creation of a larger NUCM archive than the one currently in use, and will facilitate the evaluation of the scalability of my approach. I also want to make the Web way-back machine available to a reasonably sized group of users to allow the evaluation of scalability with respect to the number of users. In addition, I expect the feedback from a diverse group of users to be very valuable in improving the design of the user interface presented in the browser.

Acknowledgements. I am greatly indebted to Jim Whitehead, Yuzo Kanomata and André van der Hoek for numerous discussions helping to shape the ideas presented in this paper. Yuzo also provided very helpful comments on earlier versions of this paper and on the prototype implementation.

I also wish to acknowledge the receipt of a generous financial scholarship from Eagle Creek Systems, Inc. in support of my research.

References

1. AltaVista, http://www.altavista.com/
2. The Apache Server Project, http://www.apache.org/httpd.html
3. Google, http://www.google.com/
4. The Internet Archive, http://www.archive.org/
5. The Internet Archive: Storage and Preservation of the Collections, http://www.archive.org/collections/storage.html

6. Kristol, D. and Montulli, L. HTTP State Management Mechanism, Lucent Technologies, Netscape, February 1997, `http://www.ietf.org/rfc/rfc2109.txt`

7. Netscape Cookies, 1997, `http://developer.netscape.com/docs/manuals/communicator/jsguide4/cookies.htm`

8. Squid Frequently Asked Questions: How does Squid work, `http://www.squid-cache.org/Doc/FAQ/FAQ-12.html`

9. Squid User Manual, `http://www.squid-cache.org/Doc/Users-Guide/`

10. Squid Web Proxy Cache, `http://www.squid-cache.org/`

11. van der Hoek, A. A Reusable, Distributed Repository for Configuration Management Policy Programming, Ph.D. Dissertation, University of Colorado at Boulder, 2000,

12. The Web Robots Pages, `http://info.we crawler.com/mak/projects/ro ots/ro ots.html`

13. Wessels, D. and Claffy, K. Internet Cache Protocol (ICP), version 2, National Laboratory for Applied Network Research, U.C. San Diego, September 1997, `http://www.ietf.org/rfc/rfc2186.txt`

14. Wessels, D. and Claffy, K. Application of Internet Cache Protocol (ICP), version 2, National Laboratory for Applied Network Research, U.C. San Diego, September 1997, `http://www.ietf.org/rfc/rfc2187.txt`

15. Why Use Google?, `http://www.google.com/why_use.html`

Web Site Interface Design: External and Internal Factors

Ahmed Mahfouz

Department of Information and Operations Management,
Mays College and Graduate School of Business Administration,
Texas A&M University,
College Station,
Texas 77843-4217, USA
amahfouz@tamu.edu

Abstract. There has been tremendous growth in electronic commerce over the past few years. This growth is expected to sustain momentum in the future. Hence, the Internet has become an essential tool for business and customers. However, unlike traditional retailers, it lacks key aspects of a shopping experience like interacting with customer sales people and being physically in a store. A well-designed user interface can overcome some of these limitations and aid customers in their search of products and services. This paper examines both the internal (to the web design) and external (to the user's environment) factors that affect user interface design on the World Wide Web. These five factors are the user's mental model, level of expertise of the user, the user's learning style, richness of the media used, and the organizational image and message. Since all factors are external with the exception of the richness of the media used, the emphasis in the paper is on external factors.

1 Introduction

Electronic commerce has exploded on the Internet over the past few years and is expected to continue growing at a phenomenal rate [1]. According to the GVU's 8th WWW User Surveys [2], the most important issues facing on-line users are privacy (31%), censorship (24%), and navigation (17%). Since user interface design impacts navigation and affects user's interaction with a web site, this paper will explore the different factors that affect user interface design on the World Wide Web. These five factors are the user's mental model, level of expertise of the user, the user's learning style, richness of the media used, and the organizational image and message. All these factors involve the internal (to the web page design) and external (to the user's environment) factors that impact user interface design on the Internet. Since all factors are external with the exception of the richness of the media used, the emphasis in the paper is on external factors.

User interface is important in relation to the World Wide Web and electronic commerce, as indicated below [3]:

S. Reich and K.M. Anderson (Eds.): OHS/SC 2000, LNCS 1903, pp. 46–56, 2000.
© Springer-Verlag Berlin Heidelberg 2000

"Issues of how people use the technology become critical as businesses and retailers attempt to exploit the boom in electronic marketing. There are large differences between a physical store and its electronic counterpart. A help button on the home page of the Web shopping site replaces the sales clerk's friendly advice and service. The familiar layout of the physical store becomes a maze of pull-down menus, product indices and search features. Now more than ever, the promise of electronic commerce and on-line shopping will depend to a great extent upon the interface and how people interact with the computer (p. 81)."

2   Literature Review

This section discusses the literature review involving user interface models and mental models. It starts out with defining the term user interface, its four types, the four levels of user interface model, GOMS model, and object-action interface models. Finally, mental models and metaphors are discussed.

2.1   User Interface Models

Four Types of User Interface. An interface is generally defined as the shared link that allows two independent systems to communicate or interact together. In computer-human interaction, it can be graphically expressed as the intersection overlapping the human and computer systems. Specifically, the interface involves all the hardware input and output devices (such as the mouse, keyboard, computer monitor, etc.) and software (operating system, application, etc.) that allow the user and the system to interact.

The user is flexible and adaptable [4]. However, the system is neither flexible nor adaptable, which in turn places the responsibility of successful interaction on the user. This responsibility makes the role of a well designed user interface an important issue in how users perceive the system. User participation and involvement towards a system affect their productivity and attitude in the workplace [5].

There are four types of user interface, as shown in Table 1: command-line, prompted, menu-driven, and graphical [6]. Command-line interface requires typing a command that follows a specific syntax and punctuation, as used in Microsoft DOS and Unix. Prompted interface asks for input from the user through the use of messages. Wizards are dominating prompted interface through the use of multi-step sequence of screens that require a response. Menu-driven interface utilizes menus and submenus for ease of use. Graphical user interface allows the computer to be accessed through graphical objects like buttons, toolbars, etc. by the means of an input device, like the mouse, or an output device, like the computer monitor.

User's involvement with the system can be expressed in two languages [7]. This interaction has differences since the needs of the user are different from the system. This communication is expressed in two languages: the action language

Table 1. Four types of user interface [6]

Type of Interface	Characteristics
Command-line	Typing of commands with specific syntax and punctuation
Prompted	Entering a response required by the system Updated through the use of wizards
Menu-driven	Utilizing menus and submenus for options
Graphical	Using graphical objects for ease of use and interaction

and presentation language. The user utilizes the action language to let the computer know what tasks or commands need to be done on the various objects and components in the system or the software package. On the other hand, the presentation language is used by the system to ask about the tasks and objects and to respond to requests with the result of the operations. Both of these languages allow interaction and communication about common tasks and domains.

Four Levels of User Interface Model. The Foley and van Dam user interface model is based on four levels [8]. The first level is the conceptual model, which describes the domain of tasks by which the human and system interact, such as objects manipulated, the relationships that exits among the objects, and the operations performed on these objects. The remaining three levels describe the semantic, syntactic, and lexical levels of both the action and presentation languages.

The semantic level defines what the words mean in the language, which is based on meanings taken from the conceptual model. This level incorporates objects that are part of the presentation language that deal with human interaction, such as menus, dialog boxes, or prompts. The physical implementation of the interface starts at this level.

The third level is the syntactic level, which describes the grammar that allows combining words into a meaningful context of sentences. Syntax for the presentation language incorporates visual arrangements, such as shape and size, and temporal arrangement, such as the appearance and disappearance of objects on the screen. On the other hand, the syntax for the action language describes the order of actions done by the user to complete the messages.

The fourth level is the lexical level, which deals with how the words in the language are expressed. In the presentation language, displayed text or various symbols and combinations of different font types, colors, lines, etc. define the words. In the action language, a word may be expressed by what the user clicks on the screen or uses the mouse to manipulate a specific object on the computer screen.

Interface consistency is an important element in user interface design [9], based on the Foley and van Dam model [8] described above. Consistency is somewhat difficult to define. Generally, it refers to how the interface is orderly, predictable, and easily defined by elements of design that make the application easy to learn and change.

Consistency can be classified into three levels: internal, analogical, and external [10]. Internal consistency refers to how the interface is consistent in design at any level of the interface inside the application itself. Analogical consistency refers to consistency of the system or the application with the user's task environment. When more than one application is involved, then external consistency refers to consistency across those applications, in all the four levels of interface design. For example, external consistency is evident in Microsoft applications, whereby Word, Excel, and to a great extent Internet Explorer share the same "look and feel" when it comes to the menus, buttons, etc.

GOMS Model. Goals, operators, methods, and selection rules (GOMS) is a cognitive model [11]. The model assumes that humans define goals, such as creating a document in a word processor, and subgoals, such as inserting words. These goals are attained by using methods or tasks, such as moving the cursor, using the four arrow keys. The operators on this context are tasks of the brain that include basic perceptual, motor, or cognitive tasks. These tasks, such as recalling a filename, moving the mouse on the screen, etc., are important in changing the user's mental state or the task environment. The selection rules are the control mechanisms for selecting among the available methods for achieving a goal, such as erasing text in a document.

Object-Action Interface Model. Shneiderman [12] redefined a user interface model he proposed earlier. The new model is called the object-action interface (OAI) model. The model emphasizes the manipulation of user objects and actions in a visual way. For example, folders of letters might be represented with envelopes (objects) and the deletion of these files (actions) could be represented with trash cans, such as the first ones introduced in the Apple Macintosh.

In the OAI model, the first step is to understand the action or task to be carried out. The task in turn is broken further into intermediate goals and individual steps. Once the task objects and actions and their decomposition have been well defined, then a metaphor can be applied. (Metaphors will be discussed in a later section of the paper.) The designer must then represent the actions visually to the user, such as the movement of the mouse as the user clicks. Since the OAI model does not rely on syntax, it is easier to learn.

The OAI model supports two components in web page design: metaphors (discussed later) and handles for interface actions. Actions in web sites can be represented using action handles: the labels, icons, buttons, images, etc. that allow the user the choice of clicks to start a specific action or sequence of actions. For example, navigation action can be represented by a turned page corner to indicate next-page action, or a magnifying glass to be used to zoom in or out of a page.

The OAI model specifies five main elements in web page design: compactness and branching factors; sequencing, clustering, and emphasis; support for universal access; good graphical design; and navigation support [12]. The first is compactness and branching factors. These refer to page length and number of links, respectively. As web pages grow and get more complex, the number of layers of index pages grows. Hence, an index is not appropriate. The solution is a higher branching factor. Good examples of web page design are the Library of Congress (LOC) home page (`http://www.loc.gov`) and Yahoo home page (`http://www.yahoo.com`). The LOC page has a compact display with 31 links to specific services instead of the original seven links to general topics. The Yahoo web site has over 100 links in a compact two-column format.

The second element is sequencing, clustering, and emphasis. Internet users expect that the most important item to be placed at the beginning of a page, which reflects the proper sequence of objects based on spatial importance. Clustering refers to grouping relevant items together to show their relationships. For emphasis, large fonts, coloring, and drawing elements could be used to have certain items stand out.

Support for universal access is the third element. Different settings, such as resolution, color, refresh rate, bandwidth, and type of browser must be taken into account by web designers. That could be achieved by building two versions of web sites: text only and graphical. This would accommodate users of differing computers and bandwidth, especially in developing countries which may lack the sufficient telecommunications infrastructure.

The fourth element is good graphical design. Several books on information presentation were written by Tufte [13]. Each design philosophy must take into account the purpose of the site, as well the users who will be visiting it. For example, Wired magazine's web site (`http://www.wired.com/`) attracts attention to certain topics by using multiple colors and multiple font sizes.

The last element is navigation support. Many sites have a site map, showing the different sites in a diagram. Others use Java to expand items into submenus when the mouse is placed on top of a specific item. As an example of an educational software, Compton's Encyclopedia uses various types of multimedia and many windows to give a rich and interactive experience of information presentation. Information presentation and display formats were shown empirically to impact user preferences and decisions [14].

2.2   Mental Models

A mental model as the domain knowledge or as "any body of information you have stored in memory about a situation, an event, a procedure, and so on can be termed a mental model in this sense" ([15], p. 561). Other synonymous terms are a user's model or user's conceptual model. For example, when someone goes to a restaurant, that person has a mental model about restaurants that may include the following: menus to select food, waiters to take orders, cooks to prepare meals, etc. Experience and further changes made to that knowledge are the sources of mental models [15].

A user's mental model will affect how the user will use an application, based on the consistency of an interface [9]. A mental model is defined as what the user knows about a particular application. Metaphors are "the cognitive lenses we use to make sense of all situations" ([16], p. 149).

Metaphors. Metaphors play an important role in defining a user's model since it represents computer components as real world objects. One of the earlier metaphors is the ledger which was used in the first electronic spreadsheet, VisiCalc. One of the most prevalent metaphors is the desktop metaphor, which was introduced by Xerox PARC and later popularized by the Apple Macintosh and Microsoft Windows. The metaphor represents documents stored in a computer as pages of paper, and storage as a filing cabinet. Metaphors affect the ease of using and learning software [17].

However, Raskin, who helped develop the Macintosh, criticized the use of the desktop metaphor [18]. First, he stated there are major problems to deal with, such as complaints from users about the functionality of the system, involving different settings that must be configured. In addition, Raskin cited cognitive psychology research that states humans can only deal with a few tasks at hand at one time [18]. The desktop metaphor consumes many of the user's resources, such as attention, since the user has to be aware of the state of the operating system and the application, which results in frustration. The solution, according to Raskin, is an interface that is operated habitually and automatically that will not take away from human attention, and is also easy to learn and to use. The research model proposed below takes into account the five factors that affect user interface, especially on the World Wide Web, that would result in an easy to use design since it takes into account the major facets that influence users.

3   Research Model

The goal of this paper is to discuss the factors that affect interface design on the World Wide Web. However, the scope of the design is not limited, like in many studies, to the internal structure of the web site design, but rather extends to the external factors (in addition to the internal ones) that impact the design process. This is a macro-level approach rather than the limited micro-level approach that deals with objects and menus, which are still discussed in the paper. It is the designer's responsibility to balance the design trade-offs and priorities of the web site for optimum effect. For example, media richness of the site would be costly to add all the various multimedia and 3D effects so that customers could "experience a product" on-line by rotating it and viewing from different angles. However, a company like Black & Decker may not see cost as a priority as much as advertising its product line very well.

Since the user's mental model was discussed earlier, this section will discuss the remaining four factors: level of expertise of the user, the user's learning style, richness of the media used, and organizational image and message. All factors are external with the exception of the richness of the media used.

3.1 Level of Expertise of the User

Users respond differently to computer systems depending on their level of expertise and knowledge with computers [19]. Users can be classified as novices with limited knowledge of the application and the domain of the system, or as experts with greater experience of the application and the domain of the system. Intermediate users would fall in the middle. Experts and novices interpret interface metaphors differently [20]. Experts rely more on abstraction while novices rely more on the physical characteristics that are more concrete.

Taking into account novices' learning curve, it was concluded that novices may not be able to distinguish the document on the Internet from the interface [21]. Using more concrete elements on a web browser, like navigation buttons, would make it easier for novices since they need less abstraction. Since novices may get overwhelmed with many tasks, the interface must be simple, broken down into simpler subtasks; on the other hand, experts prefer faster response time and the ability to do multiple tasks at one time [12].

3.2 User's Learning Style

Learning style has an impact on how users learn and interact with the user interface [22]. There are two types of learning according to Assimilation Theory: meaningful learning and rote learning (or memorization). Meaningful learning occurs when new knowledge is connected to existing information in a meaningful way to be applied to new situations and concepts. On the contrary, rote learning links old and new information in an arbitrary way, whereby memorization of new knowledge does not relate old and new knowledge in a new meaningful way. The learning style will affect how novice (versus expert) users learn and adapt to a new interface, and how they deal with its functionality.

Other learning theories, such as Kolb's learning style theory ([23], [24]) classify learning style into a four stage cycle across two modes: active experimenters (actives) and reflective observers (reflective). Kolb's cycle moves from concrete experience to reflective observation to formation of abstract concepts to testing hypotheses through active experimentation, resulting in four learning styles: diverger, assimilator, converger, and accommodator. Here there is a parallel to how novice and expert users differ: novices start with concrete concepts and progress to abstract ideas as they become experts.

User interfaces should be consistent, and a distinct visual appearance would aid users at the early stages of learning new applications [9]. Therefore, the transfer of learning would enhance a user's ability to work with a new interface or an exiting interface with new additional features [9]. Transfer of learning refers to having knowledge of one application transferred to another application. For example, learning Microsoft Word would make it easier to learn PowerPoint since they share a common "look and feel."

3.3   Richness of the Media Used

Multimedia plays an important role in the design of a web site since it adds interactivity. Entertainment value is a main factor for users' perception of a web site since users tend to favor sites that are exciting and interesting and would tend to visit them more often over poorly designed and uninteresting sites [25].

According to media richness theory, the richer or more varied the medium of communication, the richer the capabilities of information ([26], [27]). For example, using hypermedia (audio, video, and text) is an improvement over using just hypertext (plain text) to display information on a web site.

Rich media need to be used with web sites that provide information intensive products and services [28]. Information intensive products and services include those provided by such companies like insurance firms, which require the firm and in turn its web site to provide as much information as possible to assist the consumer in making a purchase decision. This allows customers to almost "test the products" on-line. For example, sites like Carpoint (`http://www.carpoint.msn.com/gallery`), a Microsoft site that sells cars online, and Sharperimage.com utilize 3-D graphics and animation so that consumers could "experience" products by viewing them from different angles and rotate them. Capabilities such as zooming in and out also allow customers to view the products from the inside, getting a closer look, such as purchasing a house on-line, using a company and its web site like `http://bamboo.com`.

Some companies have already developed fragrance cartridges that would be installed on computers and release odors depending on items shown on the screen. The web site sends a message to the computer's chip to release the appropriate smell. Other future advances in interface design would do away with the keyboard and mouse with advances in speech recognition and natural language processing, resulting in "smart interfaces" [18].

3.4   Organizational Image and Message

Organizational image should play a role in the design of the user interface. For example, a theme park like Six Flags (`http://www.sixflags.com`) would have a more playful and fun web site and image than the CIA's more serious and informative web site (`http://www.cia.gov`). A designer would need to take this into account in developing the site so that text, sound, animation, etc. are consistent with the company's image.

Metaphors which "create a personality and inviting sense of place that is consistent with company and its missions" ([25], p. 64) affect the user's perception of the site as being attractive. The domain or content of a site affects a user's mental model of the that site and the user interaction with the system through the interface [29].

Another factor linked to the organization is the message. The message refers to the purpose or goal of the site. For example, an informative site, like the Texas A&M library homepage (`http://library.tamu.edu`) would tend to have different design characteristics from a commercial site, like eBay.com. Greater use of multimedia and interaction to sell a product or service would justify the added cost of these features since the business is trying to advertise products and attract and keep customers, a characteristic of a site called "stickiness." Yahoo and Excite (`http://www.excite.com`) have transformed their sites from search engines into portals with free services like email and personal home pages to attract customers.

There are two ways to classify sites based on message: top level domain names and goals [12]. Top level domain names would indicate that a site is a commercial one (.com), an educational institute (.edu), a non-profit organization (.org), etc. The second way is to classify a site by its goal, see Table 2. A commercial site would be more eye catching in comparison with a site designed for non-profit purposes or one that is created for informative reasons.

Table 2. Goals of web sites [12]

Goal	Organization
Sell products and services	Publishers, hotels, retail stores
Market products and services	Insurance companies, car dealers
Inform	Colleges, art galleries
Give access	Libraries, magazines
Provide services	Governments, public utilities
Discuss topics	Public interest groups, newsgroups
Care for community	Political groups, professional associations

4   Summary and Conclusion

Customers who visit web sites do not get the same shopping experience as those who visit the retail store physically. In order to make up for this disparity, a web site must have a well-designed interface so that consumers can experience the products and services on-line.

Internal and external factors that affect web site design were examined in this paper. These five factors are the user's mental model, level of expertise of the user, the user's learning style, richness of the media used, and the organizational image and message. A user's mental model would affect an on-line experience, as well as how knowledgeable the user is about the application or the domain of knowledge. How a user learns an application and interacts with the interface will also have an affect. Richness of the media of a web site, which would go hand-in-hand with the organization's image and message, would be an important factor that designers must take into account in developing the web site.

References

1. P. K. Kannan, A. Chang, A. B. Whinston. Marketing Information on the I-way, *Communications of the ACM*, 41, 3 (March 1998) 35-43.
2. "GVU's 8th WWW User Surveys," (November 16, 1997), `http://www.gvu.gatech.edu/user_surveys/survey-1997-10/`.
3. G. L. Lohse, and P. Spiller. Electronic Shopping: How Do Customer Interfaces Produce Sales on the Internet, *Communications of the ACM*, 41, 7 (July 1998) 81-87.
4. D. J. Mayhew. Principles and Guidelines in Software User Interface Design, Prentice Hall, Engelwood Cliffs, NJ (1992).
5. H. Barki, and J. Hartwick. Measuring User Participation, User Involvement, and User Attitude, *MIS Quarterly*, 18, 1 (March 1994) 59-82.
6. J. J. Parons and D. Oja. Computer Concepts, Course Technology, Cambridge, MA (1998).
7. J. H. Gerlach, and F. Kuo. Understanding Human-Computer Interaction for Information Systems Design, *MIS Quarterly*, 15, 4 (December 1991) 526-549.
8. J. Foley, and A. van Dam. Fundamentals of Interactive Computer Graphics, Addison-Wesley, Reading, MA (1982).
9. J. W. Satzinger, and L. Olfman. User Interface Consistency Across End-User Applications: The Effects on Mental Models, *Journal of Management Information Systems*, 14, 4 (Spring 1998) 167-193.
10. J. Grudin. The Case Against User Interface Consistency, *Communications of the ACM*, 32, 10 (October 1989) 11-64-1173.
11. S. Card, T. Moran, and A. Newell. The Psychology of Human-Computer Interaction, Lawrence Erlbuam Associates, Hillsdale, NJ (1983).
12. B. Shneiderman. Designing the User Interface: Strategies for Effective Human-Computer Interaction, Addison-Wesley, Reading, MA (1998).
13. E. Tufte. Visual Explanations, Graphics Press, Cheshire, CT, (1997).
14. N. Tractinsky and J. Meyer. Chartjunk or Goldgraph? Effects of Presentation Objectives and Content Desirability on Information Presentation, *MIS Quarterly*, 23, 3 (September 1999).
15. M. H. Ashcraft. Human Memory and Cognition, HarperCollins College Publishers, NY (1994).
16. J. E. Kendall, and Kenneth E. Kandall. Metaphors and Methodologies: Living Beyond the Systems Machine, *MIS Quarterly*, 17, 2 (June 1993) 149-171.
17. K. H. Madsen. A Guide to Metaphorical Design, *Communications of the ACM*, 37, 12 (December 1994) 57-62.
18. J. Raksin. Looking for a Humane Interface: Will Computers Ever Become Easy to Use?, *Communications of the ACM*, 40, 2 (February 1997) 81-101.
19. M. Hamlin. Knowledge and Skill Components of Expert and Novice Software Users, University of Washington, WA (1991).
20. D. J. Gillan, B. S. Fogas, S. Aberasturi, and S. Richards. Cognitive Ability and Computing Experience Influence Interpretation of Computer Metaphors, in *Proceedings of the Human Factors and Ergonomics Society 39th Annual Meeting* (1995) 243-247.
21. J. P. Ratner. Easing the Learning Curve of Novice Web Users, in *C. Forsythe, E. Grose, and J. Ratner (Eds.), Human Factors and Web Development*, Lawrence Erlbaum Associates, Mahwah, NJ (1998).

22. S. A. Davis, and R. Bostrom. Training End Users: An Experimental Investigation of the Roles of Computer Interface and Training Methods, *MIS Quarterly*, 17, 1 (March 1993) 61-85.

23. D. A. Kolb. Experiential Learning: Experience as the Source of Learning and Development Prentice Hall, Englewood Cliffs, NJ (1984).

24. R. P. Bostrom, L. Olfman, and M. K. Sein. The Importance of Leaning Style in End-User Training, *MIS Quarterly*, 14, 1 (March 1990) 101-119.

25. J. Eighmey. Profiling User Responses to Commercial Web Sites, *Journal of Advertising Research*, 37, 3 (May/June 1997) 59-66.

26. R. L. Daft, and R. H. Lengel. A Proposed Integration Among Organizational Information Requirements, Media Richness, and Structural Design, *Management Science*, 32, (1986) 554-571.

27. O. K. Ngwenyama, and A. S. Allen. Communication Richness in Electronic Mail: Critical Social Theory and the Contextuality of Meaning, *MIS Quarterly*, 21, 2 (June 1997) 145-167.

28. J. W. Palmer, and D. A. Griffith. An Emerging Model of Web Site Design for Marketing, *Communications of the ACM*, 41, 3 (March 1998) 44-51.

29. J. D. Wells. Coupling User and Source Domains in Interface Metaphors: A Comparative Analysis, Unpublished Ph.D. Dissertation, Texas A&M University (1999).

Applying Computer Semiotics to Hypertext Theory and the World Wide Web

Moritz Neumüller

Wirtschaftsuniversität Wien
1090 Wien, Austria
moritz@altavista.net

Abstract. This paper introduces a Semiotic Approach to Hypertext Theory. Having been applied to Informatics only in recent years, Semiotics promises a broader understanding of Hypertext as a structure of signs. The rapid visualization of the World Wide Web seems to justify this approach. Using the methodology of applied Semiotics and Graph Theory, the author analyzes the challenges and restrictions of Hypertexts in general and the WWW in particular.

1 Introduction

"Computer Semiotics" is a term that has been gaining currency in recent years. Established by Peter Bøgh Andersen [1,2], it may be an emergent field of inquiry, but as of yet there is little academic consensus as to its scope. The applicability of its methods on hypertext structures has not been fully explored, partly because the methods of each academic discipline facilitate certain ways of knowing and inhibit others. Furthermore, Anderson restricts himself from the full use of the Semiotic toolkit by positing his study as part of a *European tradition* of Semiotics (evolved from the science of Linguistics) as opposed to the *American tradition* (thus being part of a much more comprehensive philosophical system). He thereby maintains a polarization which, in Semiotics itself, has long been moderated by the theories of the well-known Italian Semiotician Umberto Eco [12]. Though the scholar, himself, claims to use a dialectical approach, his followers believe that he has created a third branch of Semiotics rather than a synthesis between the two existing schools [5]. Eco, who rejects the "untenable trichotomy" of signs, icons and indices [12, p. 178], has criticized the common simplification of Peirce's classification of signs. Based on Peirce's views, Eco offers another distinction between sign vehicles; this relates to the linguistic concept of tones, tokens and types. The third classification consists in the relationship to the interpretant. The combinations of the three axes form a comprehensive classification system.

Andersen, however, shares Eco's interest in Aesthetics. Aesthetics seems a useful tool in the exploration of hypertexts: Eco points out that the Semiotic Field includes the traditional field of Aesthetics because every Code (visual codes, cultural codes, natural languages, musical codes etc.) permits an esthetic usage of its signs [12,2]. Hypertext theory has long been aware of this issue, but

S. Reich and K.M. Anderson (Eds.): OHS/SC 2000, LNCS 1903, pp. 57–65, 2000.
© Springer-Verlag Berlin Heidelberg 2000

of course the scope has widened with the growing visualization of the Web. The effects of this technical sophistication on the appearance of the medium will be treated in a forthcoming publication [31].

2   The Semiotic Approach

After speaking of language as a system of signs, the Swiss linguist Ferdinand de Saussure points out that language is only the most important of these systems and that a science that studies the life of signs within society is well conceivable [38, pp. 30-35]. This new science would be a part of social psychology and consequently of general psychology:

> "I shall call it semiology (from the Greek semeîon). Semiology would show what constitutes signs, what laws govern them. Since the science does not yet exist, no one can say what it would be; but it has a right to existence, a place staked out in advance. Linguistics is only a part of the general science of semiology; the laws discovered by semiology will be applicable to linguistics, and the latter will circumscribe a well-defined area within the mass of anthropological facts."[1]

While this definition may have inspired most semiotic research of this century, it falls short because Saussure uses the term "sign" in an unacceptably exclusive way: for him, the sign is a composition of the signifier, /horse/[2] and the signified (our idea of a horse), whereas the referent (the real animal) does not interest the linguist. Thus, many subcategories of today's semiotic studies (such as zoosemiotics or even information theory) would have to remain outside the semiotic building that Saussure sketches.

Saussure made what is now a famous distinction between *langue* (language) and *parole* (speech). Langue refers to the system of rules and conventions which is independent of, and pre-exists, individual users whereas parole refers to its use in particular instances. Applying the notion to semiotic systems in general rather than simply to language, the distinction is one between the semiotic system and its usage in specific texts [7]. The system includes rules of use which constrain but do not determine usage (this is analogous to the distinction between competence and performance in [8]). According to the Saussurean distinction, in a semiotic system such as cinema, "any specific film is the speech of that underlying system of cinema language" [23, p. 3]. The coherence in cinema shots and hypermedia components as "self standing cores" [24] has recently been underlined: "As hypertext fragments are not physically contiguous elements but rather untied units, their temporal or spatial contiguity, due to the activation of

---

[1] [38], cited in [21, pp. 34-5].

[2] It has become an academic convention among scholars to use the forward-slash character when referring to signs. Thus, /horse/ means the written or spoken word "horse" (the signifier), as opposed to the meaning of the word (the signified) and the actual object, or animal (the referent). This "semiotic triangle" has been criticized byEco [12].

a link, actually constitutes a juxtaposition, a generative combination, a connection creating meaning..." [26]. To the traditional, Saussurean semiotician, what matters most are the underlying structures and rules of a semiotic system as a whole rather than specific performances or practices, which are merely instances of its use.

Besides Saussure, the key figure in the early development of semiotics was the American philosopher Charles Sanders Peirce (1839-1914):

"I am, as far as I know, a pioneer, or rather a backwoodsman, in the work of clearing and opening up what I call semiotic, that is, the doctrine of the essential nature and fundamental varieties of possible semiosis ..." [36, 5, p. 488].

This semiosis is "an action, an influence, which is, or involves, a cooperation of three subjects, such as a sign, its object, and its interpretant, this thri-relative influence not being in any way resolvable into action between pairs." [36, 5, p. 484]. While Saussure's system needs an active sender of signals to make the semiotic process work, Peirce's semiosis-trias can be applied to phenomena that have no sender, such as natural symptoms of an illness that can be detected and interpreted by a medic [7].

Charles William Morris (1901-1979) has successfully introduced semantics, syntactics and pragmatics as semiotic subdisciplines [30]. But while Morris' semiotic view seems to be predetermined by his behavourist parameters, he has defined a broadly recognized general division of signs into simple and complex signs, where the subdivisions of the former can be applied to the latter also [30, pp. 77-80].

Formal semiotics is difficult to disentangle from Structuralism, whose major exponents include Claude Lévi-Strauss in anthropology and Jacques Lacan in psychoanalysis. However, Deborah Cameron suggests that structuralism is merely "a method you can use" in semiotics [4, p. 25]. John Hartley describes structuralism as "an analytical or theoretical enterprise, dedicated to the systematic elaboration of the rules and constraints that work [...] to make the generation of meanings possible" [35, p. 302].

Semiotics began to become a major approach to media theory in the late 1960s, partly as a result of the work of Roland Barthes. The translation of his popular essays into English in 1957, followed in the 1970s and 1980s by many of his other writings, greatly increased scholarly awareness of this approach. Its adoption in Britain was influenced by its prominence in the work of the Centre for Contemporary Cultural Studies (CCCS) at the University of Birmingham whilst the centre was under the direction of the neo-Marxist sociologist Stuart Hall in the 1960s [19]; [6].

Contemporary social semiotics have moved beyond the structuralist concern with the internal relations of parts within a self-contained system [7]. Modern semiotic theory is sometimes allied with a Marxist approach which tends to stress the role of ideology [12, pp. 168-179].

3   Definitions and Frontiers of Computer Semiotics

Just like semiotics itself, computer semiotics is not so much an academic discipline as a theoretical approach. However, what seems to be a limitation at first glance, could turn out to be of great advantage for researchers in the field of computer semiotics and hypermedia theory alike: Not only do interdisciplinary approaches to the complex subject of sign recognition and interpretation have a greater potential to lead into this dense jungle of interrelating problems. They also could help hypermedia system developers to concentrate on the ultimate goal of their efforts: Usability. Usability has been shown to be dynamic and context dependent [25], especially in the context of Web Design [32]. Thus, usability is crucial and rather directly applicable to the navigational aspect of hypermedia, e.g. [43].

Studies on the spacial and taxonomic aspects of hypermedia, however, could implement the more abstract semiotic models. The most concise brief definition of semiotics is "the study of signs" (or "the theory of signs"). It involves the study of not only what we refer to as "signs" in everyday speech, but of anything that "stands for" something else. In a semiotic sense, signs include words, images, sounds, gestures and objects. Such signs are studied not in isolation but as part of semiotic "sign systems" (such as a medium or genre), [6]; [35, p. 281].

A fuller definition of semiotics is "the study of signs, signification and signifying systems" [41, p. 1]. Semioticians are concerned not only with communication, but also with the construction and maintenance of reality. For John Fiske and John Hartley the central concerns of semiotics are the relationship between a sign and its meaning and the way signs are combined into codes [15, p. 37]. Morris divided the subject into three branches: Semantics, or the meaning of signs deals with the relationship of signs to what they stand for. Syntactics (or syntax) analyze the structural relations between signs and pragmatics the ways in which signs are used and interpreted [29, p. 7-8]; [42, p. 15]; [33, p. 50]. Whereas this terminology has been actively integrated into Computer Science, the underlying concept of this division remains to be fully applied to this discipline and, especially the field of hypermedia studies.

To establish computer semiotics as a "discipline that studies the nature and use of computer-based signs," Andersen had to adopt Morris's definition of semiotics as "the science of signs" [2, p. 1]; [29, p. 1]. However, the term *science* seems to be misleading: as James Monaco points out, semiotics "is most definitely not a science in the sense that physics or biology is a science" [28, p. 140]. It is not a strictly empirical science, though some scholars do employ empirical methods. As a result, computer semiotics is essentially also a theoretical approach to communication in that its aim is to establish widely applicable principles, [14, p. 118].

The purpose of this paper is not to contribute to the old discussion whether or not Semiotics[3] is a scientific discipline or a field of studies. I will much rather

---

[3] Note that Saussure's term, "semiology" is sometimes used to refer to the Saussurean tradition, whilst "semiotics" sometimes refers to the Peircean tradition, but that nowadays the term "semiotics" is more likely to be used as an umbrella term to embrace the whole field [33, p. 14]; [12, p. 17].

use the inherited models and theories as tools and apply them in the context of hypermedia structures. In each phase, this exercise will depend on the consistency of terminology and clear theoretic guidelines.

It is fair to say that Semiotics represents a range of studies in art, literature, anthropology and the mass media rather than an independent academic discipline. Those involved in semiotics include linguists, philosophers, psychologists, sociologists, anthropologists, literary, aesthetic and media theorists, psychoanalysts and educationalists [7]. In the field of computer semiotics, the mentioned scholars have to join their forces with computer scientists, especially system developers, hypermedia designers and information theorists.

Beyond the most basic definition, there is considerable variation amongst leading semioticians as to what semiotics involves. It is not only concerned with (intentional) communication but also with our ascription of significance to anything in the world. As it was pointed out in the previous chapter, Semiotics has changed over time, since semioticians have sought to remedy weaknesses in early semiotic approaches. But this laboration also resulted in a transformation of terminology: even with the most basic semiotic terms there are multiple definitions. Consequently, anyone attempting semiotic analysis has to make clear which definitions are being applied and, if a particular semiotician's approach is being adopted, what the source of the approach is. The frontiers of Semiotics, however, remains as a general problem out of reach [12, p. 28].

4   Beyond Graph Theory

Hypermedia structures are often referred to as aggregations of nodes (containers of information) and links (dynamic connectors). However, hypermedia designers and theorists have tried repeatedly to move beyond the directed graph concept, which defines hypermedia structures as aggregations of nodes and links. [17] folds these primitives into node/link "composites." Other approaches (summed up in [22]) distribute link functions over a taxonomy of "intensional" and "extensional" links, or envision a type scheme for link anchors as well. Proceeding from this starting point, [22] offer a critical review of two issues in hypermedia design: transition ("navigation") and information mapping. Their approach to these issues is guided by Winograd and Flores's notion of "ontological design", a design philosophy that addresses human-machine interactions in terms of complex environments instead of simple, end-directed functionality and includes an analysis of the "architectonic space" of the screen. In their view, this architectonic space is contrasted by the "semantic space" of hypertexts, "since it is deeply connected to the production of meaning, interpretation, and other activities involving symbols." Therefore, they reject the node/link model as metaphor for hypermedia and present a weighting scheme for hypertext links, similar to that incorporated in Schneiderman's HyperTIES system [39]. Besides their search for OHP and the recent struggle to extend the abstract data model with the FOHM approach, the OHSWG wants to understand how information spaces work.

5   The Hypertextual Structures of the World Wide Web

What Risak [37] calls the "Global Agora" of the Internet has often been used as a major argument for the semiotic functioning of the Internet: "Stripped of the external trappings of wealth, power, beauty and social status, people tend to be judged in the Cyberspace of the Internet only by their ideas and their ability to get them across in terse, vigorous prose." [13], cited in [9]. The World Wide Web has become the most prominent tool in so-called Cyberspace.Whereas the simplicity of HTML seems to have facilitated the immense growth of the WWW, it at the same time the reason for its limited validity as a real hypermedia system. One important feature of hypertext/hypermedia systems[4] , as they were conceptualized before anybody had heard of the WWW [18], is link classification. With the limited hypertextual toolkit of the Hypertext Markup Language, this important semantic function is deprived of its power. From today's point of view, "ideal" hypermedia systems consist of more than the navigational domain [34, 27]. Links between two nodes (or *components* [18]) can be typed, bidirectional and multiple [11]. Furthermore, they allow taxonomic and spatial organization of information [27].

There is another crucial difference between a hypertext system and the Web. A hypertext system is generally created with a single purpose or theme in mind[5] There may be several authors and development of the system may occur over several years, but there is generally a sense of unity and similarity of style throughout the system. Pages on the Web, on the other hand, share no such unity of purpose or style. An author may link with almost any other page (etiquette and legal issues aside[6]) regardless of the differences between the source and target page in terms of genre, style, intended audience, or even language or culture [16]. In the Web, all links are navigational, because their common purpose is to make it easy for the reader to move from one place to another. The author provides the link for convenience, because the link target is a likely place for the reader to want to go from the source, or to suggest to the reader that something interesting or useful can be found by following the link.

> "In this sense, we could broadly divide all links into two classes, navigation, and recommended resources. Each link anchor represents a decision point for the reader; to follow the link to the target page or to continue reading the source page. [...] Information for the decision is found in the anchor that the author provides (e.g., an icon, or text), and in the context in which the anchor is found. One possible use of link types would be to label the link anchor with an icon or symbol[7], but there is legitimate concern that a proliferation of labels would make a page unreadable." [16, p. 101]

---

[4] In this case, the distinction between text-only systems and systems containing other media, such as images, sounds and video clip is less relevant.

[5] Some examples are biblical studies, study of classic texts, virtual libraries, hypertext novels [10].

[6] In fact, there are recent cases of restraining orders that would force Web Sites to remove all links to DeCSS, a free DVD decryption code.

[7] Note the usage of icons and symbols in the terminology of Graphic User Interfaces (GUI). They are hardly compartible to the semiotic concepts of these terms. [12,2]

This concern seems to be based on technical rather than a rhetorical problem: Color coded links have also been suggested, but they would interfere with the page designers' color choices. An alternative to visible labels on links would be to have a "pop-up" label identifying the link type appear when the reader rests the mouse cursor on the anchor. As mentioned above, the extensibility of the HTM Language is limited because it does not allow users to specify their own tags or attributes in order to parameterize or otherwise semantically qualify their data. Neither does it support the specification of deep structures needed to represent database schemas or object-oriented hierarchies. Finally, HTML does not contain language specifications that allow consuming applications to check data for structural validity on importation. Despite these limitations, the World Wide Web and HTML have taken the world by storm in just a few short years. But besides these mostly un-noted insufficiencies and lost opportunities, the ever-increasing demand for more flexibility in Internet systems has XML, the Extensible Markup Language, brewing on the horizon. XML is considered a powerful tool for data representation, storage, modeling, and interoperation [3, p. 5]. Furthermore, XLink seems to have a potential ability to serve as an export format for open hypermedia links [20].

6   Conclusion

Within the range of a short analysis, I have shown the applicability of Computer Semiotic to Hypertext Theory and the World Wide Web. Further studies on recent developments of the WWW, as well as the applicability of Aesthetics and Peirce's Semiotic concepts to Hypertext Theory seem necessary to deepen this approach.

References

1. Peter Bøgh Andersen. Towards an aesthetics of hypertext systems. A semiotic approach. In *Proceedings of the ECHT'90 European Conference on Hypertext*, Designing and Reading Hyperdocuments, pages 224–237, 1990.
2. Peter Bøgh Andersen. *The Theory of Computer Semiotics: Semiotic Approaches to Construction and Assessment of Computer Systems.* Cambridge Series on Human-Computer Interaction. Cambridge University Press, updated edition, 1997.
3. Jon Bosak. XML, Java, and the future of the Web. http://metalab.unc.edu/pub/sun-info/standards/xml/why/xmlapps.ps, 3 1997. Last visited Dec. 19, 1999.
4. Deborah Cameron. *Feminism and Linguistic Theory* . Macmillan, London, 2 edition, 1992.
5. Rocco Capozzi, editor. *Reading Eco.* Indiana University Press, Indianapolis, 1997.
6. Daniel Chandler. *The Act of Writing: A Media Theory Approach.* University of Wales, Aberystwyth, 1995.
7. Daniel Chandler. Semiotics for Beginners. http://www.argyroneta.com/s4b/sem01.htm, 1998. reviewed Aug. 26, 1999.
8. Noam Chomsky. Human language and other semiotic systems. *Semiotica*, 25(31-44), 1979.

9. Carlos Colón. Semiotics in cyberspace. `http://php.indiana.edu/~ccolon/Semiotics/ccolon3.html`, 4 1995. reviewed Jun 13th, 1999.
10. Paul Delany and George P. Landow, editors. *Hypermedia and Literary Studies*. MIT Press, Cambridge, Massachusetts, 4 edition, 1995.
11. S. DeRose. Expanding the Notion of Links. In *Proceedings of Hypertext 89*, pages 249–258, Baltimore, 1989. ACM, ACM Press.
12. Umberto Eco. *A Theory of Semiotics*. Macmillan, London, 1976.
13. Philip Elmer-DeWitt. Welcome to cyberspace: What is it? where is it? and how to get there? *Times Magazine*, Spring 1995.
14. John Fiske. *Introduction to Communication Studies*. Routledge, London, 1982.
15. John Fiske and John Hartley. *Reading Television*. Methuen, London, 1978.
16. Stephanie Haas and Erika Grams. Page and Link Classifications: Connecting Diverse Resources. *Digital Libraries*, pages 99–107, 1998.
17. F. Halasz. Reflections on NoteCards: Seven Issues for the Next Generation of Hypermedia Systems. *Communications of the ACM*, 31(7):836–855, 1988.
18. Frank Halasz and Mayer Schwarz. The Dexter Hypertext Model. In *Proceedings of the Hypertext Workshop*, pages 95–133. National Institute of Standards and Technology, Gaithersburg, Md., NIST Special Publication 500-178, 3 1990.
19. Stuart Hall. Encoding/decoding. In *Culture, Media, Language: Working Papers in Cultural Studies*, pages 128–38, London, 1979. Centre for Contemporary Cultural Studies, Hutchinson.
20. Brent Halsey and Kenneth M. Anderson. XLink and Open Hypermedia Systems. A Preliminary Investigation. In Shipman et al. [40], pages 212–213.
21. Robert E Innis, editor. *Semiotics: An Introductory Reader*. Hutchinson, London, 1986.
22. Nancy Kaplan and Stuart Moulthrop. Where No Mind Has Gone Before: Ontological Design for Virtual Spaces. In *ECHT '94 Proceedings*, pages 206–216. ACM, 1994.
23. Varda Langholz Leymore. *Hidden Myth: Structure and Symbolism in Advertising*. Basic Books, New York, 1975.
24. M.C. Luesebrink. The Moment in Hypertext: A brief Lexicon in Time. In *Proceedings of Hypertext'98*, pages 106–112, New York, 1998. ACM.
25. R. Mack and J. Nielson, editors. *Usability Inspection Methods*. Wiley, 1994.
26. Clara Mancini. From Cinematographic to Hypertext Narrative. In Shipman et al. [40], pages 236–237.
27. David E. Millard, Luc Moreau, Hugh C. Davis, and Siegfried Reich. FOHM: A Fundamental Open Hypertext Model for Investigating Interoperability between Hypertext Domains. In Shipman et al. [40], pages 93–102.
28. James Monaco. *How to Read a Film*. Oxford University Press, New York, 1981.
29. Charles Morris. *Foundations of the Theory of Signs*. University Press, Chicago, 1938/1970.
30. Charles Morris. *Signs, Language and Behavior*. Prentice-Hall, New York, 1946.
31. Moritz Neumüller. *The Changed Aesthetics of the Commercialized Internet*. PhD thesis, Wirtschaftsuniversität Wien, forthcoming 2000.
32. J. Nielson. Designing Web Usability. *InFormIT*, 2000. Indianapolis.
33. Wilfrid Nöth. *Handbook of Semiotics*. Indiana University Press, Bloomington, 1990.
34. Peter J. Nürnberg and J. J. Leggett. A vision for open hypermedia systems. *Journal of Digital Information (JoDI). Special Issue on Open Hypermedia Systems*, page 2, 1 1997.

35. Tim and others O'Sullivan. *Key Concepts in Communication and Cultural Studies.* Routledge, London, 1994.
36. Charles Sanders Peirce. *Collected Papers 1931-35.* Harvard University Press, Cambridge, 1935.
37. Veith Risak. Das Internet eine globale Agora. Vortrag an der Universität Innsbruck, 21.1.98, 19h, 1 1998.
38. Ferdinand de Saussure. *Course in General Linguistics.* Fontana/Collins, London, 1974.
39. B. Schneiderman. User Interface Design for the HyperTIES Electronic Encyclopedia. In *Hypertext '87 Papers*, pages 189–94. ACM Hypertext Conference (Chapel Hill NC), 11 1987.
40. Frank Shipman, Peter Nürnberg, David Hicks, and Kenneth Anderson, editors. *HT'00. Proceedings of the Eleventh ACM Conference on Hypertext and Hypermedia*, New York, May 30-June 4, San Antonio, TX 2000. ACM.
41. Robert Stam, Robert Burgoyne, and Sandy Flitterman-Lewis. *New Vocabularies in Film Semiotics: Structuralism, Post-Structuralism and Beyond.* Routledge, London, 1992.
42. Stephen Ullmann. *Semantics: An Introduction to the Science of Meaning.* Basil Blackwell, Oxford, 1972.
43. G. Uzilevsky. Ergosemiotics of user interface research and design: Foundations, objectives, potential. *Lecture Notes in Computer Science*, 876:1ff., 1994.

Musical Part Classification in Content Based Systems

Steven Blackburn and David De Roure

Department of Electronics and Computer Science
University of Southampton, UK
sg 97r@ecs.soton.ac.uk

Abstract. In the Fourth Open Hypermedia Systems workshop, the authors presented scenarios and a set of prototype tools to explore the application of open hypermedia principles, including content-based navigation, to temporal media. The purpose of the current paper is to provide an update on this work, focussing in particular on the ongoing work on content based navigation of music. We describe the development of a system which classifies the musical parts in MIDI files. This classification is then used to enhance content based retrieval and navigation of music. The effectiveness of the various approaches to classification is evaluated with respect to both stand-alone performance and when used in conjunction with a contour database.

1 Introduction

In the paper "Amphion: Open Hypermedia Applied to Temporal Media" [2] in the Fourth Open Hypermedia Systems workshop, we presented scenarios and a set of prototype tools to explore the application of open hypermedia principles to temporal media (see also [1]). As well as hypermedia linking based on time positions and intervals, our interest continues to be in the navigation of a multimedia information space using content-based navigation; i.e. we move from multimedia content to features of that content to enhance our navigational hypermedia system. Our case study is musical information, which provides a particularly rich set of representations with which to work.

Of the many possible musical features, we have chosen melodic pitch contours as our case study. While other systems using pitch contours are aimed primarily at content based retrieval, we have addressed the particular requirements of an interactive content based navigation system. For example, the response time needs to be within acceptable bounds, so we have chosen to employ query expansion and constant-time lookup rather than fuzzy matching mechanisms.

The primary motivation for the study presented here is that informal empirical work has demonstrated a need to be able to refine our searches; e.g. we may have a query which is known to be a fragment of melody, and we wish to match this against other melodies and not all parts. This requirement is distinct from identifying instruments, which can sometimes be achieved from available

S. Reich and K.M. Anderson (Eds.): OHS/SC 2000, LNCS 1903, pp. 66–76, 2000.
© Springer-Verlag Berlin Heidelberg 2000

meta-data anyway. Analogous situations occur in other content based navigation domains such as images, where we wish to compare images of a similar type.

The main part of this paper addresses the classification problem, why it is desirable and our methodology for investigating it, using MIDI as a case study. We have employed the MIDI format as a representation from which to extract the features which in turn are used to determine the classification. MIDI files store several independent but synchronised channels each typically representing one instrument and carrying note-on and note-off information; each channel may have many notes sounding at once. We can convert digital audio to MIDI by available pitch tracking techniques, and the representations can be aligned via time-stamps and position pointers. MIDI versions of material may be available directly from the production process (synchronized with digital audio) or they may be created independently.

A secondary motivation for this study has arisen in the course of the research. Initially we regarded multimedia content as containing locations and objects to which data in a link database might refer. We now propose another view: that multimedia content can itself be regarded as a linkbase. For example, given a fragment of music played on one instrument, a MIDI file enables us to find associated fragments played by other instruments, perhaps associated text, and indeed timing information which we can use to reference synchronised media such as video.

In order to enhance our prototype system and to explore "content as link-base", we have identified a need to classify channels of MIDI data in terms of the role they have in the music. This is an instance of a general approach where one could take compound multimedia entities and classify their sub-components in order to provide meaningful navigation in that space — we believe similar issues would arise with other entities that entwine various forms of information and a coordinate system, such as digital maps.

2   Classification

Classification can improve content based retrieval systems by decreasing the amount of noise in the database. Taking retrieval of music as an example, there is little point in indexing content which is not going to be the subject of subsequent searches. Removing all but the lead (melody) line should improve the matching ability of query by humming systems.

Classification has uses in both temporal and content based navigation, although one could argue that the temporal case is a form of the latter. The classi-fication could be used as a parameter to link resolution. This enables temporal links to be authored on particular parts of the music; e.g. from 20 seconds to 30 seconds of the bass line. Similarly, content based navigation would allow an anchor to take the form of "lead lines that sound like this".

There has been little work on classifying music to assist with search, with Uitdenbogerd and Zobel [5] being notable exceptions. They tested several simple algorithms for producing a monophonic melody from a polyphonic MIDI file. A small user trial suggested that always using the top note gave acceptable results for many cases. However, this approach is obviously flawed if the melody is not the highest pitch being played.

The MIDI databases developed by Ghias et al [3], McNab [4] and Blackburn [1] make use of the General MIDI standard which defines MIDI channel 10 to be dedicated to drums. Assuming that all MIDI files adhere to the standard, which the majority do, rhythm tracks can be identified with a high degree of certainty and not added to the database.

Classification involves extracting a set of features, referred to as a feature vector, from each channel. Two feature vectors can be compared by determining the Euclidean distance between them. The Euclidean distance is found by summing the squares of the difference between each element in a vector and then taking the square root. Another function evaluates the so-called "city block" distance, which simply uses the mean difference. It is referred to as the city block metric due to the shape of the boundaries in the feature space, a diamond.

3   Part Types

For our experiments we use four musical part classes, according to how a layman listener is likely to identify each part. This approach avoids the use of any genre specific terminology and so is more generally applicable. The classifications used are: accompaniment; bass; drums / rhythm and lead.

The use of a classification to describe irrelevant parts was considered but it was decided that it would simply introduce noise into the classifiers, making identification more difficult. Having a separate "interesting / confidence" measure would be more relevant.

4   Compiling the Training Data

Classifiers require a set of files by which to evaluate their performance, and many require the same data to implement the classifier.

We selected 100 files at random from a collection of 7500 MIDI files, covering a variety of genres, found on the Internet. If it consisted solely of popular music then certain rules may be adhered to. The variable quality and variety of musical styles makes classification that much harder, but the result should be a more generally applicable classifier. The part classification for each channel was marked up manually and then extracted to individual MIDI files (so there was only one channel per MIDI file).

This resulted in a total of 535 classified musical parts: 152 accompaniment; 103 bass; 144 drums and 136 lead.

5   Musical Features

A variety of features are extracted from each training channel. These are:

- The number of notes per second
- The number of chords per second
- The pitch of notes (lowest, highest and the mean average)
- The number of pitch classes used in the channel (ie: C, C#, D, E, etc)
- Pitch classes used
- Pitch class entropy
- The length of notes (lowest, highest and mean average)
- Number of semitones between notes (lowest, highest and mean average)
- The polyphony of the channel (lowest, highest and mean average)
- How repetitive the channel is
- The number of the MIDI channel
- The instrument patches used

Repetitiveness is a number based on how many distinct n-grams there are in the primary pitch contour [1] of the channel. This is the number of distinct n-grams, represented as a percentage of the total number of pitch directions in the channel.

All of these features are normalised to a value between 0 and 1, as this is improves the performance of neural networks for classification. It also improves the effectiveness of other classification systems and makes calculation of a probability straightforward.

6   Approaches to Classification

This section discusses the three methods of classification that we have investigated.

6.1   A Simplistic Statistical Approach

We first take the simple approach of averaging each of the features for all of the channels of a common part classification. The result is four feature vectors which describe the features common to each class type.

A feature vector to be classified is compared with each of these class templates. The closest match is determined to be the classification. Although not particularly scientific, this technique can be implemented quickly and provides a benchmark by which to evaluate the more complex approaches.

6.2   Ad-Hoc Classification

The ad-hoc classifier is based on directly coding the knowledge of a musician. The classifier notes properties in a channel that would make it more or less likely to be a particular part. A probability can then be assigned to each part and the most likely chosen.

As previously mentioned, General MIDI (GM) files assign channel 10 to drums. In addition to this, there are some GM instrument numbers that are usually used for rhythm channels (i.e. timpani, taiko drum, melodic tom, synth drum, reverse cymbal and wood block). A channel exhibiting these properties is assumed to be drums. The probability of other tracks being drums is taken to be 70% of the repetitiveness measure.

A channel is more likely to be accompaniment if it only uses notes which are no more than one octave either side of middle C and is likely to be polyphonic. Bass parts tend to use the two octaves below accompaniment and is quite repetitive (a measure greater than 0.6). Bass is very likely to be monophonic and is heavily penalised if not. Lead parts often use the two octaves above middle C and is also likely to be monophonic. It is penalised for being repetitive.

The particular technique we employ in determining the probability has similar properties to comparing a feature vector, so the different distance metrics may produce different results. However, the values used in the evaluation are very coarse, so are unlikely to differ.

6.3   K-Nearest Neighbour

The k-nearest neighbour (K-NN) classification method is, theoretically at least, the most accurate one considered here. The entire training set of feature vectors is stored, along with their classification. Classification finds the example vector that best matches the unclassified one and returns the classification of that example vector.

Due to the relatively small size of the training set (hundreds instead of thousands) it was feasible to keep the entire set in memory. Searching against the set should result in a noticeable performance hit (compared to the previous two methods). No improvements to performance were considered here as accuracy was our primary concern.

7   Evaluation

We evaluate the various approaches. Primarily for accuracy, as the algorithms are not optimised for speed, although speed is interesting to note.

7.1   Comparison of Accuracy

The manual classification was compared against that given by each classification method (see Table 1). The results are broken down to identify which method performs best for each part type. The mismatches were then broken down, to show where each method gets confused — when a classification is wrong, what is it mistaken for. Both Euclidean and "city block" distance metrics were evaluated.

The K-NN classifier used 90% of the training set, so that the remaining 10% of the set could be used to evaluate its performance, allowing a more direct comparison with the other methods.

Simple Template. The statistical templates were tested against the set of channels used to calculate the templates. The results are shown in Table 2.

Table 1. Overall classifier accuracy

Classifier	Euclidean	City block
Statistical	58.88%	66.17%
Ad-hoc	71.21%	71.21%
K-NN	67.27%	72.73%

Table 2. Breakdown of statistical template classification

Part	Correct		Class when wrong	
	Euclidean	City Block	Euclidean	City Block
Acc	40.70%	53.29%	22.18%	27.62%
Bass	76.70%	80.58%	32.73%	34.81%
Drums	60.42%	62.50%	4.55%	3.87%
Lead	63.97%	73.53%	34.55%	33.70%
Overall	58.88%	66.17%		

Ad-hoc Classification. The ad-hoc classification was tested against the marked up set of channels. The results are shown in Table 3.

Table 3. Breakdown of ad-hoc classification

Part	Correct		Class when wrong	
	Euclidean	City Block	Euclidean	City Block
Acc	59.21%	59.21%	40.91%	40.91%
Bass	80.58%	80.58%	24.03%	24.03%
Drums	94.44%	94.44%	1.30%	1.30%
Lead	52.94%	52.94%	33.77%	33.77%
Overall	71.21%	71.21%		

K-Nearest Neighbour. The k-nearest neighbour method was only tested with examples not used in the feature vector table. This allows a more direct comparison with the simple template approach, although the test set is only a subset of that used for evaluating the other methods. The results are shown in Table 4.

7.2   Comparison of Speed

Timing analysis was performed by reading the set of MIDI files, used to train the classifiers, into memory. These files were then classified as many times as

Table 4. Breakdown of k-nearest neighbour classification

Part	Correct		Class when wrong	
	Eucl.	City	Eucl.	City
Acc	40.00%	53.33%	33.33%	46.67%
Bass	84.62%	84.62%	11.11%	6.67%
Drums	90.00%	90.00%	5.56%	6.67%
Lead	64.71%	70.73%	50.00%	40.00%
Overall	67.27%	72.73%		

possible in ten minutes. Tests were completed on a single user 500 MHz Pentium III running Windows NT 4. Note that K-nearest classification is not using an optimised algorithm. The results, given in Table 5, show that the k-nearest neighbour classifier is not noticeably slower than the statistical approach.

Table 5. Comparison of classifier execution time

Classifier	Euclidean	City block
Statistical	50.14 ms	50.65 ms
Ad-hoc	49.75 ms	49.83 ms
K-NN	54.90 ms	53.42 ms

7.3   Evaluation of Data Filtering on the Database

One of the reasons for classifying the channels was to improve the quality of data in a musical database. We evaluated this by building a contour database consisting of a collection of 800 MIDI files and the training set. The database was of the type described in [1] and used an atomic unit of 14 pitch directions. Secondary contours were used to both build and query the database.

Only accompaniment and lead parts were added. Ideally, only lead parts would be added, but the classification systems easily confuse lead with accompaniment, so both lead and accompaniment parts are used. The city block metric gave the best performance, so this was the one used for all classifiers. The resulting performance, considering three part classifications, is given in the Table 6.

Database queries were simulated by extracting a segment of a lead part from the training set, as the manual classification represents a realistic query. The set queries used was 500 MIDI files, each 10 seconds long, although 57 of the files had pitch contours less than 12 pitch directions and so ignored, to represent a sensible query. The rank of the file from which the query (the target file) is taken is noted, along with the total number of matches found. The test was run

Table 6. Comparison of classifer accuracy when considering three classes

Classifier	Performance
Statistical	82.24%
Ad-hoc	88.97%
K-NN	90.91%

with varying numbers of error, d, accounted for in the query. The errors are in addition to those that the pitch contour representation does not allow for (ie: more than changes in the exact pitch). Note that errors were not simulated in the query and so assumes exact pitch contour recall on behalf of the user.

The mode ranking found in all the tests was 1. This does not tell the whole story as, in the case of $d = 2$, this accounts for less than 35% of the queries. The graphs (Fig. 1, Fig. 2 and Fig. 3) show that, for $d = 0$, 90% of queries will return the target file in the top 8 files, whether a classifier is used or not. Classification does improve matching although this tends to reduce the number of false positives, rather than having a large impact on the ranking of common queries.

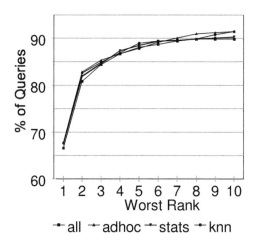

Fig. 1. Response when using exact matching $(d = 0)$

Tables 7, 8 and 9 show the average (mean) recall accuracy, taking into account any extreme results. It can be seen that the ad-hoc classifier gives consistently good average results, although the benefits of filtering only become apparent when matching allowing for larger errors.

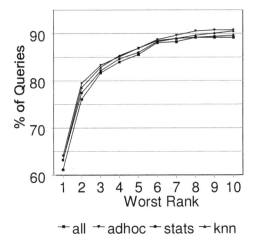

Fig. 2. Response when allowing for one error $(d = 1)$

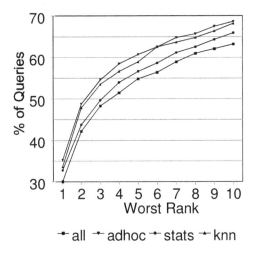

Fig. 3. Response when allowing for two error $(d = 2)$

Table 7. Ranking of targets using exact matching

Classifier	Mean rank	Mean set size
None	13.8059	46.9097
Statistical	11.3747	39.2460
Ad-hoc	10.1041	33.5056
K-NN	10.4244	35.7246

Table 8. Ranking of targets allowing for one error in the query

Classifier	Mean rank	Mean set size
None	16.5598	68.0316
Statistical	13.8623	59.8126
Ad-hoc	12.1174	50.8440
K-NN	12.5102	53.9052

Table 9. Ranking of targets allowing for two errors in the query

Classifier	Mean rank	Mean set size
None	46.605	334.461
Statistical	39.8442	319.779
Ad-hoc	32.6343	288.009
K-NN	33.7607	295.641

8   Conclusions and Future Work

We have shown the application of alternative classification techniques to improve our content-based navigation system. Some techniques are purely statistical while others attempt to bring to bear some knowledge of the nature of the content. It can be seen that classification of musical part does improve matching, more notably when performing approximate queries. The ad-hoc method appears to work best and is also the fastest.

Reliable classification can be used to enhance a content based navigation system by allowing more precise (but still general) links to be authored. For example: "bass lines like this one are linked to some information". We have yet to evaluate the recall accuracy of a link database when used in conjunction with part filtering. It should prove to be at least as useful as shown here, due to the fact that only a subset of the music is stored. The accuracy of the classifiers is shown to be extremely good when considering three types of musical part, as much as 90%. Other classifiers may perform better on the difficult problem of differentiating between accompaniment and lead. Neural networks are one method we plan to investigate, along with a hybrid classifier that uses a combination of the most accurate features of the other methods.

We have exercised the notion of "content as linkbase" in an experiment using MIDI files which contain textual representation of lyrics, enabling us to map from contour to text (and thence tools for linking with text). Future work includes building on the classification system to map from one part to another; e.g. given a chord sequence, what do we know about the corresponding bass lines within a given context? A metric for one of the characteristics of musical parts, repetitiveness, was obtained as a side effect of the content-processing implemented to compute the contour database, an aspect we hope to explore in future work.

This demonstrates a general point: content-based navigation involves features; once we have features, we have the basis for classification of components of content and of the content itself (e.g. classification of musical genre). Classification improves the effectiveness of searches; furthermore, by classifying in advance, we reduce computation at query time.

Acknowledgements. We would like to thank Pete Elsdon for his input into the ad-hoc classifier. This work was partially funded by EPSRC QuIC.

References

1. S. Blackburn and D. De Roure. A tool for content based navigation of music. In *Proc. ACM Multimedia '98*, pages 361–368, 1998.
2. D. De Roure and S. Blackburn. Amphion: Open hypermedia applied to temporal media. In *Proc. 4th Open Hypermedia Workshop*, pages 27–32, 1998.
3. A. Ghias, J. Logan, D. Chamberlin, and B. C. Smith. Query by humming - musical information retrieval in an audio database. In *Proc. Multimedia '95*, pages 231–236, San Francisco, California, November 1995.
4. R. J. McNab, L. A. Smith, I. H. Witten, C. L. Henderson, and S. J. Cunningham. Towards the digital music library: Tune retrieval from acoustic input. In *Proc. DL'96*, pages 11–18, 1996.
5. A. L. Uitdenbogerd and J. Zobel. Manipulation of music for melody matching. In *Proc. ACM Multimedia '98*, pages 235–240, 1998.

From Metadata to Links

Graham Moore[1,2] and Luc Moreau[2]

[1] STEP UK, UK, gdm@stepuk.com
[2] Department of Electronics and Computer Science
University of Southampton, UK, L.Moreau@ecs.soton.ac.uk

Abstract. Metadata systems are considered to be a powerful and generalised mechanism for extending the properties that constitute an object and for facilitating access to information. However, there is another mechanism, linking, that can also be considered as having the ability to extend the properties of an object and provide systems and users with more useful means of accessing information. In this paper, we represent both metadata and linking as abstract models and show how the metadata model may be expressed in terms of the linking mechanism. Then we discuss the benefits of the more general model of linking.

1   Introduction

Metadata systems exist for two primary reasons. Firstly, they provide a generic mechanism for the extension of an object within a system. This object need not be confined to be a document, as is classically associated with metadata systems, but should be considered to be any object [2]. The metadata mechanism works by associating a name and value pair with an object. This provides the ability to extend the attributes of an object without needing to change the object itself.

Secondly, metadata is used for grouping, sorting and providing access to objects in a system. In this scenario the metadata system can be used to provide an "Information Retrieval" service. For example, it would be possible to retrieve all objects that have a metadata value called 'date' where the value of 'date' is before '240300'.

Linking also provides us with the ability to associate objects and convey the semantics of why we associate particular objects together. Using an open-hypertext linking model [7] we can encapsulate the association information independently of the associated objects. We can search and query those data structures similarly as we do with metadata.

There are obvious similarities between links and metadata. The purpose of this paper is to investigate such similarities and better our understanding of these two models. Our first thesis is that open-linking models can express metadata functionalities and more.

Unlike the metadata model the linking model is symmetric. This is because all anchors in a link have similar "weights" and are each identified by their role. In a link, depending on a perspective[1], any anchor can be regarded as associated

---
[1] Note that we do *not* use the technical meaning of perspective [3].

S. Reich and K.M. Anderson (Eds.): OHS/SC 2000, LNCS 1903, pp. 77–86, 2000.
© Springer-Verlag Berlin Heidelberg 2000

with any other anchor. Such an association indicates the presence of information related to an object, which is precisely the idea conveyed by metadata. Thus, our second thesis is that metadata can be expressed as a perspective on typed links.

2   From Metadata to Linking

The power of an information retrieval system can be measured by how versatile the retrieval mechanism is and how explicitly it conveys the intended semantics of the user or process that built the system. In this section we present our perception of the fundamental properties of both metadata and linking systems and express them in terms of a formal model. By doing so we can decipher the power of each system and ultimately express one in terms of the other.

In this paper we perform five steps to express a metadata model in terms of an open linking model. The five steps are:

1. We define a model of metadata.
2. We summarise the simple linking model formalised in [5].
3. We show how to define the metadata model in terms of the simple linking approach. This is an enabling step towards a richer structure but we also discuss the properties of this definition.
4. We generalise the simple linking model into a notion of typed links, similar to the OHP-Nav notion of link [7].
5. We define the metadata model in terms of typed links.

The latter definition preserves the original abilities of the metadata model yet extends the power through the use of additional properties, such as role identification and association typing that are found in the linking model.

2.1   A Model for Metadata

In this section we define metadata systems, or the role of metadata, allowing:

1. New information to be associated with an object without the need to edit that object in any way.
2. Objects to be managed (grouped, sorted, navigated to) by the content of the associated metadata.

The *traditional view* of metadata is in the form of a pair, composed of an attribute and a literal value. This pair alone is inadequate to describe a metadata association. The model is completed with the introduction of the object with which the metadata pair is being associated.

In order to identify and manipulate the different components involved in a metadata system, we formalise its data model. In Figure 1, we consider a finite set of objects, where each object has the potential to be extended by metadata. Each object is identified by a unique name, belonging to the set of names *Name*. A naming function maintains the mapping between names and objects: in practical terms, given a object name, a naming function ρ is able to return the associated object.

We slightly extend the traditional view by regarding a metadata pair as composed of a metadata field and metadata name, respectively belonging to sets *Field* and *Name*. The name component of the metadata pair maps to an object. The intended meaning is that the value of this field is this object.

By defining the name aspect in a metadata pair, we are encouraging the view that metadata systems do not introduce special kinds of values but utilises the existing named object mechanism. Finally, the intent of a metadata system is to associate metadata pairs with objects. We formalise this notion by introducing a metadata association, composed of an object name and a metadata pair.

$$
\begin{array}{ll}
N \in Name = \{N_1, N_2, \ldots\} & (Object\ Name) \\
o \in Object = \{O_1, O_2, \ldots\} & (Object) \\
\rho \in Env = Name \rightarrow_f Object & (Naming\ Function) \\
\\
F \in Field = \{F_1, F_2, \ldots\} & (Metadata\ Field) \\
p \in Pair = Field \times Name & (Metadata\ Pair) \\
assoc \in Assoc = Name \times Pair & (Metadata\ Association)
\end{array}
$$

Notation:
$$
assoc := \langle N, p \rangle \\
p := \langle F, N \rangle
$$

Fig. 1. The metadata model

Now follows an example based on the abstract model defined in Figure 1. Using this example we then discuss the problems with this metadata model.

Example 1. In the following metadata representation,

$$\langle \texttt{"doc1"}, \langle \texttt{"author"}, \texttt{"graham"} \rangle \rangle,$$

`"author"` is a field, `"graham"` is the name of an object, and `"doc1"` is the name of an object (here representing a document in a document management system).

Information retrieval systems are more powerful the more they capture, express and allow for searching of the semantics that relate information. The more precise the semantics the more accurate grouping and associations can be. We now discuss the semantics expressed by the metadata model.

This metadata model requires that the semantic is implied by the 'reader', where the 'reader' may be a human or computer system. The metadata association could be read as:

$$\textit{"graham" is the author of "doc1"} \tag{1}$$

Thus the human or computer may then express:

$$\textit{"doc1" is the document that was authored by "graham"} \tag{2}$$

Sentence (2) can only be infered through the assumption that the name "doc1" maps to a document. We have defined our metadata model such that metadata can be associated with any object and not just documents. Given this we are unable to infer (2), unless we have some other mechanism for finding out the type of the object.

One such mechanism may be to access the object, but this breaks the metadata model where metadata is expressed and encapsulated independently of the object. In this case we do not have an encapsulation of the association semantics as we need to 'touch' the object in order to complete parts of the metadata structure.

In the interpretation we can see two other pieces of information that a system could query, sort on or display to the user. The two pieces of information provided are 'authored by' and 'document', respectively, the reason for the association of these objects and the role of one of the objects within the association. This infered information is not part of the metadata model, making it explicit would allows us to access and process it. □

While metadata initially appears to be a generic model for defining data associations with meaning, it transpires that the actual semantics of the metadata model are weak. Ultimately we have to question the view of metadata as a generalised association mechanism, for we have seen how assumptions lead to particular interpretation of the semantics.

2.2   Model for Simple Links

In this section we introduce the Simple Linking Model. This model will be used when we define the metadata model in terms of Linking.

In Figure 2, we present the key aspects of the simple link model, as defined in [5]. We assume that objects are identified by names, and that there is a mapping function, associating each name with an object. A link is a first-class entity, separate from objects, which we define as a pair of anchors. Anchors can be considered as handles onto the objects being associated by the link, thus they are simply defined in terms of a name.

$$
\begin{aligned}
N \in Name &= \{N_1, N_2, \ldots\} & &(Object\ Name) \\
o \in Object &= \{O_1, O_2, \ldots\} & &(Object) \\
\rho \in Env &= Name \rightarrow_f Object & &(Naming\ Function) \\
L \in Link &= Anchor \times Anchor & &(Link) \\
A \in Anchor &= Name & &(Link\ Anchor)
\end{aligned}
$$

Fig. 2. Simple Linking model

We can see that the association created by a simple link is symmetric; we will use this property in the following section.

2.3   From Metadata to Simple Links

The traditional metadata model is "readable" in one direction only and prohibits a meaningful inverse interpretation. Situations arise where it is unclear which object is the metadata and which is the data; within one association both objects could play both roles. The metadata model is not rich enough to do this but the linking model is.

In this section we proceed with the definition of the metadata model in terms of the simple linking model described in Section 2.2. The motivation for doing this is that we want to make the metadata model symmetric so that:

- The model is generic in that metadata is the combination of objects, symmetric associations and perspective.
- We can further extend it to use typed links, thus explicitly capturing the full semantics of the association.

We consider the following revised definition of the naming function:

$$Pair \subseteq Object$$
$$\rho \in Env = Name \rightarrow_f Object$$

A metadata association *assoc* of the form $\langle N, p \rangle$ can be expressed in the simple linking model by the pair $\langle N, N_p \rangle$ where N_p is a new name such that

$$\rho(N_p) = p.$$

Fig. 3. The Metadata to Linking Transformation

Figure 3 defines how the asymmetric metadata model may be transformed into the symmetric linking model. The key step is to treat the metadata pair as an identifiable object within the system. Thus, metadata pairs are defined as being a subclass of *Object*. This then allows an anchor, via its name, to be mapped using the standard naming function to a metadata pair.

Example 2. If "doc1" is the name denoting a document, and "p" the name denoting a pair $\langle$"author", "graham"$\rangle$, then $\langle$"doc1", "p"$\rangle$, is the representation of the metadata seen in Example 1 in terms of a simple link. □

This definition is a step towards a model of typed links that can explicitly expose the full semantics of an association. However, this intermediate model is worth discussing because of the following properties:

1. Now that the metadata pair is an object, it is necessary to understand the internal structure of this object in order to access and interpret the metadata. In the same way that the previous example required us to 'touch' the object to find out it was a document this model requires us to fetch and interrogate an object in order to discover the metadata field and object value name.
2. Also similar to the metadata model, the semantics for the association are embedded within an object as opposed to being encapsulated within the association itself.
3. The third issue with this model is that it provides no mechanism for expressing the meaning of the association and of *all* components in the association (e.g, here the role of "document" is not explicit).

This simple linking model does not provide greater expressiveness than the metadata model and additionally requires us to fetch and examine an object. However, moving from an asymmetric to a symmetric model enables us to define the metadata model in terms of typed links, which we do in the following section.

2.4   Model for Typed Links

Having now developed a symmetric model from the asymmetric metadata model we have seen that there is more work to be done. In this section we extend the simple linking model to have typed links. Later we will see that by using this model we can fully define the semantics of the association and the roles of the anchors within it.

The extension of the linking model introduces the ability to specify the semantics that describe the reason for associating objects together and allow for the role within the link of each participating anchor to be defined.

In Figure 4, we generalise the notion of simple links by the notion of typed link. A typed link is a triple formed of a type and two anchors. Each anchor contains the name of an object and its role in the link. For example, a directional link for navigation may give the role of source and destination to the two anchors in the link.

$$
\begin{aligned}
ta &\in TypedLink = Type \times Anchor \times Anchor \quad (Typed\ Link) \\
a &\in Anchor = Name \times Role \qquad\qquad\quad (Anchor\ with\ Role\ Type) \\
r &\in Role = \{R_1, R_2, \ldots\} \qquad\qquad\quad (Role) \\
t &\in Type = \{T_1, T_2, \ldots\} \qquad\qquad\quad (Link\ Type)
\end{aligned}
$$

Fig. 4. The Typed Link Model

We have introduced the typed linking model such that we can fully convey the intended semantics that caused these objects to be associated. Now that we have such a mechanism our systems can provide more refined object-retrieval as there is valuable information that can be processed. The next stage is to show how the metadata model can be mapped into this one, thus giving the new metadata system the equivalent power of this typed linking model.

2.5   From Metadata to Typed Links

We have shown how the metadata model is not as general as first thought and that the semantics it communicates are not rich enough. Therefore the value of an information system built on top of such a mechanism is questionable. It should be noted that we do not discard the value of this kind of system, we are merely illustrating that more valuable semantics can be added while providing an equivalent metadata model.

In Figure 5, we construct a typed association from three of the components of a metadata association, namely a name N, a field F and its associated name N'. The transformation requires us to identify two further components: T the type of the association and R^N the role of N in the association of type T. They may be used to construct an instance of typed link, explicitly containing the name N and N' and the field F, which were part of the initial metadata association.

Let us consider a metadata association *assoc* of the form $\langle N, p \rangle$, with p of the form $\langle F, N' \rangle$.
Let R^N be the role of the object named N in an association of type T.
We can construct an instance of *TypedLink* representing *assoc* as follows:

$$\langle \langle N, R^N \rangle, \ \langle N', F \rangle, \ T \rangle.$$

Fig. 5. The Metadata to Typed Link Transformation

The key aspect about the definition in Figure 5 is that the metadata model of Figure 1 is not rich enough to populate the typed link model, yet the typed link is powerful enough to express all the aspects of the metadata model. Given this, information systems could define metadata in terms of linking and then fill in the undefined semantics to provide a richer model. The example below illustrates a metadata to linking transition.

Example 3. Let us reconsider the metadata introduced in Example 1.

$$\langle \texttt{"doc1"}, \langle \texttt{"author"}, \texttt{"graham"} \rangle \rangle$$

We can transform this example into the typed link model as shown below. Note, we have left question marks where the metadata model is insufficient to fully utilise the typed link model.

$$\langle \langle \texttt{"doc1"}, ? \rangle, \langle \texttt{"graham"}, \texttt{"author"} \rangle, ? \rangle.$$

Finally, we instantiate the missing semantics. We now have a model that encompasses what was originally expressed but has additionally provided richer association semantics.

$$\langle\langle\texttt{"doc1"},\texttt{"document"}\rangle,\langle\texttt{"graham"},\texttt{"author"}\rangle,\texttt{"DocumentAuthoredBy"}\rangle$$

Figure 6 shows a graphical representation of the previous link, the roles it contains and its type. □

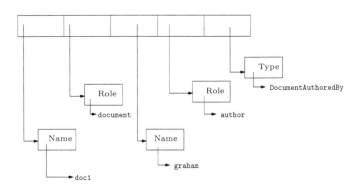

Fig. 6. Metadata as Typed Link

The next example illustrates that due to symmetry of the linking paradigm we can now consider metadata to be typed links and perspective.

Example 4. In the following link example the object whose name is `"luc"` plays several roles in different associations. Depending on a given perspective the object named `"luc"` can be considered as metadata to the object named `"graham"` and the object named `"doc2"`.

$$\langle\langle\texttt{"doc2"},\texttt{"document"}\rangle,\langle\texttt{"luc"},\texttt{"author"}\rangle,\texttt{"DocumentAuthoredBy"}\rangle$$
$$\langle\langle\texttt{"graham"},\texttt{"supervisee"}\rangle,\langle\texttt{"luc"},\texttt{"supervisor"}\rangle,\texttt{"Supervises"}\rangle \;\square$$

This section has shown how the metadata model can be defined in terms of typed links and that this step leads to a more expressive model. Secondly, we have shown by the use of examples how metadata can be viewed as typed links and perspective.

3   Discussion and Related Work

The Open Hypermedia Systems Working Group (OHSWG) was formed to coordinate the efforts of the community in creating standards that would address interoperability issues. Among the output of this working group, we find the

Open Hypermedia Protocol (OHP). In particular, OHP [7] defines a data model, identifying all the data structures necessary to represent information about "hyper links" and associated primitives. Furthermore, OHP aims at providing a medium to promote interoperability between hypertext domains. From the data model specified by OHP, a fundamental open hypertext model (FOHM) [4] was formally defined and showed to support interoperability.

In this paper, we have assumed the existence of a linking data model to express the notion of metadata. We can show that this model is entirely compatible with the FOHM model. Indeed, we observe the following correspondence:

Metadata Linking Model	FOHM
typed links	associations
role	feature
link type	relation type

As a result, we conclude that the OHP and FOHM data model are powerful enough to encode the type of metadata that we have presented in this paper.

As an exercise in the study of our model's expressiveness, we can show how to encode real world metadata systems such as the Dublin Core [2]. Each field value pair could be encoded as a binary typed link, as describe above; the record itself could be represented by a n-ary link, where each anchor references a binary typed link. It should be noted that we do not want to prescribe an implementation technique, but that we are merely investigating the respective expressiveness of linking and metadata by using encodings.

Structural computing [6] has emerged as an alternative approach to unify hypertext domains, including domains such as spatial and taxonomic hypertexts. The support of our metadata by structural computing would require the definition of a new "middleware" able to handle metadata appropriately. Lessons from our experiments can benefit the design of such middleware. In particular, symmetry in the link between the metadata and the object it refers to should be preserved in order to allow for powerful queries over metadata.

This paper has highlighted a number of issues that could provide a basis for further work. The introduction of names to replace objects has allowed us to think and model in more generic terms. It would be interesting to investigate the use of named objects as the role and type parts of a typed link. Continuing this theme, a more detailed investigation into the nature of a system where links are members of the set of objects could produce some interesting results. Showing this would allow links to associate links together; could this be used as a formal model for standards such as Topic Maps [1] ?

4   Conclusion

This paper has shown how the metadata model can be defined in terms of both a simple and typed linking model. Defining metadata using simple links did not enrich the model but illustrated that it was possible to make a metadata model symmetric. Knowing this, we defined the metadata model in terms of the typed linking model. This definition showed how the metadata model was less expressive than the linking model, and how the typed linking model was capable of capturing the intent of the original metadata association. Given the linking model was more expressive we showed how the missing additional semantics could be added in order to complete the enrichment of the original metadata association. Our second thesis, that metadata can be expressed as a perspective on typed links, was shown by defining the metadata model in terms of typed links and that examples in this typed link form could be seen as metadata when viewed from a given perspective.

References

1. Michel Biezunski, Martin Bryan, and Steve Newcomb. Topic maps. ISO/IEC FCD 13250:1999.
2. Dublin Core Metadata Initiative. `http://purl.oclc.org/dc/`.
3. Catherine C. Marshall and Frank M. Shipman. Spatial hypertext: Designing for change. *Communications of the ACM*, 38:88–97, 1995.
4. David Millard, Luc Moreau, Hugh Davis, and Siegfried Reich. FOHM: A fundamental open hypertext model for investigating interoperability between hypertext domains. In *Proceedings of the '00 ACM Conference on Hypertext, May 30 - June 3, San Antonio, TX* (2000), pp. 93–102.
5. Luc Moreau and Wendy Hall. On the Expressiveness of Links in Hypertext Systems. *The Computer Journal*, 41(7):459–473, 1998.
6. Peter J. Nürnberg, Kaj Grønbæk, Dirk Bucka-Lassen, Claus A. Pedersen, and Olav Reinert. A component-based open hypermedia approach to integrating structure services. *New Review of Hypermedia and Multimedia*, 5:179–207, 1999.
7. Siegfried Reich, Uffe K. Wiil, Peter J. Nürnberg, Hugh C. Davis, Kaj Grønbæk, Kenneth M. Anderson, David E. Millard, and Jörg M. Haake. Addressing interoperability in open hypermedia: The design of the open hypermedia protocol. *New Review of Hypermedia and Multimedia*, 5:207–248, 1999.

Weaving the Pervasive Information Fabric

Mark Thompson, David De Roure, and Danius Michaelides

Department of Electronics and Computer Science,
University of Southampton, UK
{mkt,dder,dtm}@ecs.soton.ac.uk

Abstract. As the pervasive computing infrastructure emerges, we consider the impact on information applications and their middleware requirements – what we call the pervasive information fabric. In particular, we consider the evolution of hypermedia link services to support the structuring of ad hoc information spaces. We describe a prototype implementation of an ad hoc distributed link service using a tuple-space model.

1 Introduction

Advances in network technologies and miniaturisation of computing devices are providing us with a new target architecture for computer science and engineering, with devices embedded in our environment, in wearable computers and potentially in everyday artefacts. Mobility of users and devices is a particularly profound paradigm shift; it also introduces a new type to our information space, i.e. location information. This pervasive computing infrastructure is with us now, with increasing numbers of devices available, motivated for example by the needs of the mobile e-business user. We now anticipate the gradual disappearance of the general purpose 'personal computer' in favour of task-specific devices that we will not think of as computers at all.

Meanwhile, the majority of hypermedia systems that we work with are intranet based with a traditional client-server model based on large servers accessed by many clients and interconnected by a static network. Activities such as WAP (Wireless Application Protocol) [5] and JINI [8] are establishing an infrastructure for the mobile and pervasive computing environments, but we believe that the information perspective, in particular the hypermedia perspective, is one that has been little explored thus far.

We focus here on one particular aspect of pervasive computing: ad hoc networking. In this scenario, a number of devices that happen to be in the same physical space can establish communication and provide exchange of information. The network technologies and protocols to support this are becoming established. Above this level, we regard hypermedia link resolution as a basic service that helps applications provide customised information spaces. Hence the focus of our investigation is the provision of link services in the ad hoc setting, in order to provide hyperstructure to facilitate navigation of the available information space.

S. Reich and K.M. Anderson (Eds.): OHS/SC 2000, LNCS 1903, pp. 87–95, 2000.
© Springer-Verlag Berlin Heidelberg 2000

This paper motivates the study and describes some aspects of our research agenda to create this pervasive information fabric. In section 2 we discuss the fabric, followed in section 3 by a motivational scenario, which leads us to the ad hoc information space discussed in section 4. Section 5 focuses on link service issues, and section 6 presents a prototype implementation. Finally we describe future work with the system and where it interacts with existing projects within our laboratory.

2   The Pervasive Computing Fabric

The pervasive computing vision was established by work at Xerox around 1989 on 'ubiquitous computing' and brought to public attention through Weiser's Scientific American article [15] and Communications of the ACM [12,16]. The last few years have seen the infrastructure technologies emerge. Next generation Internet Protocol (IPv6) supports many aspects of pervasive computing, including the address space for large numbers of devices, and there is ongoing activity at IETF (Internet Engineering Task Force) in support of mobility, ad hoc networking, service discovery and automatic configuration of devices.

This same period has seen a huge increase in the availability, diversity and richness of digital content, compounding the difficulties of content delivery in this increasingly pervasive setting. WAP addresses delivery of content, and techniques for dealing with adaptive and scalable delivery of multimedia content is attracting much attention (e.g. [11]). This technology is a further constituent of the pervasive multimedia computing infrastructure.

3   An Ad Hoc Linking Scenario

What are the applications that will employ these underlying devices, protocols techniques for content processing and delivery? Our particular focus here is on information applications that take advantage of a hyperstructure. In particular, we adopt the open hypermedia model, whereby links are first class citizens and we can readily work with linkbases and linkbase fragments.

Imagine you are walking along a corridor, you look at a poster on the wall and the text and images on the poster prompt you to think of a number of associated things. Think of this as having a few collections of hypermedia links (the sets of associations) active in your mind. In our scenario, a wearable computer behaves in a similar way, reifying and augmenting our mental linkbases with various personal linkbases, a linkbase associated with your current task and one associated with the building you are in. This highly dynamic, highly context-sensitive and ad hoc situation is what we are trying to realise through the hypermedia link services in our pervasive information infrastructure.

We extend this vision to a collaborative setting: you walk into a meeting room and sit down with several other people. Everyone is carrying computing devices and these form a shared workspace of documents relevant to the meeting; perhaps each has a Web server. How is this information space structured?

Imagine everyone has linkbases that they publish – then we have an ad hoc aggregation of linkbases to assist in constructing the hyperstructure for the shared information space. Looking at the agenda of the meeting, you now have links available according to the linkbases of everyone in the room. Even if you do not use these directly, your agent may wish to – perhaps, trivially, for search purposes, or in general to answer a context-sensitive query.

The key notion here is that the topology of the underlying network is not predetermined or particularly organised, rather it is self-organised and ad hoc. Also, the location and availability of network services (web servers, etc.) are fluidic in nature.

4   Ad Hoc Information Space

Whilst the meeting is in progress, users can browse documents present on the collection of web servers in the meeting. Any of the published linkbases can also be applied to these documents, rendering an augmented view, specialised to the meeting at hand. Once the meeting is over, the hyperstructure that has been created in the meeting through the amalgamation of linkbases, documents and interactions (our ad hoc information space) is deconstructed.

In order to preserve the space, documents, linkbases and accompanying information, data shared during the meeting would have to be mirrored. Many tools exist to perform the mirroring of entire documents present on web servers; however it may be the case that only a summary of the document is required to be taken away, or that the document exists on the globally accessible Internet and thus an entry in a linkbase will suffice.

One approach to mirroring linkbases is to export the complete repository to a persistent entity, in a format that can either be re-loaded into the application at a later date, or into other link services at a different location. This same process enables the merging of multiple linkbases into a conglomeration of links pertaining particularly to the meeting that has just expired. More complicated merging can be achieved by combining linkbases using linkbase algebra, for example, merging only links that specifically relate to a particular set of documents.

5   Mobile and Ad Hoc Linking

Without studying specific application requirements, we have a notion here that the hypermedia middleware – the link service – needs to support ad hoc networking by supporting ad hoc combination of linkbases. But first it must also support mobility of linkbases, sharing and mobile access to linkbases. These then are the goals in our next iteration on the architecture of the Distributed Link Service (DLS) [1,3], our proven infrastructure for hypermedia linking.

Carrying a linkbase is as simple as carrying any data, but the provision of access requires protocols. The model whereby linkservers can be accessed with HTTP is well established in DLS, but we have recently produced a version using LDAP (Lightweight Directory Access Protocol) as this permits the use of standard infrastructure and deals with some scalability and update issues. We have also implemented effective query routing for multiple link servers [2]. In support of the collaborative scenario above we draw on our experience of collaborative filtering [4] on an Intranet, and look to existing hypermedia models supporting collaboration such as activity spaces [13,14].

LDAP is well suited as the communications protocol to manage and query the numerous linkbases present in the scenario. It is an existing, off-the-shelf technology with multiple language bindings and multiple server implementations. The protocol itself deals with the issues of scalable access, whilst not strictly relevant to this particular scenario this is an important feature should the techniques developed here be deployed in wider-area information spaces.

The flexible design of LDAP facilitates complex filter-based directory querying (including phonetic matching) and a readily available, extensible data model. The naming scheme employed by LDAP enables scoped directories, which is paramount in this scenario where we have many linkbases being built and distributed between potentially many link servers.

Also, through our collaboration with IBM Hursley Labs, we have introduced Tspaces [17] as a link repository and messaging infrastructure. TSpaces, conceptually nothing more than a communications buffer with database capabilities, enables inter-application messaging in a network of heterogeneous devices and operating environments. Besides the simple primitives of `write`, `read` and `take`, borrowed from its Linda background, TSpaces is an interesting platform for DLS implementations in that it provides event notification services, offers user-definable operations on the repository and has the ability to store arbitrary sized objects (e.g. document chunks), all enabling unique approaches to this DLS scenario. TSpaces is small in memory-, processor- and disk-usage, thus fits well with the long-term target architectures for Pervasive Computing. That is to say it brings the power of the network to palm devices, making them fully-fledged network computers.

6 Prototype System

We have built a system comprising a modified DLS implementation and an application that generates the linkbases automatically in the ad hoc setting. Users submit documents they deem relevant to the meeting via a shared resource; the application then extracts linking information that is made available to the DLS as a custom linkbase for the meeting. In an initial implementation, users at the meeting set their web browser clients to use the DLS as their web proxy; as a result, documents they browse throughout the meeting have the newly created links inserted where relevant. The proxy is also able to record the users' trails and we intend these to be a source of further navigation support in later systems. The second phase of prototyping introduced a local Meeting Participant (MP) "agent" to which the local web-browsers and other Internet applications are pointed. The MP module is then responsible for the interactions of the user with the meeting space, including all resource discovery, service interaction and management.

Extraction of link information from HTML documents is a straightforward task, and when working with open hypermedia systems the separate link databases are already available. The link extraction mechanism used in this prototype is a tool that parses a set of documents, saving link data generated by a specified criteria – for example, by keyword match – in a relational database and making local copies of the documents with the anchors (HREFs) rewritten. The SQL database facilitates the subsequent generation of multiple linkbases. The initial implementation was based on libwww from W3C and ran on FreeBSD and Linux.

In our prototypes, a linkbase is a repository of four-tuple Link objects, with a well-defined set of operations for Creation, Destruction and Query for links and Initialisation, Extend-by-import and Publish for linkbases. Unlike other DLS implementations, the interaction with linkbases is distributed, as are the linkbases themselves. The linkbase algebra is trivial, yet flexible, in that links are added to the linkbase "piecemeal", through submission of grounded tuples; destroyed by "filter", where the filter components are conjunctive; and navigated or resolved by "query", where the exactness of a link can vary from fully grounded (exact match required to verify an existing link against an existing linkbase) to completely vague (just matching on a selective keyword, or the source document location).

In order to enable the different component applications of our scenario, the interface to the DLS has to be specified and well known so as to enable interoperability, and in the extended prototype, automated service discovery. For the purposes of these experiments, this interface is partially defined as follows:

Both the LDAP and TSpaces implementations implement a link service using this interface. The LDAP implementation maintains the repository of links where each link originates from a particular linkbase and has an id within the linkbase. In LDAP terminology, this gives a Distinguished Name for the object, for example 'lid=1., lb="Links about LDAP"'. The actual information associated with a link become attributes of the LDAP object. To facilitate link algebra, other attributes such as user could be associated with a link. The methods defined by the LinkService interface map to various LDAP operations, for example the destroyLink method implementation for an LDAP link server is a direct wrapper around the LDAP delete operator, qualified by LDAP search filters generated from the arguments.

The TSpaces implementation has links represented as Tuple objects in their own namespace, with additional namespaces used for housekeeping data. This differs from the LDAP approach in that each linkbase is a separate tuplespace, containing Link objects. As with the LDAP implementation of the link service interface, the TSpaces version is a glue-layer to API calls, which result in either a query over a network socket connection or a direct intra-application call. This is dependent on whether the TSpaces server is executing in the same JVM as the client application, as may be the case if participating clients are executing their own link servers locally.

```
interface LinkService {
  oolean authorLink( Link lnk);
  oolean destroyLink( Link lnk);
  oolean destroyLinkSource( String src);
  oolean destroyLinkTarget( String tgt);
  oolean destroyLinkType( String typ);
  void resetLink ase( );
  oolean importLink ase( URL src, Format fmt );
  void export (PrintStream out, Format fmt);
  void exportBySource( PrintStream out, Format fmt,
                       String src);
  void exportByTarget( PrintStream out, Format fmt,
                       String tgt);
  void exportByType( PrintStream out, Format fmt,
                     String typ);
  Link queryBySource( String src);
  Link queryByTarget( String tgt);
  Link queryBySelection( String sel);
  Link queryByType( String typ);
}
```

Fig. 1. Standardised LinkService Interface

The interface chosen enables linkbase publication to a number of different formats, including LDIF, TSpaces tuples, Webcosm [7] linkbase and human-/browser-readable bookmark formats. The choice of format is exposed through the defined LinkService API such that Meeting Participant agents can expressly request the most suitable export format for their user's need. This permits integration into other DLS implementations, and also is the mechanism used by the prototype system to off-line snapshots of the current live set of linkbases known by a MP node at runtime. Conversely, the import function as implemented reads a linkbase in from a given URL and linkbase format. Whilst this is fine for a prototype implementation, additional mechanisms for the bulk update of linkbases, other than over HTTP connections, would be required for a production service.

The initial prototypes require each client user to manually configure their web browser's proxy settings to point to a location (host-port pair) that executes the link service web proxy. The proxy is controlled through a web form interface that configures which linkbases to include when answering HTTP queries from a particular IP address, thus specialising the response per participant machine. The triggers to import and export linkbases were also buttons on this form, which inadvertently became the user interface to the application.

Later prototypes introduce the notion of a Meeting Participant agent, which is a local piece of code that the user's applications are proxied through. This application is lightweight in that it does not have all of the DLS implementation that the full prototype has behind it, only the session management and service discovery functionality. Its task is to discover what other DLS services are available in the ad hoc network at meeting-time and offer these additional resources to the local user. It is also the endpoint for communications from other Meeting Participant agents at other clients. Naturally, should the local client also be running a DLS service, its presence will be discovered by the MP agent and made available locally.

The automation required of the MP agent implies a need for some level of service discovery mechanism, finding the relevant resources on the network for the meeting. A trivial implementation of this utilising network sockets is to broadcast or multicast a request packet on a well-known port such that all the available services can reply, announcing their presence and available resources. A more appropriate mechanism is to use a standardised service discovery protocol, such as the IETF SLP [6], or Sun's Jini Lookup Service [8]. The approach taken by this work to define a standardised LinkService interface readily enables the use of Jini-style service lookup based on template matching in that specific requests for specific services can be made, for example to search for a LinkService that implements an export to HTML function.

7   Further Work

This is work in progress, with implications on other projects that the IAM group at Southampton is actively researching. Part of the further work with these prototype applications is to integrate the architecture developed here into the other frameworks available.

In adopting standard infrastructure components to build the prototype we have not talked explicitly in terms of building a multi-agent system; however, it is entirely possible to caste the prototype in that paradigm. This builds on the concept of software agents both as personal information assistants and as autonomous components of a distributed system in which they collaborate and negotiate to perform their tasks. Future work includes an implementation of the scenario within SoFAR, the Southampton Framework for Agent Research [10]. We also wish to consider this work in the light of the FOHM model [9].

Section 4 above discusses the need to mirror documents when deconstructing the information space at the close of the meeting, i.e. when the resource is about to become unavailable. Where current technologies permit relatively low bandwidths for wireless access, the power capability of the client's device may be such that only part of the document, or even a generated executive summary of the document should be transferred. Techniques for doing this are well known and employed in on-line information navigation systems, such as Refindment [7]. Summarisation and semantically relevant keyword matching are two extended features that would enrich the architecture under development in this work.

As a precursor to any work integrating this system with the SoFAR activity, it is likely that the subscription facilities permitted by TSpaces could be used to add additional functionality to the system. For example, by implementing a module that listens to instances of new links being inserted into a linkbase, the authoring event can be replicated on another DLS instance, thus providing a passive mechanism for linkbase mirroring. The target DLS in this case does not necessarily have to be another TSpaces DLS implementation, just one that implements the LinkService interface as defined.

8   Summary

The pervasive computing infrastructure has many research challenges, including scalability of interactive applications. In this paper, we have illustrated a holistic approach that enables scenarios to be developed to define and exercise these enticing challenges. By extending the distributed link service into this pervasive setting we hope to establish a pervasive information fabric to enable a new class of applications.

The prototypes developed within the presented scenario are designed under the premise that centralised control (i.e. a "Meeting Manager") is not acceptable, that the infrastructure should be self-forming as much as possible. Local processes, including the user, always manage local data such that access permissions, publication rights and document selection can be controlled with a high degree of confidence – especially important in commercial meeting environments.

This research is near-term in that enabling technologies for local area wireless networking and low-juice, medium-power handheld devices are available now, permitting ad hoc environments incorporating laptops, pads and PDAs with wireless interconnect. One key requirement at present, however, is the efficient management of bandwidth. The architecture under development here is flexible such that rather than entire documents being transferred between participant devices, either links to (in the case that the document is published on an accessible Internet) or summaries of the document can be generated and transferred in situ. The longer-term aspect of this is that as current trends continue, the wireless bandwidth will grow as power consumption decreases and bigger documents/media types emerge to "use up" the advances, this architecture can still apply.

Acknowledgements. This research is partially supported by the EPSRC Link Me project and the IBM University Partnership Programme. We are grateful to our colleagues at IBM Hursley Park, particularly Adrian Colyer and Colin Bird, for helpful discussions. The LDAP and query routing experiments were supported by British Telecom Laboratories and we are grateful to Nigel Walker for his participation in this exercise.

References

1. L.A. Carr, D.C. De Roure, H.C. Davis, and W. Hall. Implementing an open link service for the world wide web. *World Wide Web Journal*, 1(2), 1998.
2. D. De Roure, N. Walker, and L. Carr. Investigating link service architectures. In *Proceedings of the Hypertext Conference HT'00*, May 2000.

3. D.C. De Roure, L.A. Carr, W. Hall, and G.J. Hill. Enhancing the Distributed Link Service for multimedia and collaboration. In *FTDCS 97 - Proceedings of the Sixth IEEE Workshop on Future Trends in Distributed Computing Systems*, pages 330–335. IEEE, October 1997.

4. S. El-Beltagy, D.C. De Roure, and W. Hall. A multiagent system for navigation assistance and information finding. In *PAAM 99 - Proceedings of the Fourth International Conference on the Practical Application of Intelligent Agents and Multi-Agent Technology*, pages 281–295, April 1999.

5. WAP Forum. Wireless Application Protocol. http://www.wap.net/.

6. E. Guttman, C. Perkins, J. Viezades, and M. Day. Service location protocol (SLP), version 2. Technical Report Request For Comment number 2608, Internet Engineering Task Force, June 1999.

7. Multicosm Ltd. http://www.multicosm.com/.

8. Sun Microsystems. The Jini lookup service specification (LU), version 1.0.1, November 1999. http://www.sun.com/jini/specs/lookup101.html.

9. D.E. Millard, L.A.V. Moreau, H.C. Davis, and S. Reich. FOHM: A fundamental open hypertext model for investigating interoperability between hypertext domains. In *Proceedings of the '00 ACM Conference on Hypertext, May 30 - June 3, San Antonio, TX* (2000), pp. 93–102.

10. L.A.V. Moreau, N.M. Gibbins, D.C. De Roure, S. El-Beltagy, W. Hall, G.V. Hughes, D.W. Joyce, S. Kim, D.T. Michaelides, D.E. Millard, S. Reich, R.H. Tansley, and M.J. Weal. SoFAR with DIM agents: An agent framework for distributed information management. In *The Fifth International Conference and Exhibition on The Practical Application of Intelligent Agents and Multi-Agents*, Manchester, UK, 2000.

11. J.R. Smith, R. Mohan, and C. Li. Scalable multimedia delivery for pervasive computing. In *Proceedings ACM Multimedia 99*, pages 131–140, Orlando, October 1999.

12. M. Spreitzer and M. Theimer. Scalable, secure mobile computing with location information. *Communications of the ACM*, July 1993.

13. W. Wang and J. Haake. Supporting user-defined activity spaces. In *Proceedings of ACM Hypertext'97*, Southampton, April 1997.

14. W. Wang and J. Haake. Flexible coordination with cooperative hypermedia. In *Proceedings of the ninth ACM Conference on Hypertext and Hypermedia*, pages 245–255, Pittsburgh, June 1998.

15. M. Weiser. The computer for the twenty-first century. *Scientific American*, pages 94–104, September 1991.

16. M. Weiser. Some computer science problems in ubiquitous computing. *Communications of the ACM*, pages 74–83, July 1993.

17. P. Wyckoff, S.W. McLaughry, T.J. Lehman, and Ford D.A. TSpaces. *IBM Systems Journal*, 37(3), August 1998.

Introduction to SC2

Kenneth M. Anderson

Department of Computer Science
University of Colorado, Boulder
ECOT 717, Campus Box 430
Boulder CO 80309-0430
kena@cs.colorado.edu

The hypermedia community has engaged in open hypermedia research for well over a decade. Open hypermedia is an approach to providing hypermedia services to multiple users over heterogeneous information managed by an open set of applications. However, the conceptual foundations of open hypermedia—its underlying structures and behaviors—have all focused on supporting one task: *information navigation*. While these structures are flexible enough to be applied to other domains, the mappings are often inefficient and unsatisfying. In fact, concurrent with open hypermedia research, several researchers were exploring domains such as spatial hypermedia and taxonomic hypermedia that required conceptual foundations markedly different from those used to support navigational hypermedia.

As a result of this situation, a new approach has emerged that attempts to unify these, and other, disparate domains under a common conceptual foundation that allows the lessons learned from conducting over a decade's worth of research on open hypermedia to be applied to problems in these new domains. This approach is called *structural computing*. Structural computing "asserts the primacy of structure over data" [1] and aims to develop a set of principles, techniques, and technology that can be used by developers as resources for developing applications in new domains.

The First International Workshop on Structural Computing (SC1) was held as part of the 1999 ACM Conference on Hypertext [2]. At that workshop, a variety of researchers representing various areas of study presented requirements placed on the new field of structural computing by their respective domains. Collecting these requirements is an important activity for the structural computing field and, as such, requirements papers for the Second International Workshop on Structural Computing (SC2) were encouraged. However, SC2, also solicited the submission of papers concerning the application of structural computing ideas to real problems, as well as work reporting on experimental prototypes of structural computing infrastructure.

The goal, then, of the SC2 was to bring researchers interested in structural computing together for intense discussion of its ideas and techniques.

Kenneth M. Anderson was the organizer of the workshop and Uffe K. Wiil chaired the event in San Antonio.

The papers presented in this proceedings can be grouped into several topic areas. These topic areas formed the basis of presentation and discussion

S. Reich and K.M. Anderson (Eds.): OHS/SC 2000, LNCS 1903, pp. 96–97, 2000.
© Springer-Verlag Berlin Heidelberg 2000

sessions at the workshop. The first topic area includes papers that discuss requirements for structural computing from the perspective of a particular domain. Jim Rosenberg focuses on the domain of hypertext writers. Jörg Haake addresses the collaborative work domain, and Simon Buckingham Shum presents the domain of scholarly work. The second topic area includes papers on formal models for structural computing. David Millard's paper presents a new formal model for structural computing known as the Fundamental Open Hypermedia Model. Kenneth M. Anderson's paper identifies the need for additional formal models in structural computing and identifies two promising areas for such models. The third topic area includes papers on structural computing tools. Uffe Wiil's paper describes the Construct Development Environment, which can auto-generate structure service skeletons from IDL specifications. Manolis Tzagarakis described recent developments of the Callimachus open hypermedia system aiming at providing support for development of new structure services from a structure specification.

Finally, the fourth topic area includes papers that focus on the future of structural computing. David Hicks' paper raises a fundamental question of whether structural computing should be viewed as a natural evolution from past open hypermedia system development work or should it be seen as a revolutionary new way to think about structure and build systems? While Peter Nürnberg's paper addresses the fundamental thinking behind the ideas of structural computing.

The Third International Workshop on Structural Computing (SC3) will be held at the next Hypertext conference in Århus, Denmark, August 14-18, 2001. Manolis Tzagarakis will be the organizer of this event. It is anticipated that SC3 will see additional work in each of the four topic areas — requirements, formal models, tools, and future directions — and that this newly emerging field of computation will continue to evolve and begin to provide useful techniques and technology to developers working in multiple computing domains.

References

1. Peter J. Nürnberg, John J. Leggett, and Erich R. Schneider. As We Should Have Thought. Proceedings of the Eighth ACM Conference on Hypertext and Hypermedia (HT '97), Southampton, UK. ACM Press: New York (1997) 96–101.
2. Peter J. Nürnberg (ed). Proceedings of the First Workshop on Structural Computing. Technical Report AUE-CS 99-04, Department of Computer Science, Aalborg University Esbjerg, Denmark (1999) (see <http://www.cs.aue.auc.dk/publications/>).

Domain Requirements for a Cybertext Authoring System

Jim Rosenberg

Grindstone, PA
jr@amanue.com
http://www.well.com/user/jer/

Abstract. This paper presents requirements for a cybertext authoring system in the literary domain. Issues discussed include a drawing framework; pluggable objects; openness to a variety of different types of structure, including piles, relations, sets, links, and composites; flexible behavior (extensibility and tailorability); dependency control; non-binary file formats for export and import; web-enabled player; and portability. Issues relevant to structural computing appear throughout, as structural computing is the only paradigm likely to support all of these requirements.

1 Introduction

This paper considers the requirements for an authoring system to meet the needs of cybertext writers, particularly those pursuing literary aims.[1] Throughout, the discussion will speak about "the system", without presupposing whether that system consists of a single "monolithic" program or multiple cooperating separate programs. The needs of cybertext authors can be satisfied equally by either. To the degree that these requirements can be met by many small programs each providing a limited functionality, there is an advantage to the user in allowing for a marketplace where there are alternative choices. However, there is a large risk in such an approach: if the software engineer simply assumes "someone else" will provide a particular functionality (e.g. fonts allowing multiple-resolution rendering, royalty-free distribution, etc.) the result may be that *no one* provides that functionality; if this functionality is deemed crucial to a work by a cybertext author, it may leave that author without support at all. Accordingly, we will speak of an authoring system as if it were provided by a single-source *provider*, even though the details of where the boundaries are on particular components will be left unspecified as an implementation detail.

While it may not seem that the subject of structural computing is addressed directly in this paper, in fact its contribution is crucial. Existing commercial hypertext systems and Web authoring systems tend to embed a fixed vocabulary

---

[1] This paper is a revised version of a submission to an on-line discussion group for the conference *Technology Platforms for 21st Century Literature* held at Brown University, April 1999.

S. Reich and K.M. Anderson (Eds.): OHS/SC 2000, LNCS 1903, pp. 98–107, 2000.
© Springer-Verlag Berlin Heidelberg 2000

of structural elements that may not be sufficient for cybertext authoring. It is assumed throughout this paper that structural computing will be required to meet the kind of structure openness discussed in 4 below.

2   Drawing Framework

It must be possible to approach the work through an object-oriented drawing interface in which text spaces are "visual first". Text objects must be visually placeable anywhere, not restricted by a "word processing" framework. Visual word spaces will of course need to be related by structure operations; see 4 below. To the extent that text objects have time requirements, a timeline should be an optional property of the individual object; the visual structure of a complete document must not be subject to an overall timeline unless the author specifically elects to attach a timeline to the entire document.

The drawing framework requires:

2.1   Virtual Pages

The cybertext author must be able to construct text spaces which act as *virtual pages*. The authoring system should place as few limits as possible on the size of these pages; it must be possible to construct virtual pages which are several times the size of the user's physical screen. Some form of zooming interface (similar to e.g. Pad++ [3]) is highly desirable. The issue of how to render in the face of zooming is similar to the problem of rendering across a wide variety of possible screen resolutions; although as of this writing screen resolution has been nearly stagnant for decades, this situation is likely to change.

2.2   Font Support

It is typical for software designers to leave the issue of fonts to third party vendors and end-users. The cybertext author needs the ability to deploy fonts that will render properly across a variable set of resolutions, with the ability to maintain a very exacting control over text appearance, and without making assumptions about what fonts are installed on the end-user's system. Pad++ renders fonts graphically at intermediate resolutions using a form of bitmap interpolation which is visually very unappealing. By contrast, PDF technology [1] allows scalable font rendering which can employ font outlines to render acceptably across a range of resolutions; unfortunately PDF is far too restrictive in the structures and behaviors allowed to be suitable as the "entire" file format for any but a very narrow range of cybertexts. The concept implemented in the forthcoming MacOS X of using PDF for *individual objects* rather than as a "closed" format for an entire document illustrates how font support might be accomplished. A cybertext run-time system needs to have *its own* font system which has a very deep interface to the event system that allows the developer to trap the zoom-resolution (see above) and relate resolution to point size for scalable fonts *or* permit the Pad++ "bit-map" style of font rendering, under scriptable control.

The run-time license must include the rights to distribute whatever font objects are required to get a document to "play".

3   Pluggable Objects

When a text object is placed in a visual space by the author, it must be a genuine object. Ideally this means author-definable classes, in the technical sense. (Whether the *reader* should be able to define classes is an interesting question; this should be considered a special case of the more general question of the extent to which the reader is empowered with full authoring ability.) It may be possible for some authors to get by with a lighter-weight system—some sort of grouping—but the authoring environment must allow pluggable text objects to be indefinitely complex, with their own user interface, consisting of components that are likewise as complex. This means a text object may have sub-objects which include handlers that exhibit *behavior*. As an example, a text object may include a whole set of dynamically rendered "on mouseOver" areas that "follow" the object.

Pluggable text objects should have a simple user interface in which they can be placed just like any other object in an object-oriented drawing program. They should work in the clipboard via cut copy and paste, and when pasted the behavior and sub-object structure must come with them.

4   Structure Openness

The system of pluggable objects in visual text spaces must be open to the full range of structure abstractions already investigated in the hypertext research community and must somehow allow new ones to be invented. For a discussion of several aspects of allowing arbitrary structures in hypertext, see [15]; we will adopt the terminology of that paper (e.g. *scope* — the extent of an object — and *valence* — the schema for how other objects are plugged into an object) in the following discussion. Structure abstractions supported should include:

4.1   Piles

A pile is a spatially overlaid implicit structure, as in VIKI [10]. A pile is an object with a spatial scope and undifferentiated valence. Piles have special user interface requirements, which have not all been adequately addressed by existing systems. Among the requirements for piles are:

4.1.1 Spatial Parsing. When the user has enabled spatial parsing, objects which are placed in close proximity should be recognized by the system as belonging to a pile, simply by virtue of how they are placed and without the user specifically "registering" an object as belonging to a pile.

4.1.2 Open/Close Behavior. Objects in a pile may spatially overlay one another, to the point that some objects may be entirely invisible. Existing systems tend to assume that opening an object is accomplished by selecting a member of a pile, thereby bringing it to the top, and then specifically opening it, e.g. by double-clicking. This does not solve the problem of opening an object which is 100members of the pile. [13] introduced a system of "proximity hot-spots" for navigating members of a pile. The problem of visualizing occluded members of a pile is discussed in 4.1.3 below.

Behaviors of this kind raise a special challenge for structural computing. It is frequently assumed that structural computing will be implemented using "structure servers". When a new structure is invented that requires special behavior of the kind discussed above, where is that behavior to be implemented? Lodging all structure functionality at the server poses severe complications for novel user interface behavior required by objects which are instances of the new structure. Of course, a structure server could also serve *code* which implements behavior. This would require some significant design to achieve a protocol regarding such issues as the dependency framework. (See the discussion in section 5 below.)

4.1.3 Membership Visualization. As above, 100% occlusion of a pile member may prevent the user from even knowing the object is there as a pile member. The system needs to have a method for the user to be able to see what members a pile contains. (E.g. the user interface in [13] provides pop-up frame outlines to delineate members of a pile.) The problem of visualizing occluded members of a pile will likely require dynamic behaviors not often found in current software. For instance, if objects occupy rectangularly bounded regions, the user could engage a behavior in which each object in a pile is rendered as an empty transparent rectangle the size of the bounding box. This would allow selection of a bounding box in the same way this occurs in object-oriented drawing programs. Another method for discovering occluded objects might utilize a variable-sized region surrounding the cursor; when the cursor hovers, a pop-up menu could appear with the names of all objects intersected by the region surrounding the cursor.

4.2   Relations

Relations were first pioneered in Aquanet [9], and have not been supported by subsequent systems. A relation is somewhat like an *n*-ary link. A relation may be thought of as an abstraction that has some number of *slots*; these slots may or may not be typed. A relation has specified valence; scope is determined by the scope of all of the slots. Among the user interface requirements:

4.2.1 Graphical Rendering of the Relationship. The system should provide for the ability of the objects that go in the slots to be rendered in such a way that their participation in the relation is indicated graphically. (E.g. the Toulmin diagram notation shown in the Aquanet paper, the relational diagram notation of [12], etc.) This requires draw objects that are "smart" about the connections. Given that the object plugged into a relation slot may be deeply embedded in some other object, user interface ramifications here may be tricky.

4.2.2 "Multi-open"/"Multi-close" of All the Slots at Once. When a relation is "opened", the user interface must provide the ability to open all the slots at one time. (A scheme of "serial visitation" of slots — a *tour* perhaps — might also be available to the document author, but should not be mandatory as the only way of opening slots.) This has several user interface ramifications. The opened slot objects have a dependency relationship (see 6 below). For navigation purposes, "location" is *non-unitary:* one is not necessarily located in a single relation slot one at a time (though that should be available as an option) — one may be "located in" *all the slots at once.* (For a discussion of non-unitary location see [15].)

4.3   Sets

Sets as a hypertext structure primitive were introduced in [11]. A set has exactly specified scope and undifferentiated valence. User interface requirements for sets are an open issue. Presumably sets should have an open/close operation, and have membership visualization issues similar to piles. When an object is inserted into a set, there needs to be some canonical method for how to determine "where it fits". Sets and piles have a close relationship. A pile could be considered to be a particular form of set; however spatial proximity is implied for piles, but sets could have members with arbitrary location. Some authors may need some form of "auto-arrange" display behavior for the members of a set.

4.4   Links

Links are provided by nearly all hypertext systems. It is worth pointing out that much research in the hypertext community supports implementing links via an external link base, as opposed to embedding links within the text, as is typical with HTML. It is an open question whether writers have specific needs in this regard.

4.5   Composites

Composites [5] are a hierarchical grouping of objects, and were recognized as an important part of the Dexter Hypertext Reference Model [6]. A composite has precisely specified scope and precisely specified valence. It is frequently assumed by Dexter proponents that some of the structure categories mentioned above, e.g. piles and relations, can be implemented as composites. This paper considers composites as a generic form of grouping, without specific behavior requirements. Behavior requirements for piles and relations are discussed above. They are different both from each other and from the generic requirements of composites.

5   Flexible Behavior

The system must allow the author to create whatever forms of behavior of interactive word objects can be imagined. Some authors will want complex animations
under programmatic control, perhaps mediated by interactive choices of the reader. This may have serious consequences for the user interface. For instance, if
the author wants to use animation for some particular artistic purpose, and the
system designer also wants to use animation for some purpose (e.g. "fluid links"
[16]) these might conflict. It is exactly such artistic conflicts that can render
an otherwise eminent multimedia system *unusable* for a particular work by a
particular artist.

Behavior flexibility includes the following requirements:

5.1   Extensibility

There is simply no possible way a system designer can anticipate every kind
of artistically desired behavior; some form of scripting language is absolutely
essential.

5.2   Tailorability

It should be possible for the document author to *intervene* in built-in behavior
in those circumstances where that behavior conflicts aesthetically with the aims
of the author. This has a direct impact on the kind of extensibility strategy
implemented. Multimedia tools often use the "Scripted Articulation Points" [14]
strategy for extensibility. This strategy typically fails completely to provide tailorability. Published source code provides "complete" tailorability, though this
presents the document author with a very high programming demand, and is
likely to be unacceptable to commercial developers unwilling to follow the so-
called "Open Source" model. Tailorability is possibly the single most difficult
issue from the standpoint of resolving artistic requirements by individual authors vs. the economic requirements of commercial software companies.

6   Dependency Control

Interactive word objects will have complex dependencies. E.g. in the case discussed above of opening all the slots of a relation at once, the objects occupying
the slots are all dependent on the relation object. If the relation object is closed, all of its slots must be closed. Ideally a tool set should include some kind
of generalized framework for handling dependencies. Such frameworks, e.g. the
Model View Controller Paradigm (MVC) [7] tend to be complex and obscure.
MVC has surely not universally established itself as the method of choice for or-
ganizing dependencies, but no comparable alternative has emerged either. (It is
worth noting that pluggable objects was an explicit goal of MVC and the results
achieved in that regard were impressive, including pluggable behaviors as well

as pluggable structures.) Dependency control must interact with the framework for pluggable objects. When an object is plugged into a "slot", the dependency frameworks for the parent object and child object must be connected. Exactly how this is to be achieved while allowing structure extensibility is an interesting challenge.

If multimedia systems designers leave this issue completely in the hands of document authors to create their own dependency framework themselves "by hand", the result will most likely be no dependency framework at all. This particularly affects the authors of very large works. An author may get away without having a dependency framework "in the small", but as the size of a work scales up, this is likely to be painful.

7   Exportable/Importable File Formats

Some form of binary file format may be necessary for performance reasons, but at a minimum it must be possible to export to and import from a standard widely-*readable* file format. A suitable XML [4] DTD is an obvious choice. (It should be emphasized that in this connection XML would be used as "tomorrow's ASCII" to merely provide an external data format, in lieu of a proprietary binary format; the XML tags would in no way "be" the structures represented. I.e. XML would be used for syntactic rather than semantic purposes.) Such an export format is necessary for several reasons:

7.1   Amenability to Open Tool Sets

A file in a format such as XML can be processed not only by specific XML tools, of which there are likely to be a great number, but also the kind of generic tools UNIX programmers use to solve a myriad of problems.

While it is important for a cybertext authoring system to include its own graphics framework (1 above), there is so much material that might need to be incorporated from "outside" sources that it is crucial that there be a variety of export/import formats.

7.2   Suitability for Preservation Purposes

A "closed" binary file format — such as the HyperCard stack format — becomes a serious obstacle to preservation of artistic works if the software platform having that file format goes out of use. The XML DTD concept is particularly interesting: in contrast to a file format for which *no description is available*, XML attempts to be self-describing. Such a file is much more likely to achieve preservation than a proprietary undocumented binary file format. Continuation of such closed binary formats as the only mechanism by which artistic works may be preserved is simply no longer acceptable. Serious thought must be given to the issue of "preservation languages" for literary cybertext. It is possible this will turn out to be a separate problem from the problem of devising the most effective "presentation languages".

7.3   Versioning

(This is actually a special case of 7.1.) Cybertext tools currently in use by literary authors currently give very poor support for versioning. Ideally, strong versioning would be built in to an authoring environment. Versioning is needed not only by the scholarly community to study the evolution of works in the author's hands; as programmers know from countless hours of practical experience, versioning is a safety net by which an author can recover from potentially catastrophic mistakes. Exportability to standards-based file formats allows a wide range of external versioning tools to be used.

8   Web-Enabled Player

Some form of run-time mechanism that operates over the Web is an absolute necessity. This could be achieved in a number of ways, e.g. a browser plug-in, a run-time generator that emits Java bytecodes instead of a proprietary "play object" (e.g. "stack"), implementing the run-time engine entirely in Java, or a sufficiently enhanced native Web browser.

9   Portability

In the world of commercial software it is fashionable to ignore the portability problem and consider that Windows is the only necessary platform. In the creative community, use of the Macintosh is still strong. Portability in a GUI world is admittedly difficult, but the effort to achieve it will produce better software. There is a strong similarity between the abstractions needed to support GUI portability and those needed to support such issues as arbitrary structure and dependency control discussed above.

A related point: to be of any use to authors, authoring software must work on "consumer grade" computing equipment. Many of the most exciting research hypertext systems have gone almost completely untouched by cybertext authors because they required a computing environment typically available only in a research setting. If a system requires e.g. a Sun Workstation or Smalltalk image, these are not likely to be available to cybertext authors.

10   Related Work

There are many points in common between these requirements and those in [2]. In particular, Anderson's call to support composites and extensible behaviors are similar to points covered above. The Hypertext Writers Workshops have produced requirements documents (e.g. [8]) which have some similarities to this paper.

Acknowledgments. I would like to thank Kenneth M. Anderson for his extensive comments on an earlier draft of this paper.

References

1. Adobe Systems Incorporated, *Portable Document Format Reference Manual*, Fourth Edition, San Jose, 1999,
   `http://partners.ado e.com/asn/developer/acrosdk/DOCS/pdfspec.pdf`.
2. Kenneth M. Anderson. "Software Engineering Requirements for Structural Computing", *Proceedings of the First Workshop on Structural Computing*, Nürnberg, Peter J. editor, Technical Report AUE-CS-99-04, Aalborg University, Esbjerg, 1999, pp. 22-26.
3. Benjamin B. Bederson and James D. Hollan. "Pad++: A Zooming Graphical Interface for Exploring Alternative Interface Physics", *Proc. ACM UIST'94*, ACM, New York, 1994.
4. Tim Bray, Jean Paoli, and C. M. Sperberg-McQueen. *Extensible Markup Language (XML) 1.0*, W3C, REC-xml-19980210, Cambridge MA, 1998, `http://www.w3.org/TR/1998/REC-xml-19980210`.
5. Kaj Grønbæk."Composites in a Dexter-Based Hypermedia Framework", *European Conference on Hypermedia Technology 1994 Proceedings*, ACM, New York, 1994, pp. 59-69.
6. Frank G. Halasz and Mayer Schwartz. "The Dexter Hypertext Reference Model", Hypertext Standardization Workshop, NIST, 1990.
7. G. E. Krasner and S. T. Pope. "A Cookbook for Using the Model-View-Controller User Interface Paradigm in Smalltalk-80", *Journal of Object Oriented Programming*, August/September, 1988, 26-49.
8. Deena Larsen. "Providing Flexibility Within Hypertext Systems: What We've Learned at HT Workshops, CyberMountain, and Elsewhere", *Proceedings of the Eleventh ACM Conference on Hypertext and Hypermedia*, ACM, New York, 2000, pp. 268-269.
9. Catherine C. Marshall, Frank G. Halasz, Russell A. Rogers and William C. Jr. Janssen. "Aquanet: a hypertext tool to hold your knowledge in place", *Proceedings of Hypertext 91*, ACM, New York, 1991, pp. 261-275.
10. Catherine C. Marshall, Frank M. III Shipman and James H. Coombs. "VIKI: Spatial Hypertext Supporting Emergent Structure", *European Conference on Hypermedia Technology 1994 Proceedings*, ACM, New York, 1994, pp. 13-23.
11. H. Van Dyke Parunak. "Don't Link Me In: Set Based Hypermedia for Taxonomic Reasoning", *Proceedings of Hypertext 91*, ACM, New York, 1991, pp. 233-242.
12. Jim Rosenberg. "The Interactive Diagram Sentence: Hypertext as a Medium of Thought", *Visible Language* 30.2, Rhode Island School of Design, 1996, pp. 103-116 `http://www.well.com/user/jer/VL.html`.
13. Jim Rosenberg. *The Barrier Frames: Finality Crystal Shunt Curl Chant Quickening Giveaway Stare*, Eastgate Systems, Watertown, MA., 1996.
14. Jim Rosenberg. "Locus Looks at the Turing Play: Hypertextuality vs. Full Programmability", *Hypertext 98: The Proceedings of the Ninth ACM Conference on Hypertext and Hypermedia*, ACM, New York, 1998, pp. 152-160, `http://www.well.com/user/jer/LLTP_out.html`.

15. Jim Rosenberg. "A Hypertextuality of Arbitrary Structure: A Writer's Point of View", *Proceedings of the First Workshop on Structural Computing*, Nürnberg, Peter J. editor, Technical Report AUE-CS-99-04, Aalborg University, Esbjerg, 1999, pp. 3-10, `http://www.well.com/user/jer/HAS.html`.

16. Polle T. Zellweger, Bay-Wei Chang and Jock D. Mackinlay. "Fluid Links for Informed and Incremental Link Transitions", *Hypertext 98: The Proceedings of the Ninth ACM Conference on Hypertext and Hypermedia*, ACM, New York, 1998, pp. 50-57.

Structural Computing in the Collaborative Work Domain?

Jörg M. Haake

GMD - German National Research Center for Information Technology
IPSI - Publication and Information Systems Institute
Dolivostr. 15, D-64293 Darmstadt, Germany
haake@darmstadt.gmd.de

Abstract. Structural computing is a new paradigm for developing applications in new domains. One of its benefits is that adaptation of behavior—as a consequence of changes of the structures used to model the application—becomes easier. In this paper, the collaborative work domain—in particular the task of coordination—is examined as a potential application area for structural computing. Coordination behavior shows high variability, depending on the ever-changing requirements of cooperative work processes. This makes frequent adaptation of the coordination behavior necessary. To support this adaptation, a structural computing approach is described in this paper, which (1) explicitly models processes, teams, and content as part of a shared workspace, and (2) dynamically defines coordination support as behavior (i.e. computations over the above structure). Finally, some requirements on structural computing, which result from this work, are presented.

1 Introduction

As Ken Anderson points out in his introduction to the 2nd International Workshop on Structural Computing (San Antonio, Texas, June 3rd, 2000), structural computing "asserts the primacy of structure over data and aims to develop a set of principles, techniques, and technology that can be used by developers as resources for developing applications in new domains" (as introduced by Nürnberg et al, [16]). In this position paper the domain of collaborative work is examined as a potential application area for structural computing.

In the past, research on collaborative work has focused either on understanding how people work together (e.g. using computers as supporting tools or as a medium) or on how to develop computer-based tools for teams (e.g. groupware). Most researchers looked at specific tasks or domains, where people need to work together. As a result, some tasks can now be supported by specific groupware tools or environments. Other researchers focused on identifying general tools, which address basic tasks to be performed in any collaboration (such as communication, coordination and manipulation of shared artifacts). As a consequence of the generic approach, these generic tools usually need to be adapted to the

S. Reich and K.M. Anderson (Eds.): OHS/SC 2000, LNCS 1903, pp. 108–119, 2000.
© Springer-Verlag Berlin Heidelberg 2000

domain or task at hand. Otherwise, they usually lack a specific ease of use (e.g. due to missing domain specific support).

Adaptation of generic tools to a specific task is not easy. This problem becomes even more critical when properties of the task are frequently changing, and these properties changes should be reflected in new adaptations. In this case, adaptation becomes a moving target.

One such task is coordination in shared workspaces, where teams create and manipulate shared artifacts to solve a complex problem (e.g. to develop software, to design a product, or to write a research paper). As described above, dedicated collaboration environments (e.g. collaborative software development environments, or shared document editors) have traditionally supported such tasks. However, the task of coordination is still a problem.

One possibility of supporting coordination in such a shared workspace arises when looking at the coordination problem from the structural computing point of view. The shared workspace may capture shared artifacts describing (partial) solutions as well as plans and arguments of how to achieve the final result. Events raised by actions of co-workers change the state of the shared workspace. Coordination can then be described as the task of minimizing differences between the actual state and the terminal state to be achieved over a number of steps (occurring over the lifetime of the collaboration). Letting the structure of the workspace and the structure of the events being executed on that workspace drive the coordination support might actually devise a new approach to coordination of shared work.

In this paper, first the properties of the coordination task in shared workspaces are analyzed. Then, previous approaches to coordination are summarized. Next, some possibilities of supporting the coordination task with a structural computing approach are examined. Finally, some conclusions for future work are presented.

2   The Coordination Task in Shared Workspaces

Haake [9] defined a "shared global workspace" as an arbitrary hypermedia structure, which is used by multiple teams or users to facilitate asynchronous and synchronous collaboration. Not all hypermedia objects in such a shared global workspace are in use all the time. Generally, the users may use parts of the shared global workspace as shared local sub workspaces. A shared local workspace can be used for supporting either synchronous collaboration (i.e. a shared workspace offering synchronous sharing of objects and views) or asynchronous collaboration (i.e. only one user works on the objects in the local workspace and other users will access the results only later).

Work in a shared global workspace can be viewed as a sequence of state transitions over time. Each state describes the current properties of the shared global workspace such as the individual states of nodes and links (e.g. information objects, documents and their relationships) contained in the workspace, and where users are currently working. State transitions are triggered by actions performed by the users of the shared global workspace (such as modifying content of nodes or adding links). In addition, state transitions can also be triggered by time-dependent actions (such as reaching a deadline). In order to orient themselves in such a shared global workspace, which is used over a longer period of time, users need to find out about the past, present and future of the workspace:

1. Comprehending the past (history) of the shared global workspace requires understanding the current state of the global workspace (in terms of structure and content) and understanding the changes and sometimes also why and when and by whom they occurred.
2. To be able to coordinate activities with others one must be able to assess the present, i.e. the current state of the shared global workspace (who is doing what right now).
3. To be able to recognize conflicts and opportunities for synergy requires being able to make informed decisions about the future, i.e. what to do next. This requires knowledge about current tasks to be performed in the group and about relevant parts of the shared global workspace.

Answers to these three groups of issues need to take into account the dynamic nature of cooperative work in a shared global workspace. Tasks and plans might change or even evolve in the course of collaborative work, and opportunities for synergy and conflict usually develop unplanned and in unforeseeable ways.

Also, not all aspects are equally important to users all the time. When making a decision about which task to work on next, users need knowledge about the current state (in terms of who is currently working on which tasks) and about the planned tasks for the future. However, when working on a task, users are more likely to need knowledge about people working on tasks or objects "relevant" to their own work. Thus, they may need a different kind of overview of the shared global workspace than they would need for working on a new task. This general problem can be considered to be a problem of dealing with information overload.

Coordination in such a shared workspace, where teams create and manipulate shared artifacts to solve a complex problem (e.g. to develop software, to design a product, or to write a research paper), needs to deal with:

– Work planning:
  Here, planning of how to achieve the common goal (e.g. by creating tasks, relating them to each other and to deliverables and schedules) is important. As experience shows, task planning cannot be done once for all at the beginning. Rather, it is an ongoing activity, where the team continuously refines the task plan and adjusts it to changes in the environment and according to the progress of knowledge in the team. Task planning is a way of achieving coordination between team members by agreeing on how to split and integrate individual work.
– Work execution:
  Here, coordination is needed when actually carrying out the work. This does not only address the need of selecting tasks to be worked on in a meaningful

way, but also addresses the need for coordination between people working on related tasks or working on the same objects/resources in different tasks. These dependencies partially arise at run-time. They should not only be seen as a threat to consistent work, but also as an opportunity for achieving synergy in the team.

- Work monitoring:
  In work monitoring the task is to get an overview about the "state of affairs". Are tasks progressing as planned? Do things fit? Is there a need to change the plan?
- Consistency management:
  This may be seen as a part of work monitoring (i.e. to maintain consistency between the work plan and the actual performance of the work). Alternatively, one can see consistency management as a general problem, which also addresses consistency between tasks and their results, and how work performance, work plan, and the overall goals relate to each other.

Overall, current approaches to implement shared workspaces only address some of these issues.

Previous work focused either on providing means for coordination or on supporting overviews. Approaches to coordination in shared workspaces include the provision of group awareness, intra- and inter group conventions [12], documentation of previous states (as in versioning systems, or using log files such as in NoteCards [22]), process support (such as shared plans or workflow management) or communication support. Means for retaining overviews include fisheye views, flexible Diff-ing [14] or shared task lists. However, previous approaches do not address all the requirements of supporting overviews in shared workspaces.

3   Previous Approaches

Coordination in shared global workspaces is a known problem in the CSCW area. Previous approaches include

- provision of group awareness in shared workspaces,
- provision of direct communication channels between collaborators (e.g. notifications, messaging services, informal communication via computer-supported conferences), and
- provision of explicit process support (e.g. workflow management, task-based versioning).

Group awareness [4] facilitates the assessment of the present state (who is doing what) in a shared workspace. It is usually a concept that is applied to shared local sub workspaces in order to help synchronously cooperating users to coordinate their activities. It also supports - to some degree - making informed decisions about what to do next (based on knowledge about who is working in which part of the shared local workspace, thus showing some opportunities for synergy or conflict). However, it does not support finding out about the past, and it does not explicitly address current tasks and plans of the group. Most systems in this area provide local awareness [9]. Examples are applications implemented in GroupKit [19] and Suite [3] as well as SEPIA [21], DOLPHIN [20], Team-Rooms [18], and ShrEdit [11]. These examples used user lists, activity markers, shared views, and telepointers. Some other systems also provided tools for global awareness [9]. Examples include task lists as in CoAUTHOR [10] or workflow management systems, radar views as in SEPIA, or history logs as in NoteCards [22]. BSCW [1] provides workspace awareness through a user presence and activity monitor since version 3.2. This tool shows the presence of participating users in the workspace. It also facilitates communication among users. In addition, BSCW provides access control, simple versioning of documents in a workspace, and asynchronous workspace reports. ORBIT [13] organizes a shared workspace using the locales concept (as a means to communicate tailored awareness) and supports global awareness on other locales through a "navigator". The RICH system provided hierarchical view filters as a means for searching hypermedia networks for content and change related predicates [23]. However, RICH does not support search for collaboration related predicates. Another interesting approach is to provide activity awareness between different individual workspaces as in the Interlocus system [15]. Here, notifications and awareness functions provide asynchronous workspace awareness. However, synchronous awareness and assessment of future activities are not supported. Finally, GroupDesk [5] provides presence awareness and activity awareness in a shared workspace. It uses the concepts of work situation and interest context to distribute events in the shared workspace.

Direct communication channels may be used to provide some group awareness (e.g. informing collaborators about ongoing activities via notifications) and may also help to assess the current state and potentials for synergy and conflict. An example is NSTP [2], which provides an infrastructure e.g. to share meta-information about a shared workspace. Here, workspace structure and content are described as places, things, and facades, to enable sharing and navigation in the shared workspace. However, NSTP itself does not offer awareness functions to applications. Using informal communication collaborators may determine which tasks or parts of the document they should work on next. However, assessment of past changes and finding out about parts of the shared global workspace relevant to the task at hand is not supported.

Explicit process support such as WFM type systems (e.g. GroupDesk [5]) and task-based versioning (e.g. CoVER [6] and Verse [7]) facilitate informed decisions about the future (based on currently active tasks, or tasks to be activated next). Also, the past can be assessed (in terms of activities finished or active, their states, and the respective versions of the shared global workspace). However, these systems require detailed planning in advance and usually cannot deal very well with frequent changes and emerging structures. In addition, finding out about relevant parts of the shared global workspace, which were not initially modeled as part of the process structure, is not supported. Also, these systems largely focus on asynchronous collaboration (with the exception of the versionedSEPIA system [6]).

As a result of this analysis we can state that previous approaches do not address all the aspects of coordination in shared global hypermedia workspaces. In the next section the potential of structural computing for addressing the coordination problem is examined.

4   Supporting Coordination by Structural Computing?

An interesting possibility of supporting coordination in such a shared workspace arises when looking at the coordination problem from the structural computing point of view. In this case, one could view the shared workspace as a medium for collaboration and coordination. The shared workspace may

1. capture shared artifacts describing objectives as well as plans and arguments of how to achieve the final result (i.e. address work planning).
2. support actual performance of work by providing team members with access to tasks, to their related information resources and tools, and to information about ongoing work in other tasks, which might be of potential interest to the current task (i.e. address work execution). This can even include active suggestions about which people to contact for coordination purposes. Obviously, supporting work execution requires integration of all resources required for tasks. For this reason, the open hypermedia systems approach [17] seems highly useful in this domain.
3. enable monitoring of work by providing access to overviews about completed and active tasks, and their relationship to the work plan.
4. support consistency between the components of the shared workspace.

When developing such a shared workspace environment, which could provide the above functionality, the main problem lies in the interdependency between

- the actual content of the workspace (e.g. objectives, plans, task descriptions, and results, as well as the description of the team including members, roles, and organizational hierarchies) and
- the coordination behavior necessary to let the collaborative work progress smoothly.

Both aspects influence each other, and are highly fluent (i.e. changing continuously). Plans might trigger users to do certain actions, actions of co-workers change the state of the shared workspace, and these changes might require different coordination behavior. Here, coordination can aim at the global level or at the local level:

- Coordination on the global level (global coordination) can be defined as the task of minimizing differences between the actual state of the workspace and the terminal state to be achieved over a number of steps (occurring

over the lifetime of the collaboration). Constraints such as "all deliverables have been produced", "deadlines have been met", etc may characterize the terminal state.
– Coordination on the local level (local coordination) aims at aligning activities of team members working on different parts of the project (e.g. on different tasks, on different documents). Some needs for local coordination may arise from the global coordination need (e.g. caused by dependencies between tasks), while other needs for local coordination may arise from user behavior (such as navigating in the shared workspace, or having special expertise).

So, how can we build such a system? Clearly, the open hypermedia systems approach [17] can help to easily integrate information. However, it does not support the continuous change of coordination support adapted to the situation at hand. It is here were structural computing can potentially help.

Figure 1 shows the three main components of the shared global workspace, which have been proven useful to facilitate coordination:

– Content structure,
– Team structure, and
– Process structure.

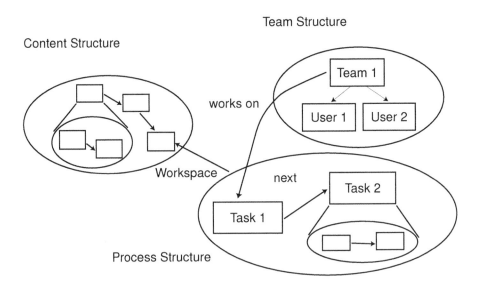

Fig. 1. Example components of the shared workspace; nesting of composite nodes is indicated by showing dashed lines between nodes (indicated by rectangles) and the subnetwork they contain (indicated by ovals).

The content structure models the content of the shared global workspace (i.e. the artifacts and their relationships) using typed hypermedia nodes (atomic and composite nodes) and hypermedia links. Different node and link types are supported, which can be used to express domain semantics as well as constraints. Using an extensible type system ensures that emerging task-oriented structures can be supported. For more details see [8].

The team structure models users and teams working in the shared global workspace using again hypermedia objects and representing relationships between users, teams and artifacts using typed hypermedia links. Examples for such relationships are teams being composed of users, users owning pages, and teams working on pages. This dual use of hypermedia supports simple editing and browsing of organizational as well as content structures in the global workspace. Note that content and team structures are connected via relationships (such as, a user owns a node). These relationships can be represented as links.

The process structure models tasks and activities performed in the shared global workspace. It uses nested hypermedia nodes (of type "task") and represents dependencies (such as temporal order, control flow and data flow among tasks) between them using hypermedia links. Again, the process structure is connected with the content structure (e.g. a task uses a node as its work area) and the team structure (e.g. a task is performed by a team or a user).

In our approach we assume that the shared global workspace is in principle available to all group members all of the time. This requires means for synchronous access to the shared global hypermedia workspace such as, e.g., implemented in the DOLPHIN [20] and the CHIPS [8] system. However, since group members may join and leave the workspace asynchronous work can also be supported.

Since all three aspects of the shared global workspace (its content, its users, the way it is used) are represented in the shared hypermedia workspace, tools can be provided that exploit the joint data model to facilitate orientation and coordination (for more details on these tools, cf. [9]).

The open issue is now how to support the adaptation between the content of the shared hypermedia workspace and the coordination functionality. Letting the structure of the workspace and the structure of the activities being executed on that workspace drive the coordination support might actually devise a new approach to coordination of shared work. In this approach, the structures present in the shared workspace are regarded as building blocks, on which behaviors (i.e. computations over structure) can be used to express structural semantics (i.e. coordination behavior matching the needs of the structure). Potential structures in a shared hypermedia workspace include:

- Process structure:
  Task networks (describing pieces of work to be done as well as flows of control and information) can be used to define coordination behavior aimed at presenting users with information regarding the context of their work, including:
  - Task structure (predecessor-successor tasks, work decomposition hierarchy, and previous results which should be reflected in their work)
  - Concurrent activities in related tasks

- Team Structure
  Teams composed of users carrying roles reflect organizational dependencies. The connection between team structure and process structure can be used to define coordination behavior aimed at presenting users with information regarding e.g.

  - Responsibility of teams and users
  - Competencies of teams and users (which may be deduced from previous tasks that have been tackled by the users)

- Content structure
  The content structure models the content of the shared global workspace (i.e. the artifacts and their relationships) using typed hypermedia nodes (atomic and composite nodes) and hypermedia links. Using the relationships between process structure, team structure, and content structure coordination behavior can be defined, which aims at presenting users with information regarding e.g.

  - Other tasks related to the same document
  - Other people related to the same document
  - Other documents, which may be related due to their use in related tasks or teams.

Now, structural computing could help to facilitate coordination by deriving the required coordination functionality from the above structures, which are present in the shared workspace. Local coordination could be supported by behaviors over the above three structures, which would present the above kinds of information to users in awareness or coordination tools (which need to be provided on the shared workspace) or as part of existing tools to manipulate these structures in the shared workspace. The latter would require including special awareness or coordination widgets.

Defining behaviors that test and reflect the dependencies between objectives and planned tasks (as part of the process structure) and content structure (respectively the content of the tasks being executed) could support global coordination. However, at this point it is unclear how these constraints could be defined (e.g. as static rules or as meta-rules defining how the actual behaviors are computed from the structures present in the shared workspace).

Implementing above functionality define some requirements for structural computing:

- The respective computations need to be defined, which derive the needed coordination behavior from the hypermedia structures in the shared workspace. Such coordination behavior requires (1) the selection of the appropriate user interface elements or tools (on the appropriate objects), and (2) the creation of new hypermedia objects in the shared workspace, which provide derived information (e.g. new versions, references to interesting objects, notifications of relevant users).

- Coordination behavior depends on the teams and users of the shared workspace, and their preferences etc. Thus, these aspects need to be modeled as structures in the shared workspace, too, so that they can influence the coordination behavior exhibited by the workspace.
- Since coordination behavior also depends on current use, information such as the users currently logged in, the sessions they work in collaboratively etc. must be represented as structures in the shared workspace, too.

5   Conclusions

In this paper, properties of the coordination problem in shared hypermedia workspaces were analyzed. Based on the deficits of existing approaches to local and global coordination, the potential of using a structural computing approach was discussed. The main benefit of such a structural computing approach, which explicitly models processes, teams, and content as part of a shared workspace, is that behavior (i.e. computations over structure) can be used to dynamically define coordination support.

However, up to this point there exist no implementation of such an approach. Thus, next steps include a proof-of-concept implementation of the approach as well as design considerations for the user interface of such a system. Application domains for this approach include extended enterprise engineering, a discipline where independent companies combine their resources (i.e. including their work processes) to deliver new products in a short time frame. Here, process structure and coordination requirements cannot be defined up front, and they are likely to change fast over the execution of such a project.

Acknowledgements. Many thanks are due to Ken Anderson for his detailed comments on earlier versions of this paper.

References

1. R. Bentley, T. Horstmann, J. Trevor. The World Wide Web as enabling technology for CSCW: The case of BSCW, Computer-Supported Cooperative Work: Special issue on CSCW and the Web, Vol. 6 (1997), Kluwer Academic Press.
2. M. Day, J. F. Patterson, D. Mitchell, D. The Notification Service Transfer Protocol (NSTP): Infrastructure for Synchronous Groupware. Proc. of 6th International WWW Conference, April 7-11, 1997, Santa Clara, USA. http://atlanta.cs.nchu.edu.tw/www/PAPER80.html.
3. P. Dewan, R. Choudhary. Flexible User-Interface Coupling in Collaborative Systems. In Proc. of ACM CHI'91 Conference, April 1991, pp. 41-49.
4. P. Dourish, and V. Bellotti. Awareness and Coordination in Shared Workspaces. In Proc. of the ACM 1992 Conference on Computer Supported Cooperative Work, Toronto, Nov. 1-4, pp. 107-114.
5. L. Fuchs, U. Pankoke-Babatz, W. Prinz. Supporting Cooperative Awareness with Local Event Mechanisms: The GroupDesk System. In Proc. of the 4th European Conf. on CSCW (ECSCW'95), Stockholm, September 10-14, 1995, pp. 247-262.

6. A. Haake, J. Haake. Take CoVer: Exploiting Version Support in Cooperative Systems. In Proc. of InterCHI'93, Amsterdam, April 26-29, pp. 406-413.

7. A. Haake, D. Hicks. VerSE: Towards Hypertext Versioning Styles. In Proc. of 7th ACM Conference on Hypertext, Washington, March 16-20, pp. 224-234.

8. J. M. Haake, and W. Wang. Flexible support for business Processes: Extending cooperative hypermedia with process support, Proceedings of Group'97, Phoenix, November 16-19, 1997, pp. 341-350.

9. J. M. Haake. Facilitating Orientation in Shared Hypermedia Workspaces. In: Stephen C. Hayne (Ed.): Group'99. Proceedings of the International ACM SIG-GROUP Conference on Supporting Group Work (November 14-17, 1999, Embassy Suites Hotel, Phoenix, Arizona, USA), pp. 365-374, New York, ACM Press, 1999.

10. U. Hahn, M. Jarke, K. Kreplin, M. Farusi. CoAUTHOR: A hypermedia group authoring environment. In Proc. of the 1st European Conference on Computer Supported Cooperative Work (EC-CSCW'89), Gatwick, U.K., September 13-15. Computer Science House: Sloug.

11. L. MacGuffin, G. M. Olson. ShrEdit: A Shared Electronic Workspace. Technical Report No. 45, University of Michigan, Cognitive Sciences and Machine Intelligence Laboratory. 1992.

12. G. Mark. Merging Multiple Perspectives in Groupware Use: Intra- and Intergroup Conventions. Proceedings of Group'97, Phoenix, November 16-19, 1997, pp. 19-28.

13. Tim Mansfield, Simon Kaplan, Geraldine Fitzpatrick, Ted Phelps, Mark Fitzpatrick, Richard Taylor. Evolving Orbit: a progress report on building locales. Proc. of Group'97, ACM Press, Phoenix, AZ, Nov 1997.

14. C. M. Neuwirth, R. Chandhok, D. S. Kaufer, P. Erion, J. Morris, D. Miller. Flexible Diff-ing in a Collaborative Writing System. In Proc. of the ACM 1992 Conference on Computer Supported Cooperative Work , Toronto, October 31-November 4, pp. 147-154.

15. T. Nomura, K. Hayashi, T. Hazama, S. Gudmundson. Interlocus: Workspace Configuration Mechanisms for Activity Awareness. In Proc. of the ACM 1998 Conference on Computer Supported Cooperative Work (CSCW'98), Seattle, Washington, November 14-18, 1998, pp. 19-28.

16. P. J. Nürnberg, J. J. Leggett, E. R. Schneider. As we should have thought. Proceedings of ACM HT'97, pp. 96-101.

17. S. Reich, U. K. Wiil, P. Nürnberg, H. C. Davis, K. Grønbæk, K. M. Anderson, D. E. Millard, J. M. Haake. Addressing Interoperability in Open Hypermedia: The Design of the Open Hypermedia Protocol. The New Review of Hypermedia and Multimedia 5 (1999), 207–248.

18. M. Roseman, S. Greenberg. TeamRooms: Network Places for Collaboration. In Proceedings of the ACM CSCW '96, Boston, November 1996, pp. 325-333.

19. M. Roseman, S. Greenberg. GroupKit: A Groupware Toolkit for Building Real-Time Conferencing Applications. In Proc. of the ACM 1992 Conference on Computer Supported Cooperative Work (CSCW'92), Toronto, October 31-November 4, pp. 43-50.

20. N. Streitz, J. Geissler, J. Haake, J. and Hol. DOLPHIN: Integrated meeting support across local and remote desktop environments and liveboards. In Proc. of ACM CSCW'94 (October 1994), pp. 345-358.

21. N. Streitz, J. Haake, J. Hannemann, A. Lemke, W. Schuler, H. Schütt, and M. Thüring. SEPIA: a cooperative hypermedia authoring environment. In Proceedings of ACM Hypertext'92 (1992), pp. 11-22.

22. R. Trigg, L. Suchman, F. Halasz Supporting Collaboration in NoteCards. In Proc. of the ACM Conference on Computer Supported Cooperative Work (CSCW'86), Austin, December 3-5. Pp. 153-162.
23. W. Wang, and R. Rada. Structured Hypertext with Domain Semantics, ACM Transactions on Information Systems, Vol. 16, No. 4 (Oct. 1998), pp. 372-412.

Scholarly Discourse as Computable Structure

Simon Buckingham Shum, John Domingue, and Enrico Motta

Knowledge Media Institute, The Open University
Milton Keynes, MK7 6AA
UK
{Buckingham.Shum, J.B.Domingue, E.Motta}@open.ac.uk
<http://kmi.open.ac.uk/projects/scholonto>

Abstract. In their initial proposal for structural computing (SC), Nürnberg et al. [18] point to hypertext argumentation systems as an example of an application domain in which structure is of first-order importance. In this paper we summarise the goals and implementation of a knowledge based hypertext environment called ScholOnto (for Scholarly Ontologies), which aims to provide researchers with computational support in representing and analysing the structure of scholarly claims, argumentation and perspectives. A specialised web server will provide a medium for researchers to contest the significance of concepts and emergent structures. In so doing, participants construct an evolving structure that reflects a community's understandings of its field, and which can support computational services for scholars. Using structural analyses of scholarly argumentation, we consider the connections with structural computing, and propose a number of requirements for generic SC environments.

1 Introduction

Structural Computing (SC) has been proposed as a new paradigm which generalises hypertext's interest in explicit, computable structure to a philosophy for computing more widely. The approach is distinguished by its assertion of the primacy of structure over data: "Structure should be the ubiquitous, atomic building block available to all systems at all times and from which other abstractions (including data) are derived" ([18], p.96). Services for detecting, analysing and manipulating structure should therefore be represented using abstractions that transfer across domains and systems. We find SC an interesting proposal with strong connections to our own work. In this short paper, we outline a knowledge based digital library server currently in development, which focuses on the representation of scholarly claims and discourse as semantic structures (see [7] for details). Specifically, we show the connections between this specific domain and SC, and propose several requirements that analyses of our system motivate for generic SC systems.

S. Reich and K.M. Anderson (Eds.): OHS/SC 2000, LNCS 1903, pp. 120–128, 2000.
© Springer-Verlag Berlin Heidelberg 2000

2   Scholarly Publishing, Literature Analysis, and ScholOnto

2.1   Representing Discourse Structure to Assist Scholarly Analysis

We are concerned with future infrastructures for *scholarly publishing*, by which we include scientific, technical and medical research in both academia and industry. Scholarly publishing technologies are currently focused on using networks to access *digital analogues of paper, bibliographic metadata*, and *databases*. Whilst interoperable repositories make such information increasingly accessible, they provide no analytical leverage for *interpreting* the information. The power of the network (i) as a medium for scholarly discourse, and (ii) as a representation for conceptual structures and perspectives within a research community's digital library remains unexplored.

Support is needed for researchers who, typically, are interested in the following kinds of phenomena (exemplified with queries):

- The *intellectual lineage* of ideas: e.g. where has this come from, and has it already been done? (*"Are there any arguments against the framework on which this paper builds?"*)
- The *impact* of ideas: e.g. what reaction was there to this, and has anyone built on it? (*"Has anyone generalised method M to another domain?"* "Has anyone extended Language L?")
- *Perspectives*: are there distinctive schools of thought on this issue? (*"Has anyone proposed a similar solution to Problem P but from a different theoretical perspective?"*)
- *Inconsistencies*: e.g. is an approach consistent with its espoused theoretical foundations?; is there contradictory evidence to a claim? (*"Are there groups building on Theory T, but who contradict each other?"*)
- *Convergences*: are different streams of research mutually reinforcing in interesting ways? (*"Who else uses Data X in their arguments?"*)

Currently, researchers have no way to articulate such questions in a library, analogue or digital. Current metadata initiatives are focused on the encoding of *primary content attributes* to improve retrieval and interoperability. Inconsistencies and interpretations in encoding at this level are considered undesirable in order to assist machine processing. In contrast, these are precisely the features that a system needs to support the *interpreted, knowledge level*, as researchers contest the significance of data, and the concepts which it underpins. The ScholOnto project seeks to address the fundamental requirement for an ontology capable of supporting scholarly research communities in interpreting and discussing evolving ideas: overlaying *interpretations* of content, and supporting the emergence of (possibly conflicting) *perspectives*.

2.2   Hypertext Argumentation

In their initial proposal for structural computing, Nürnberg et al. point to hypertext argumentation systems as an example of an applications domain in which structure is of first-order importance. Argumentation schemes make use of semantic networks of typed nodes such as *Claims, Arguments, Evidence* and *Theories* (e.g. [14], [15], [20]), and computer-supported collaborative argumentation (CSCA) continues as an active research and development field [11]. CSCA does however have important cognitive and social dimensions which if ignored, lead to end-user rejection of systems. Our own research into hypertext support for argumentation, e.g. [3,4,5,6] emphasises that any discourse structuring scheme intended for untrained users must carefully balance simplicity with expressive power, and provide computational services in order to balance the cost/benefit tradeoff. Applied to scholarly discourse, the social fabric of a research field will influence, and in turn be influenced by, the explicit declaration of claims and relationships between researchers' work. The vocabulary provided must be sensitive to this, and be customisable to the language of different communities.

2.3   Towards Ontologies for Scholarly Discourse

Research disciplines are in constant flux and by definition lack consensus on many issues. Whilst this renders futile the idea of a "master ontology/taxonomy" for a discipline, there does appear to be one stable dimension, namely scholarly discourse—the way in which new work is expressed and contested. Thus, it is hard to envisage when researchers will no longer need to make claims about a document's *contributions* (e.g. "this is a new theory, model, notation, software, evidence..."), or contest its *relationships* to other documents and ideas (e.g. "it applies, extends, predicts, refutes...").

Our approach provides an environment for scholars to make claims about concepts in documents, both their own and those of others. Decoupling concepts from claims about them is critical to supporting the emergence and co-existence of multiple *perspectives*. The kind of ontology that we are moving towards is outlined in Figure 1, suggesting concepts and relationships suitable for a wide range of disciplines. This generic scheme already enables inter-operability between different domains, but we also envisage that different disciplines might re-express or specialize concept or relational types, e.g. an experimental field might specialize *predicts* into *hypothesises*. Details and examples of modelling are presented in [7]. It is important to emphasise that our ontology is not merely a taxonomy or metadata scheme. We use a rich modelling language (OCML, see below) to provide both declarative and operational semantics for the concepts and relationships required to deliver ScholOnto's services (discussed below).

As a simple example, using a web form, a researcher R1 might summarise a document's contributions as follows:

```
R1{{Language L uses/applies      Model M}
   {Model M     modifies/extends Theory T}}
```

However, a researcher R2 (or, significantly, a software agent monitoring the network) might challenge R1, in this case reasoning by a model of consistency grounded in the ontology's relational types:

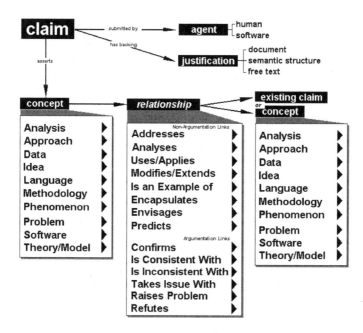

Fig. 1. The structure of a scholarly *Claim* in the ontology. All claims are owned by an agent, and have some form of justification. Claims assert new relationships with other claims, or between concepts. It is hypothesised that such a scheme could be customised and adopted by research communities, whilst maintaining technical interoperability, and hence opening new possibilities for interdisciplinary discourse.

```
R2{{Model M modifies/extends Model N}{Model N refutes Theory T}
    is-inconsistent-with {Model M modifies/extends Theory T}}
```

Structured discourse only pays off when the benefits outweigh the effort. In principle, discourse primitives such as those above would on their own support the emergence of useful networks and support a range of novel queries, but additional representational power is derived when they combine to form "compound structures" corresponding to a range of interesting phenomena in a literature. Such structures could be declared meaningful by researchers, but in principle could also be identified by agents through structural computation.

2.4   Current Status

ScholOnto is implemented as an application of several generic knowledge modelling technologies. Motta's *OCML* knowledge modelling language integrates both specification and operationalization, thus allowing seamless ontology specification, instantiation and integration with reasoning components [16], whilst Domingue's suite of Java tools [12], [17] provide graphical user interfaces onto an OCML knowledge base: *WebOnto* makes it possible to browse, edit, search, share and visualize knowledge models over the Web; *Knote* provides interactive forms to guide the process of populating the knowledge base, and *Lois* generates contextualised search forms for querying knowledge bases. A skeletal prototype has been implemented, and seeding with concepts has begun to validate the design of the ontology and to elicit requirements for a user interface for non-knowledge engineers.

3   Structural Computing in ScholOnto

3.1   Knowledge Based Hypertext and Structural Computing

Implicit in ScholOnto (and SC) is the machine's ability to reason about structure. ScholOnto's knowledge base is a large, semantic network of typed concepts and relationships, plus rules for reasoning about the structure. The reasons for implementing in OCML (apart from local expertise) were the ease of defining semantic schema (as in Aquanet [15], or Germ [2], the meta-environment of which gIBIS was one application). It is thus simple to represent structural patterns of interest, and write inference rules (OCML is Lisp-based) to link system action to structure, or to compute new structures. Clearly there are many ways to implement structural reasoning capability, but we suggest that the overlap between knowledge based systems, semantic hypertext, and SC adds an interesting dimension to the SC initiative, especially where "knowledge level" processing and interactive systems are combined.

The following sections illustrate the kinds of structural computing that ScholOnto will perform. With each example, broader implications for SC systems are highlighted as an "SC requirement". Whether these should be regarded as fundamental or merely desirable requirements is open for discussion.

3.2   Detecting Contrasting Perspectives

Perspectives within a literature could correspond to clusters of documents aligning for/against clusters of concepts. A ScholOnto agent could therefore be set to monitor the network for *contrasting perspectives* defined as structures where *≥3 documents support ideas of type A and challenge ideas of type B, and ≥3 documents do the converse.* The ontology thus provides the basis for detecting the emergence of "camps" within a literature in which the basis for one cluster of documents is attacked by another cluster. If SC environments are to be customisable by non-programmers, structure and behaviours need to be accessible. One requirement might therefore be:

– SC Requirement: High level scripting languages and user interfaces for end-users to define structures of interest (e.g. for searches or agents)

The detection of structural corrollaries of perspectives would make use of *link families.* An example would be "difference of opinion" with a concept or perspective, that is, relationships varying in strength from *raises issues with* or *is inconsistent with*, to *challenges* and *refutes*. Such a family could be usefully defined in order to cover relational sets that are of interest (e.g. "show me any papers that 'have problems' with this theory"). In addition, if a query is posed to the system that implicates the milder *raises issues with* relationship, it is reasonable for the system also to infer that the stronger *refutes* relationship will also be of interest, and use this to retrieve potentially relevant material. This level of knowledge also enables the computation of links that may not have been explicitly declared.

– SC Requirement: Generalization and specialization of relational types (e.g. enabling reference via a parent to a whole set of relational types, or "intelligent inference" based on known relationships between types)

Link families are a specialised kind of composite structure that aggregate links.

3.3   Perspectives and Composite Structures

Scholarly perspectives themselves emerge from, and come to represent, a configuration of concepts (that normally has established a following). An example might be the debate between those who subscribe broadly to symbolic processing approaches to AI, and those who work from a situated cognition perspective (for instance, we could imagine a properly elaborated model of the exchanges in [9]). Closer to home, the *As We Should Have Thought* paper seeks to establish *structural computing* as a coherent perspective on the design of systems by drawing on existing work, and the purpose of these SC workshops is to map out in more detail the conceptual roots of this perspective, and its ability to solve persistent problems. There would be a need within ScholOnto to be able to refer to *structural computing* as a perspective in a simple way that encapsulates this community. We are talking of course about the need for *composite nodes*, as proposed by Conklin [10] and reiterated recently by Anderson [1] in his SC analysis of software engineering environments (although composite nodes are more usefully conceived as composite structures within an SC paradigm).

– SC Requirement: Composite structures that encapsulate sub-structure for ease of human/machine reference/processing.

3.4   Arbitrary Granularity: Micro- and Macro-Argumentation

Argumentation/discourse is conducted at many levels of detail, so (in concert with composite structures) ScholOnto must support arbitrary granularities of structure (another of the SC requirements noted in [1]). At present, ScholOnto has been designed for "macro-level" discourse (emphasising key claims and relationships *between* documents), bearing in mind the lessons from previous hypertext argumentation systems which indicate a reluctance or inability on the part of untrained users to make the structure of too many ideas and concepts explicit.

Even at this level, we envisage the need for shades of discourse level (implied by the need for composites). However, closely related work on hypertextual argumentation by Kolb [13] and Carter [8] describes the reification of argumentation structure at a finer granularity, suggesting possible uses of ScholOnto if there was the demand for its ontology to be refined to support fine-grained argumentation. This corresponds to a requirement to represent *intra-document* as well as inter-document structure. To summarise,

- SC Requirement: Support the expression of multiple levels of structural granularity, enabling common structural reasoning capabilities to be applied at multiple levels of analysis.

3.5   Conflicting Structures

A research discipline's raison d'être is to debate and evaluate conflicting views. As a medium for making claims and engaging in argumentation, ScholOnto must support this process, and thus is fundamentally perspectival in philosophy. The ontology therefore permits conflicting links to be made between concepts, regarding them as *claims* associated with a person, and open to contest. This is of course very different to systems seeking to maintain structures for machine interpretation only, or for applications where inconsistency is undesirable. Current web metadata and ontological annotation initiatives fall into this category, being focused on the encoding of primary content attributes to improve retrieval and interoperability. Inconsistencies and interpretations in encoding at this level are considered undesirable in order to assist machine processing. In contrast, these are precisely the features that ScholOnto needs for human interpretation.

What are the implications for generic SC environments? There are no doubt other application domains where multiple, logically conflicting, structures need to co-exist. A collaborative SC environment should support this, at least when end-users expect plurality of perspectives, and need to negotiate the meaning of structures. Avoiding premature commitment to structure was, after all, precisely the motivation behind spatial hypertext systems such as VIKI [19] which are a prime application for structural computing.

- SC Requirement: Support the emergence, co-existence, and analysis of structures contributed by multiple authors, which may conflict logically.

3.6   Structural Patterns Signalling Inconsistency

With many research groups working with shared concepts, possibly across different disciplines, these concepts are invariably misunderstood, or mutate as they are better understood. Authors may ignore, or not be aware of each other (publications might be years apart, or in different fields), but ScholOnto's model of the network enables one to trace consistency (as defined by the ontology). It would be useful for researchers to explore "what if" scenarios for new ideas (for instance publishing a draft concept map in a personal space to see what the system came back with in terms of inconsistencies or related work). Or, we can imagine a journal reviewer testing the ideas in a paper for consistency with the concepts on which it claims to build.

The ScholOnto functionality deployed here is the ability to use the ontology to define arbitrary principles (e.g. "consistency"), and heuristics to detect possible violations of that principle (e.g. "existence of both positive and negative relationships between two concepts"—where link families have been defined, as discussed above). The generic SC requirement motivated by this example might be expressed as:

– SC Requirement: Support the definition of arbitrary criteria and provide a means to validate structures against those criteria.

4 Conclusion

To summarise, our analysis of the computational work that the ScholOnto system must perform confirms that it is an application that falls squarely in the domain of structural computing. Our representation, through the use of an ontology for scholarly claims and argumentation, highlights the fruitful overlap between knowledge based hypertext and structural computing, and raises for discussion several new requirements for generic structural computing environments.

References

1. Anderson, K. Software Engineering Requirements for Structural Computing. In First International Workshop on Structural Computing, Darmstadt (Feb. 21), 1999, Technical Report, Dept. Computer Science, Aarhus University, DK <http://www.daimi.au.dk/~pnuern/sc1/su missions/anderson.html>.
2. Bruns, G. Germ: A Metasystem for Browsing and Editing. Microelectronics and Computer Technology Corporation, Technical Report STP-122-88, 1988.
3. Buckingham Shum, S. Analyzing the Usability of a Design Rationale Notation. In Design Rationale: Concepts, Techniques, and Use, Moran, T.P. and Carroll, J.M., (Eds.), Lawrence Erlbaum Associates: Hillsdale, NJ, 1996, pp. 185–215.
4. Buckingham Shum, S. Negotiating the Construction and Reconstruction of Organisational Memories. Journal of Universal Computer Science (Special Issue on Information Technology for Knowledge Management), 3, 8, 1997, pp. 899–928 <http://www.iicm.edu/jucs_3_8/>.
5. Buckingham Shum, S. and Hammond, N. Argumentation-Based Design Rationale: What Use at What Cost? International Journal of Human-Computer Studies, 40, 4, 1994, pp. 603–652.
6. Buckingham Shum, S., MacLean, A., Bellotti, V. and Hammond, N. Graphical Argumentation and Design Cognition. Human-Computer Interaction, 12, 3, 1997, pp. 267–300 <http://kmi.open.ac.uk/kmi-a stracts/kmi-tr-25-a stract.html>.
7. Buckingham Shum, S., Motta, E., and Domingue, J. ScholOnto: An Ontology-Based Digital Library Server for Research Documents and Discourse. International Journal on Digital Libraries, Aug./Sept., 2000 <http://kmi.open.ac.uk/projects/scholonto/>.

8. Carter, L.M. Arguments in Hypertext: A Rhetorical Approach. In Proc. Hypertext 2000, San Antonio, TX, 2000, ACM: New York.

9. Cognitive Science (Special Issue on Symbolic Reasoning and Situated Action), 17, 1993, pp. 1–133.

10. Conklin, J. and Begeman, M.L. gIBIS: A Tool for All Reasons. Journal of the American Society for Information Science, 40, 1989, pp. 200–213.

11. Computer-Supported Collaborative Argumentation Resource Site. Knowledge Media Institute, Open University, UK ¡http://kmi.open.ac.uk/sbs/csca¿.

12. Domingue, J. and Motta, E. PlanetOnto: From News Publishing to Integrated Knowledge Management Support. IEEE Intelligent Systems (Special Issue on Knowledge Management and Knowledge Distribution over the Internet), in press.

13. Kolb, D. Scholarly Hypertext: Self-Represented Complexity. In Proceedings of The Eighth ACM Conference on Hypertext, Southampton, 1997, pp. 29–37.

14. Lee, J. SIBYL: A Tool for Managing Group Design Rationale. In Proc. Computer Supported Cooperative Work, Los Angeles, CA, 1990, ACM Press: New York, pp. 79–92.

15. Marshall, C.C. and Rogers, R.A. Two Years before the Mist: Experiences with Aquanet. In Proc. Fourth ACM Conference on Hypertext, 1992, pp. 53–62.

16. Motta, E. Reusable Components for Knowledge Modelling. IOS Press: Amsterdam, NL, 1999.

17. Motta, E., Buckingham Shum, S. and Domingue, J. Ontology-Driven Document Enrichment: Principles and Case Studies. International Journal of Human-Computer Studies, 2000, in press
`<http://kmi.open.ac.uk/projects/scholonto/>`.

18. Nürnberg, P.J., Leggett, J.J. and Schneider, E.R. As We Should Have Thought. In Proceedings of Hypertext'97: 8th ACM Conference on Hypertext, Southampton, 1997, pp. 96–101
`<http://journals.ecs.soton.ac.uk/~lac/ht97/pdfs/nuern.pdf>`.

19. Shipman, F.M. and Marshall, C.C. Formality Considered Harmful: Experiences, Emerging Themes, and Directions on the Use of Formal Representations in Interactive Systems. Computer Supported Cooperative Work, 8, 4, 1999, pp. 333–352.

20. Trigg, R. and Weiser, M. TEXTNET: A Network-Based Approach to Text Handling. ACM Transactions on Office Information Systems, 4, 1, 1983.

Navigating Spaces: The Semantics of Cross Domain Interoperability

David E. Millard and Hugh C. Davis

Intelligence, Agents, Multimedia,
University of Southampton, Dept. of Electronics and Computer Science,
Southampton, UK
{dem97r, hdc}@ecs.soton.ac.uk

Abstract. The Open Hypermedia Protocol (OHP) developed by the Open Hypermedia Systems Working Group (OHSWG) allows components of a system to discuss Navigational Hypermedia, but it does not yet address the needs of other hypertext domains. The focus of Structural Computing has been to recognise the need for structure at all levels of computing, if OHP could express the structure of multiple domains then it could be used to facilitate this goal. The Fundamental Open Hypermedia Model (FOHM) has been developed to incorporate other domains into the OHP data model, forming a semantic language that can potentially be used to discuss any structure. In this paper we look at the 'cross-domain fertilization' that takes place when several domains are brought together in this way and describe what it means to encounter structures from one domain in another.

1 Background

The Open Hypermedia Systems Working Group (OHSWG) has been working on the problem of interoperability between hypermedia systems and has produced the Open Hypermedia Protocol (OHP), an evolving standard by which such systems can communicate. Originally this work focused on Navigational Hypertext, but recently the group has been attempting to extend OHP to apply to other Hypertext Domains (such as Spatial and Taxonomic Hypertext). Focus has also shifted to the paradigm of structural computing, where the issues of Navigational Hypermedia have been recognised as part of a wider problem domain, that of managing structure throughout a computer system.

The authors have been working on the **F**undamental **O**pen **H**ypertext **M**odel (FOHM), which extends the OHP data model to apply to these other domains. FOHM considers each domain as a particular way of using the same basic associational structures. Combining all three views results in a model that could be used as an exchange format between components of differing domains and could theoretically form a basis for multi-domain knowledge transfer in future systems.

Because FOHM encompasses the functionality of all three domains, when using the model in any particular domain one must handle the structures normally unique to the others. Initially this was seen as a problem as it introduced

S. Reich and K.M. Anderson (Eds.): OHS/SC 2000, LNCS 1903, pp. 129–139, 2000.
© Springer-Verlag Berlin Heidelberg 2000

unnecessary complexity into each domain, but surprisingly it has resulted in each domain growing in a useful manner. We have described this as *cross-domain fertilisation*. In essence FOHM has become more than the sum of its parts.

In this paper we explore this cross-domain fertilization and look at what structures are supported in FOHM as a result.

2   An Overview of Hypertext Domains

In its work on interoperability the OHSWG has been considering the requirements of several domains. The three most frequently mentioned were Navigational, Spatial and Taxonomic Hypertext. Before we can examine FOHM it is necessary to define these domains.

2.1   Navigational Hypertext

Navigational Hypertext is the most traditional domain of hypertext, exemplified in Open Hypermedia Systems such as Chimera [1], DHM [5], HyperForm [15], Microcosm [3] and the HB/SP series [13]. It is also used by the World Wide Web (WWW) [2] which has resulted in a generation of people becoming comfortable with the point and click interface commonly associated with it.

FOHM is strongly based on the OHP data model of navigational hypertext [4], demonstrated by Figure 1.

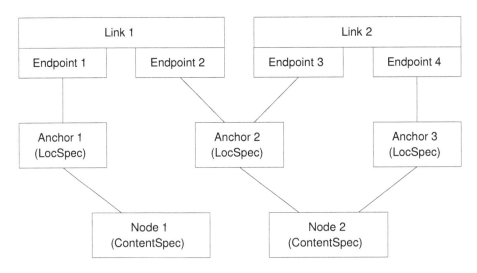

Fig. 1. The OHP Node Link model

A link is a defined relationship between zero or more endpoints, where each endpoint references an anchor. These are objects that attach the link to other objects, typically nodes (wrappers for documents). An anchor can attach either to the whole object or to a location inside that object. Multiple anchors can attach to the same thing and multiple endpoints can reference the same anchor.

The endpoint contains information that is separate from the anchor itself but is useful for a link. Typically this is a direction attribute, such that in any link an endpoint may be a source, destination or bidirectional endpoint. This is then used in the Follow Link operation that a user invokes to navigate the structure.

2.2   Spatial Hypertext

Spatial Hypertext systems allow users to organise their information visually in a process known as 'Information Triage' [7]. Relationships between nodes are expressed by their visual characteristics such as proximity, colour or shape. This results in some interesting properties. If for instance a node is slightly misaligned with other nodes then this might express an uncertainty about whether the node is actually part of the relationship. In other words it expresses classification within relationships, where some nodes are 'more' related then others.

Spatial hypertext systems are therefore ideal for an evolving organisation of data. Examples of such systems include VIKI [6] and CAOS [12].

2.3   Taxonomic Hypertext

Taxonomic Hypertext is the categorisation of information, called artifacts, into sets. Applications can allow users to navigate the information space by moving between overlapping sets and can also reason about the relationships that nodes have with one another, represented by the sets. In addition it expects there to be differing views on how the information is to be categorised and defines perspectives, objects that allow the categorisation hierarchy to split according to the views of differing users.

Figure 2 gives an example of a Taxonomy. Here two people have categorized five artifacts. They both agree that all five lie within category one and that artifacts one and two also lie within sub-category two. However they disagree on how the remaining three artifacts should be split up. The two perspective objects represent the branching point of the categorisation tree.

3   A Common Model

3.1   FOHM and Structural Computing

FOHM makes no assumptions about the protocol it is running over or the systems that are using it. It is a semantic language that requires an implementation in a syntactic language before it can be used. We currently have one implementation of FOHM running across the SoFAR agent framework developed at Southampton [9]. In this implementation FOHM is described in an ontology which is then discussed over the agent infrastructure.

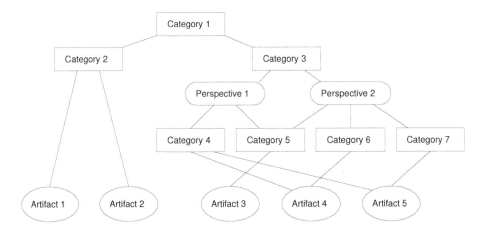

Fig. 2. Example Taxonomy

Structural Computing "asserts the primacy of structure over data" [10], as such it is concerned with looking at how structure can be discussed and managed at all levels of computing. FOHM is a semantic language for the discussion of structure. Although other structural languages exists they tend to contain very little semantic information (e.g. XML) and suffer performance penalties as a result of their generality [11].

3.2   A Description of FOHM

In FOHM we describe four objects that are analogous to objects in the OHP-Nav data model [8]. An *association* contains a feature space; a list of features that all the objects in the association must map to. It also contains a set of *bindings*, these attach *datarefs* to the association via a feature vector that describes how the dataref maps to the feature space. Finally FOHM has a notion of a *data* object, this is a wrapper for some piece of data that lies outside the scope of the model, normally a document although it could represent any file or stream.

Figure 3 shows a possible FOHM structure. Bindings map DataRefs to the Navigational Link on the left by defining their direction and to the Spatial List on the right by defining their position. The DataRefs either reference a whole item of Data or point into that Data (e.g. to reference a particular region).

3.3   Levels of Structure in FOHM

Between them the domains modelled support three levels of structure:

1. *Explicit External Structure.* By creating typed associations between data, FOHM allows explicit relationships to be expressed. This is analogous to taxonomic categorisation, where we say that an object (or data) belongs in one category or another.

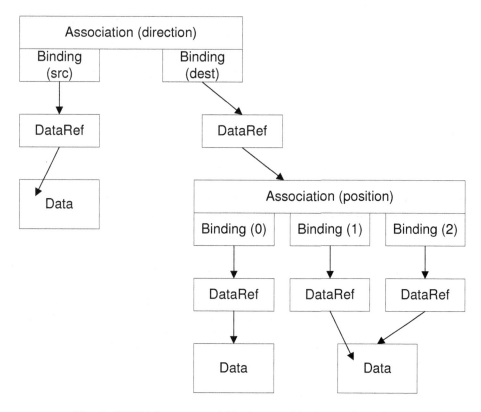

Fig. 3. FOHM Structures: A Navigational Link to a Spatial List

2. *Implicit External Structure.* This is classification within a relationship, defined by the feature space of an association and the corresponding feature
   vectors. E.g. in Spatial Hypertext an association may contain a set of data
   objects, each one of which is given a Red/Green/Blue (RGB) value. Objects
   which are similar in some way will be more alike in colour.
3. *Internal Structure* is the structure of the information actually inside individual data objects. For example a film can be viewed as a collection of many
   scenes, a user viewing the film follows a path or trail through those scenes.
   Typically this is not the way a film is stored due to file size and performance
   restrictions. Thus at some level we no longer handle structure externally and
   instead handle it internally via a proprietary data format. Datarefs allows
   FOHM's external structures to reference the internal structure of data (e.g.
   link to the seventh scene of a film).

One of the most important aspects of FOHM is that if a client does not totally
understand the semantics of the structure it is given it may still understand a
portion of it. For example imagine an association that represents a company.
This association may have a feature space with a single feature 'role'. All data

that binds to this association must have a vector that maps to that feature, in effect stating what the role of that data object is in the company.

Should this structure be served to a client that understands the feature space 'role' then that client will appreciate all of the meaning of that structure. However if it was served to a client that didn't understand the feature then that client would at least still understand that a relationship exists, could display the relationship to the user and otherwise manipulate the association as normal.

4   The Contribution of the Domains

Each domain brings something unique to the FOHM model. In this section we will look at what is brought to FOHM from each domain and discuss how each of the domains are extended to handle the extra structure.

4.1   Navigational Hypertext: Introducing the Anchor

In many ways Navigational Hypertext is the simplest of the three domains. Its notion of directed links can be easily modeled in FOHM by a single feature 'direction' to which nodes are bound with either a 'source', 'destination' or 'bi-directional' value. The anchor object allows external linking structure to point into otherwise opaque data, it is this mechanism that allows the referencing of *internal structure* as mentioned above. However neither Spatial or Taxonomic Hypertext has such a mechanism.

In FOHM the anchor is replaced by a dataref object. This object is also accessible by Spatial and Taxonomic clients enabling those domains to reference internal structure as well. This is useful to both domains and allows spaces and categories to refer to parts of a data object as well the object in its entirety.

4.2   Spatial Hypertext: Classification within Relationships

At a superficial level it is possible to view Spatial Hypertext as a presentation layer on top of Navigational Links. For example a link may have some attributes that determine that when viewed spatially it appears as a red square. However this is to miss the important notion of *implicit external structure* as described above. In a Spatial Hypertext System the visual attributes of the various objects actually form extra structural information about those objects, one of the applications of which is to allow fuzzy membership of an association.

Spatial Hypertext Systems rely on users to understand the visual clues supplied. E.g. they can express that one object is redder than another but no semantic reason is given, the user must interpret that information themselves. In FOHM we use the feature space to contain all the spatial features that datarefs may bind to, e.g. colour, shape, size, etc. A binding maps values to those features, therefore describing a datarefs position in the space. An interesting consequence of this approach is that as FOHM has no restriction on the feature spaces used it is possible to replace spatial mappings with semantic ones. In effect allowing the system, as well as the user, to appreciate fuzzy membership.

As an example consider a set of nodes that represents dangerous animals. In a Spatial Hypertext system we may colour the animals such that red indicates danger. When rendered the user can see what the nodes represent and they can also see that some are redder than others, but the understanding of what red represents is lost. However in FOHM we could replace the colour with a different feature that explicitly defined that semantic, e.g. 'danger', which has defined values ranging from 'harmful' to 'deadly'. A system that understands the meaning of the 'danger' feature has a true understanding of how the animals relate to one another. The disadvantage of this is that it is probable that more systems understand colour than a specific feature like 'danger'.

The feature space is a very powerful way of binding objects to an association, however we must extend Navigational and Taxonomic Hypertext to deal with these powerful bindings.

With Taxonomic Hypertext this is a fairly trivial operation, the *implicit external structure* simply becomes an extension of the categorisation process, where the fuzzy membership of a category becomes possible. In addition if the people creating a taxonomy disagree on this implicit structure then they can divide the taxonomy at that point using the perspective feature as normal.

Navigational Hypertext has many more issues to deal with because it relies on the feature space to enable the navigation of associations. There are two ways to cope with the 'pollution' of the feature space.

1. Ignore it. A Navigational client can assume that if there is no direction feature then all members of an association can be treated as bi-directional for purposes of navigation.
2. Extend the navigation model. We can make the same assumption as above but also extend our model of navigation so that it understands some of the common features that would be used by the other domains and allows them to alter the effect of navigation.

In actual fact this is a decision that is beyond the scope of the model, however it is important to think about the consequences of a client taking the second approach. If we had a standard definition of what it means for a client to navigate a list (as opposed to a link) then hypertext designers could build their hypertexts to take advantage of that functionality.

There are two places were the structure of an association could become important. The first is during *traversal*, applying a Follow Link operation to an association, the second is *arrival*, where following a link results in another link, rather than a document. This behaviour remains beyond the scope of the model, but still requires definition if interoperability is to be achieved at a useful level. Some example definitions are given in [8].

4.3   Taxonomic Hypertext: Perspectives and Context

Although the OHP-Nav data model has no notion of context, context has long
been an important issue in navigational systems, allowing a user to see different versions of documents or hyperwebs according to a particular viewpoint.
In Taxonomic Hypertext context is realised via the use of a perspective object.
These are designed to be placed in a categorisation hierarchy at the point where
it splits according to the views of the authors. The context of the viewer will
determine which perspective (branch of the taxonomy) that they see.

When implementing a perspective in FOHM one could use an association of
type 'perspective'. However this does not fit in very well with the rest of the
model. This is because the semantics of what a perspective does to traversal and
arrival functionality has to be understood by the association containing those
perspectives and not by the perspectives themselves. In addition what would it
mean for that parent association to have structure? What is the meaning of a
list of perspectives as opposed to a set?

Fortunately there is a way of shifting this knowledge back into the perspective object itself. Rather than a category containing perspectives representing a
branch, in FOHM we say that a perspective object *is* the branch. If there were
two versions of a data object you would create a perspective association that
contained both versions. Now the arrival semantic of a perspective is to choose
one of the data objects to reveal and the traversal semantic is essentially the
question 'what other views are there on this object?'

Figure 4 shows these alternative implementations of perspective. Note that
in the FOHM model there are two versions of Category 1 – the result of viewing
that Category in different contexts.

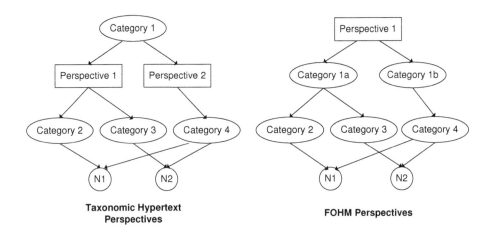

**Taxonomic Hypertext
Perspectives**

FOHM Perspectives

Fig. 4. Alternative implementations of perspective

The FOHM model of perspective contains some properties that are very desirable when dealing with contextual systems:

1. The ability to link to a specific node, whatever the contextual considerations (linking across context). This is achieved by linking to the node itself.
2. The ability to link to a node that is determined by context. This is achieved by linking to the perspective that contains the choice of nodes.
3. Everything about the structure can change in context. Including the type of that object! (e.g. linking to a perspective could result in a data object in one context but result in an association object in another)

However FOHM only gives a framework in which context can operate, it does not define context itself. A context is an object that contains contextual information. FOHM assumes the existence of two types of context.

1. *User Context*. This is an object that defines the state of the user. This could include information about the user (such as age and job position) as well as information relating to their interaction with the system (trails etc.). In addition it may include temporary user specified information that will help the user filter the information space (e.g. today I am interested in cars).
2. *Data Context*. This is an object that describes a data object. This could include information about the object (such as the date of its creation), versioning information as well as a description of to whom the object would be interesting.

In addition FOHM assumes the existence of a 'magic function' that compares a user context to a data context and decides if they match. A simple implementation could define a the contexts as lists of keyword value pairs and then the function would choose an object based on the number of matching values.

5   Conclusions

FOHM is a semantic language in which associational structures can be discussed. In this paper we have shown how those structures draw from the three original domains that FOHM was based on. Enabling structure to be represented at many levels and providing a framework for context. However there remain a number of non-trivial issues to be resolved.

FOHM allows the definition of structure in the form of associations across objects (other associations or data). It controls the access to those associations via the feature space and the accompanying feature vectors. A client that does not understand the feature space should not edit the association as they do not understand the implications of their changes or additions. However FOHM has no easy way of controlling macro-structures formed out of associations, structures formed in the hyperweb itself.

A taxonomic hierarchy is an example of such a structure, one which has strong rules about circularity and branching that cannot be conveyed in the

FOHM model (instead they must be enforced at the server end). It is not yet known whether this will be a serious problem to applications that use specific macro-structures.

There also remains a great deal of work to be done on standard feature spaces. An initial set of feature spaces with arrival and traversal semantics is needed. In addition although FOHM represents a powerful framework for the implementation of context we have yet to define a universal context object (either for a user or for data).

The development of FOHM is a step towards a future where structure is as important as data and can be discussed by a variety of different components over a global information network. The authors believe that the infrastructure for that discussion is only now being developed [9] [14] and that FOHM represents the semantic layer that could run over such an infrastructure. One which brings together and extends the traditional information domains.

References

1. Kenneth M. Anderson, Richard N. Taylor, and E. James Whitehead. Chimera: Hypertext for heterogeneous software environments. In *ECHT '94. Proceedings of the ACM European conference on Hypermedia technology, Sept. 18-23, 1994, Edinburgh, Scotland, UK*, pages 94–197, 1994.
2. Tim Berners-Lee, Robert Cailliau, A. Luotonen, Henrik Frystyk Nielsen, and A. Secret. The World Wide Web. *Communications of the ACM*, 37(8):76–82, 1994.
3. Hugh C. Davis, Simon Knight, and Wendy Hall. Light hypermedia link services: A study of third party application integration. In *ECHT '94. Proceedings of the ACM European conference on Hypermedia technology, Sept. 18-23, 1994, Edinburgh, Scotland, UK*, pages 41–50, 1994.
4. Kaj Grønbæk. Interoperability - issues beyond the protocol. In *Proceedings of the 4th Workshop on Open Hypermedia Systems, ACM Hypertext '98 Conference, Pittsburgh, PA, June 20-24*, pages 33–38, 1998.
5. Kaj Grønbæk and Randall H. Trigg. Design issues for a dexter-based hypermedia system. *Communications of the ACM*, 37(3):40–49, February 1994.
6. Catherine C. Marshall and Frank M. Shipman. Spatial hypertext: Designing for change. *Communications of the ACM*, 38:88–97, 1995.
7. Catherine C. Marshall and Frank M. Shipman. Spatial hypertext and the practice of information triage. In *Proceedings of the '97 ACM Conference on Hypertext, April 6-11, 1997, Southampton, UK*, pages 124–133, 1997.
8. David E. Millard, Luc Moreau, Hugh C. Davis, and Siegfried Reich. FOHM: A fundamental open hypertext model for investigating interoperability between hypertext domains. In *Proceedings of the '00 ACM Conference on Hypertext, May 30 - June 3, San Antonio, TX* (2000), pp. 93–102.
9. Luc Moreau, Nick Gibbins, David DeRoure, Samhaa El-Beltagy, Wendy Hall, Gareth Hughes, Dan Joyce, Sanghee Kim, Danius Michaelides, Dave Millard, Sigi Reich, Robert Tansley, and Mark Weal. SoFAR with DIM agents. An agent framework for distributed information management. In *PAAM 2000. The Fifth International Conference and Exhibition on The Practical Application of Intelligent Agents and Multi-Agents. April 10 - 12, 2000, Manchester, UK* (Apr. 2000), pp. 369–388.

10. Peter J. Nürnberg, John J. Leggett, and Erich R. Schneider. As we should have thought. In *Proceedings of the '97 ACM Conference on Hypertext, April 6-11, 1997, Southampton, UK*, pages 96–101, 1997.

11. Siegfried Reich, Jon P. Griffiths, David E. Millard, and Hugh C. Davis. Solent — a platform for distributed open hypermedia applications. In *Database and Expert Systems Applications. 10th Intl. Conference, DEXA 99, Florence, Italy* (Berlin/Heidelberg/New York, Aug. 1999), T. Bench-Capon, G. Soda, and A. M. Tjoa, Eds., vol. 1677 of *LNCS*, Springer, pp. 802–811.

12. Olav Reinert, Dirk Bucka-Lassen, Claus A. Pedersen, and Peter J. Nürnberg. CAOS: A collaborative and open spatial structure service component with incremental spatial parsing. In *Proceedings of the '99 ACM Conference on Hypertext, February 21-25, 1999, Darmstadt, Germany*, pages 49–50, February 1999.

13. John L. Schnase, John L. Leggett, David L. Hicks, Peter J. Nürnberg, and J. Alfredo Sánchez. Open architectures for integrated, hypermedia-based information systems. In *HICSS 94 — 37th Annual Hawaii International Conference on System Science.*, 1994.

14. Jim Waldo. Jini architecture overview. Technical report, Sun Microsystems, Inc., 901 San Antonio Road, Palo Alto, CA 94303 U.S.A., 1998.

15. Uffe Kock Wiil and John J. Leggett. HyperForm: using extensibility to develop dynamic, open and distributed hypertext systems. In *ECHT '92. Proceedings of the ACM conference on Hypertext, Nov 30-Dec 4, Milan, Italy*, pages 251–261, 1992.

Structural Computing Requirements for the Transformation of Structures and Behaviors

Kenneth M. Anderson

Department of Computer Science
University of Colorado, Boulder
ECOT 717, Campus Box 430
Boulder CO 80309-0430
kena@cs.colorado.edu,
http://www.cs.colorado.edu/users/kena/

Abstract. The field of structural computing is a new paradigm of computation based on structure as opposed to data. Initial work in this area has suggested the need for the transformation of structures, especially when considering the interpretation of a structure from domain A within domain B. This work examines the need for formal mechanisms to specify both structures and the legal ways in which structures can be transformed from one structure to another. We motivate this discussion with an example from the domain of programming languages. In addition, we briefly present an example from the domain of genetic algorithms that suggests the need to consider transformations on behaviors as well. We conclude by enumerating the benefits to structural computing if such formalisms are developed and suggest possible first avenues of exploration.

1   Introduction

Structural computing is an emerging field of research exploring a new paradigm of computation based on structure as opposed to data. In the original conceptualization of structural computing [5], Peter Nürnberg emphasizes this point of view by stating that structural computing "asserts the primacy of structure over data" and that computing should be performed on entities that are intrinsically structured. Stated another way, the "atoms" of structural computing should have the ability to both contain (structured) information and participate in arbitrary structural relationships. In this view, data can be viewed as "degenerate structure" e.g., an atom that does not make use of its ability to participate in structural relationships. In addition, Nürnberg asserts that structure and behavior should be separated, such that developers have the ability to apply multiple behaviors to a single structure or the ability to apply a single behavior to multiple structures. The idea is that a behavior can be "structure-aware" with the ability to examine structures to see if they contain or participate in relationships that it can manipulate or otherwise process.

Initial work in structural computing has fallen into one of two categories. The first category concerns itself with examining domains that may benefit from this

S. Reich and K.M. Anderson (Eds.): OHS/SC 2000, LNCS 1903, pp. 140–146, 2000.
© Springer-Verlag Berlin Heidelberg 2000

new paradigm of computation and analyzing them for the requirements they place upon structural computing. Example domains include argumentation support [8], spatial hypermedia [3], taxonomic reasoning [6], linguistics [5], software engineering [1], and literary hypertext [7]. The second category produces prototype techniques and tools for experimentation and evaluation of the utility of structural computing. In particular, structural computing has identified the need for a structural computing infrastructure. Such an infrastructure will consist of a set of structure servers, where each server is responsible for managing access to a particular set of related structures.

This paper is an example of a new category; one which deals with establishing theoretical foundations for structural computing.

In particular, we identify a need for formal techniques in specifying (1) structure and (2) transformations on structure. We also indicate the need for similar mechanisms for transformations of behavior by considering the domain of genetic algorithms. Developing formalisms to specify these transformations enables the design and construction of generic mechanisms to support structural and behavioral transformations within future structural computing infrastructure.

The rest of this paper is organized as follows. Section 2 defines the requirements for structural transformations and grounds these requirements with a few examples. Section 3 provides a motivation for developing similar requirements for behavioral transformations. We then present our conclusions in Section 4.

2   Structural Transformations

In order to realize its true potential, a structural computing infrastructure must be able to support the specification of structure and the ability to transform a structure into other types of structure. Formal specifications for specifying structures and their transformations can provide developers of structural computing infrastructure with mechanisms for sharing structures between structure servers and automating the transformation of structures to avoid errors.

One domain that may provide useful techniques to structural computing developers is the domain of compiler construction. Compiler construction tools must deal with the specification of programming language structures and how they can be transformed from unstructured input text to structured parse trees to (ultimately) executable code. Traditionally a compiler performs three operations: lexical analysis, syntactic analysis, and semantic analysis. Lexical analysis scans the input text and converts it into a stream of language-specific tokens. Syntactic analysis converts the stream of tokens into a parse tree (which follows the rules of a particular language's grammar). Semantic analysis "decorates" the parse tree with information that allows the parse tree to be converted into executable code. This information concerns identifying names, types, and operators and ensuring that they conform to the semantic rules of the language. Relevant to the topic of this paper is the fact that some compiler construction tools (such as Eli [9]) make use of an abstract grammar that deals with the construction of parse trees in a general way. Users of the compiler construction tool concern themselves with specifying the mapping (or transformation) of their language's concrete grammar into the abstract grammar and the compiler construction tool can then automatically construct a parse tree for the user's language. This feature can greatly reduce the complexity of the work that must be performed by the user of the compiler construction tool and argues for similar mechanisms for structural computing developers to aid in the task of sharing structures between structure servers.

We envision a language that will allow structural computing developers to specify the form of a structure. A specification written in this language (which we will call the structure definition language or SDL) can be automatically processed by a structure server in order for it to allocate space to store instances of the described structure and to make it available for associating behaviors with it.[1] We expect that SDL will make use of existing programming language conventions for defining structures and therefore existing techniques in the compiler construction domain can be used to aid a structure server in processing SDL specifications.

In addition, we envision a language that will allow structural computing developers to specify transformation operations on structures defined in SDL. A specification written in this language (which we will call the structure transformation language or STL) can be written by a developer to specify how a structure server can manipulate an instance of one structure to produce an instance of some other structure (also defined by SDL). STL specifications can then be used by a structure server to automate the conversion of one structure into another or to automate the import of a set of external structures into internal structures that it can manipulate. We envision STL to be an imperative language that provides operations such as delete field, create field, associate structure, etc. in order to manipulate the form of a structure and type conversions such that the values associated with structures can be manipulated during structure transformation. An STL specification (we envision) would typically involve importing a set of SDL structure definitions, specifying a structure as the input for the transformation and then specifying one or more programs for creating instances of the remaining structures which are the possible outputs of the transformation.

In the conclusions, we briefly touch on some of the benefits that would result if SDL and STL languages for structural computing are actually developed. We now turn our attention to the transformation of behaviors and the associated implications such a concept has on structural computing.

---

[1] In structural computing, behaviors are separated from structure. Therefore, the structure definition language does not concern itself with specifying the behaviors of a structure. Instead behaviors must be specified separately and then associated with structures using an interface that is provided by the structure server for that purpose.

3   Behavioral Transformations

Structural computing infrastructure may need to support the transformation of behaviors in addition to the structural transformations discussed above. For instance, flexible transformation of behaviors provides considerable power to the domain of evolutionary computation [4]. One approach to evolutionary computation is a technique known as genetic algorithms. Genetic algorithms can be viewed as computations that randomly walk around the design space of a problem looking for a solution. Typically, a genetic algorithm is fed a set of example problems and solutions to those problems. It then attempts to generate a program that given one of the example problems can automatically generate its solution. This program is generated by applying a set of pre-defined operations in various sequences and then mutating those sequences according to the principals of evolution. Genetic algorithms will construct thousands of these programs in multiple generations looking for a program that can produce the solutions of all of the example problems. This requires the definition of a "fitness" function that given one of the generated programs can judge how well its solutions "fit" the problem being solved.

Brumby et al. [2] applied genetic algorithms to the domain of detecting water in high-resolution satellite images of the earth. The genetic algorithm is trained with a set of images in which a human user shades water on an image as green and land as red. The algorithm then tries to generate a water detection algorithm using sequences of image manipulation primitives. These sequences were evolved by the genetic algorithm using mutations (in which an operation is randomly replaced by another operation) or by adding or removing operations from the sequence in subsequent generations. The algorithm produces multiple generations of water detection algorithms until one of them matches the desired characteristics of the fitness function (such as being able to detect 95 percent or more of the water on all of the training images). At that point, the "winning" algorithm can be used to detect water on images outside of the original training set. Brumby et al. [2] reported that the genetic algorithm developed a water detection algorithm in a matter of a few hours that exactly reproduces an algorithm developed by humans over a much larger time frame!

The lesson for structural computing is that great power can be gained by first class support for behavioral transformations. While structural computing is not necessarily addressing domains that are amenable to the techniques of evolutionary computation, nevertheless the ability to transform the operations of a behavior in response to external factors such as environmental constraints (e.g. low memory situations) or application demands (e.g. an application suddenly demanding more resources as its user applies it to a complex or large-scale problem) can provide structural computing developers with the flexibility they need to produce powerful infrastructure and applications.

We believe it will be useful to specify structural computing behaviors in a fashion that makes it straightforward to specify variant sequences of operations that will allow a behavior to be customized in response to a variety of non-functional constraints. For instance, a behavior that computes the transitive closure of a set of structures by navigating their relationships may automatically reduce the amount of information generated when confronted with a low memory situation. For instance, it could decide to limit the number of "hops" it uses to compute the closure or it could compute the closure of one structure, return the results to the client, free up resources from that computation, and compute the closure of the next structure.

As such, we envision the need for two types of specifications associated with behaviors. The first specification needs to express the algorithm of the behavior including the pre-conditions that a structure needs to pass before the behavior can be applied to it. The second specification needs to describe variants of the original specification in response to non-functional constraints. For instance, such a specification may suggest substitutions of particular operations contained in the original specification based on how much memory is available to the operation at run-time. The two specifications, in practice, may be able to be combined into one formal notation, however they each address distinct aspects of a behavior. A structure server will then need to be able to interpret these specifications in order to dynamically compose the optimal set of operations to execute a behavior given the constraints of its invocation environment.

4 Conclusions

This paper has identified the need for formal models of structural computing that enable the transformation of structure and behavior within structural computing infrastructure. In particular, this paper has put forth a proposal that structural transformations should be formalized using declarative and operational specification techniques represented in a notation that can be interpreted by future structure servers. In particular, the types supported by a structure server can be communicated to other servers via these specifications. In addition, the legal transformations on a server's types would also be specified. This would enable an external structure server to transform a given type into something it can process, or alternatively allow it to transform its types into something that can be processed by the original server.

The benefits of formalizing structural computing types and their transformations are significant:

– Types become explicit named entities that can be shared among structure servers; standard type checking techniques can be reused in the structural computing domain to ensure that a structure is valid before a structure server makes use of it
– Formal specification of type transformations can automate the process of type conversion and minimize errors that may otherwise occur if a structure server made use of, for instance, an API to convert an external server's types into something that it can use

– Inference engines can make use of type and transformation specifications to automatically create information within a structural computing infrastructure. For instance, a rule that specifies how an instance of type A and an instance of type B can be transformed into an instance of type C can be used to populate a structure server managing instances of type C by automatically accessing structure servers that contain instances of types A and B.

With respect to behavioral transformations, this paper has identified the need for supporting applications that require the ability to transform the services they provide to their clients. The domain of genetic algorithms was briefly introduced to serve as an example, however the applicability of behavioral transformations is much broader. For instance, the ability to specify behavioral transformations for a structure server provides developers significant power to customize the server for a variety of situations. For instance, a developer can have a server query its environment to determine characteristics such as processor power, disk space, memory, network connections, etc. and access specifications that transform its behaviors to optimize performance. Or, for instance, an application built on top of a structure server can transform its behaviors to adjust for the skill level of a particular user. Formalizing the specification of these transformations can lead to similar benefits as cited above for structure transformations. In particular, transformations can be specified ahead of time and then flexibly and dynamically applied by a structure server at run-time as needed.

The work in this paper represents a new category of structural computing research; work that begins to formalize the theoretical foundations of this new approach to computation. Indeed, having identified the need for these formalisms and touched on some of their requirements, our future work will involve specifying prototype languages such as the SDL, STL, and behavioral transformation specifications and creating tools that will enable the exploration of the associated research issues. We will do this work in the context of our initial attempts to create a structural computing infrastructure. The need for formalisms is clear: In the very near future, significant amounts of structural computing infrastructure will be created by the structural computing community and structure servers created by different research groups will need to interoperate. Having common formalisms will pave the way for this critical interoperability to be achieved.

References

1. Anderson, K. M. (1999). Software Engineering Requirements for Structural Computing. In *Proceedings of the First International Workshop on Structural Computing*. Darmstadt, Germany. February 21, 1999.
   <http://www.cs.colorado.edu/users/kena/papers/workshops/sc1.html>.

2. Brumby, S. P., Theiler J., Perkins S., Harvey N., Szymanski J. J., Bloch J. J., and Mitchell M. (1999). Investigation of Image Feature Extraction by a Genetic Algorithm. In Proceedings of SPIE (International Society for Optical Engineering), Volume 3812, Special Issue on the Applications and Science of Neural Networks, Fuzzy Systems, and Evolutionary Computation II, Bosacchi, Bruno, Fogel, David B., Bezdek, James C. (eds.), November 1999.

3. Marshall, C. C., Shipman, F. M., III, and Coombs, J. H. (1994). VIKI: Spatial Hypertext Supporting Emergent Structure. In *Proceedings of the Sixth ACM Conference on Hypertext*, pp. 13-23. Edinburgh, Scotland. September 18-23, 1994.

4. Mitchell, M. and Taylor, C. E. (1999). Evolutionary Computation: An Overview. In *Annual Review of Ecology and Systematics*, 20:593-616.

5. Nürnberg, P. J., Leggett, J. J., and Schneider, E. R. (1997). As We Should Have Thought. In *Proceedings of the Eighth ACM Conference on Hypertext*, pp. 96-101. Southampton, UK. April 6-11, 1997.

6. Parunak, H. V. D. (1991). Don't Link Me In: Set Based Hypermedia for Taxonomic Reasoning. In *Proceedings of the Third ACM Conference on Hypertext*, pp. 233-242. San Antonio, Texas, USA. December 15-18, 1991.

7. Rosenberg, J. (1999). A Hypertextuality of Arbitrary Structure: A Writer's Point of View. In *Proceedings of the First International Workshop on Structural Computing*. Darmstadt, Germany. February 21, 1999.

8. Smolensky, P., Bell, B., Fox, B., King, R., and Lewis, C. (1987). Constraint-Based Hypertext for Argumentation. In Proceedings of the First ACM Conference on Hypertext, pp. 215-245. Chapel Hill, NC, USA. November 1987.

9. W. M. Waite. (1992). ELI: A Complete, Flexible Compiler Construction System. In *ACM Computing Practices*, Vol. 35, No. 2, February 1992

Using the Construct Development Environment to Generate a File-Based Hypermedia Storage Service

Uffe Kock Wiil

Department of Computer Science
Aalborg University Esbjerg
Niels Bohrs Vej 8, 6700 Esbjerg, Denmark
ukwiil@cs.aue.auc.dk

Abstract. The Construct development environment is targeted at the construction of different types of hypermedia services. The primary goal of the environment is to ease the construction of component-based open hypermedia systems by providing development tools that assist system developers in the generation of the set of service components that make up a hypermedia system. This paper explains how the Construct development environment was used to generate a file-based hypermedia storage service.

1   Introduction

Development of a state-of-the-art component-based open hypermedia system (CB-OHS) is a very difficult and time-consuming task. The system developers must deal with many non-trivial issues such as Internet distribution, process architecture, multi-user and collaboration support, structural abstractions, and storage management [1,2,3].

The Construct development environment is targeted at the construction of different types of hypermedia services. The primary goal of the environment is to ease the construction of CB-OHS's by providing development tools that assist system developers in the generation of the set of service components that make up a hypermedia system. This paper explains how the Construct development environment (in particular, the Construct Service Compiler) was used to generate a file-based hypermedia storage service. The generated storage service is now part of the set of services available in the Construct development environment.

The environment has built-in solutions to many of the difficult issues involved in building CB-OHS's such as inter-process communication, naming and location, and storage management. Both predefined and generated services are encapsulated inside service components that can operate in a massively distributed environment such as the Internet. The development tools can generate a skeleton service from a graphical UML diagram or from a highlevel service specification written in IDL (see Figure 1). The system developer only needs to fill in the semantic parts of the generated skeleton (the service's method bodies).

S. Reich and K.M. Anderson (Eds.): OHS/SC 2000, LNCS 1903, pp. 147–159, 2000.
© Springer-Verlag Berlin Heidelberg 2000

Thus, the level of expertise needed to construct a state-of-the-art CB-OHS component with the Construct development environment is considerably lower than the level of expertise needed to build a similar component from scratch.

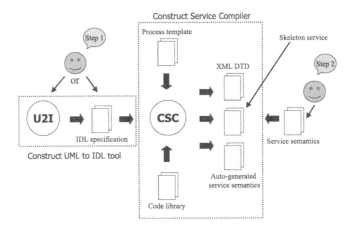

Fig. 1. The Construct development environment. Circles indicate tools (processes), rectangles indicate service specifications or source code, and dotted lines indicate tool boundaries.

The paper argues that a development environment reduces the effort to build hypermedia services both with respect to development time and complexity. The argument starts with a description of previous work and continues with a short overview of the Construct development environment. The main part of the paper is a detailed example of how a storage service can be developed. The paper finishes with a conclusion.

2   Previous Work

Many of the ideas behind the current work were conceived in the HOSS [4] and Hyperform [5] projects as well as the ongoing work in the Open Hypermedia System Working Group (OHSWG) [6].

Hyperform (from the early 1990's) is both a hypermedia system development environment and a hypermedia system execution environment. The focus was on rapid prototyping of hypermedia services such as system architectures, data models, and entire hyperbase configurations. Hyperform provides a set of editors that allow hypermedia services to be specified and installed in the environment at runtime.

HOSS (from the mid 1990's) focused on providing tools that ease the task of generating new hypermedia services. Examples of development tools in HOSS are the Protocol Definition Compiler and the Generalized Process Template.

Experiences from HOSS indicate that about 90% of the code base of a typical hypermedia system can be auto-generated based on high-level service specifications.

The OHSWG started its work on open hypermedia interoperability and standards in March 1996 [3]. The first few years of OHSWG effort focused on defining standards that allowed for interoperability between existing open hypermedia systems (OHS). The first standard that was defined covered the navigational hypermedia domain (called OHP-Nav) [1,2].

Construct is a CB-OHS [7] developed as the common code base successor of the DHM [8], HOSS, and HyperDisco [9] systems. It is a major goal of the Construct project to be fully OHSWG standards compliant. For example, Construct provides a complete implementation of the OHSWG navigational interface standard (OHP-Nav). One important lesson from this work is that a standard goes through several iterations before it is ready to use. In every single one of these iterations, parts of the interface are updated. The result is that all systems that wish to comply with the standard must be updated several times as the standard evolves.

Our background with the HOSS and Hyperform systems led us to believe that a development environment with a set of basic development tools can help reduce the effort to develop new standards and the effort for system developers to comply with these standards.

3   Overview of the Construct Development Environment

The environment is aimed at the development of services. A service in our terminology is the basic building block of a hypermedia system. We distinguish between different kinds of services such as frontend services (e.g., an application wrapper), middleware services (e.g., a navigational hypermedia server), backend services (e.g., a hyperstore), and infrastructure services (e.g., naming and location) – see Figure 2. We even view our development tools as services.

The "Construct UML to IDL tool" (U2I) is a graphical tool with which the system developer can draw UML diagrams. The U2I can generate an IDL specification matching the UML diagrams. The "Construct Service Compiler" (CSC) takes an IDL specification as input and generates several forms of output: an XML DTD, a skeleton service, and a small set of auto-generated service semantics. These semantics (a command line interface and method bodies that print out the method parameters) allow the skeleton service to be tested. The CSC uses a general process template and different types, predefined services, etc. from its code library to generate the skeleton services and the CB-OHS environment in which they run.

The development cycle for a service is depicted in Figure 1. The first step is to generate an IDL specification describing the required service. This can be done either by hand or by using the U2I. The IDL specification is then fed into the CSC, which generates a skeleton service. The skeleton service consists of a set of classes specifying a set of methods. The bodies (semantic parts) of these methods are empty. Hence, the second (and final) step for the system developer is to fill in the semantic parts of the methods. The service is now ready to use. The experiment described in the next section provides additional insights into the CSC and how it is used in hypermedia service generation.

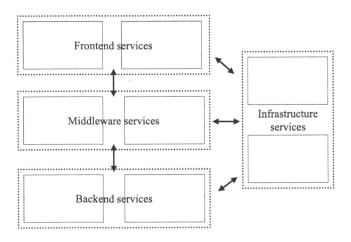

Fig. 2. Conceptual system architecture of the Construct development environment. Development tools are not shown.

Generated services become part of the Construct development environment. A generated service is encapsulated in a Construct service component that can operate in the environment and make use of existing services (see Figure 2). The developer decides what type of communication should be used to interact with other Construct services (components). Currently, the Construct development environment supports shared memory communication and socket (TCP/IP) communication. We are currently working on other means of communication such as HTTP tunneling. The full range of options will allow the developer to built a wide variety of system architectures ranging from single process (single machine) systems to massively distributed multi process systems.

The Construct development environment is coded in Java. The UML tool is still under development. We expect to have this tool ready during the summer of 2000. The first running version of the CSC was operational in January 2000. This version generates service skeletons in Java. The first "auto-generated" services will be demonstrated at Hypertext 2000.

4 Development of a File-Based Hypermedia Storage Service

This section gives a detailed description of the first real development undertaken with the CSC. We had two specific goals in mind when we performed this experiment:

- **Specification of a common hypermedia storage interface**. We wanted to use this opportunity to work towards a common hypermedia storage interface for CB-OHS's. The idea was to refine a specification of a storage interface in several iterations and propose the interface specification to the OHSWG as a first standard proposal for a hypermedia storage interface (see [10] for details). A standard storage interface is a first step towards interoperability at the middleware level in CB-OHS's (i.e., interoperability between a navigational and a spatial hypermedia service).
- **Development of a file-based implementation of the interface**. We wanted to make a specific file-based implementation of the interface specification, which, after its development, would become a natural part of the Construct development environment. A storage service is an essential component in a hypermedia system. Provision of such a component would obviously increase the usefulness of the Construct development environment.

This paper focuses on describing the work related to the second of the two goals. We will simply show the interface specification without any explanation of how it was generated and without any argumentation of why it contains what it does. Instead, we will explain how we, based on the interface specification, used the CSC to assist us in the generation of an implementation of the interface specification. The description is broken into three parts: a description of the approach; a description of the actual CSC experiment; and, a summary of lessons learned.

4.1 Approach

The experiment was carried out in a way that allows us to generate statistical information about the effort involved in hypermedia service development with the CSC versus development without the CSC. First, we developed a standalone version of a file-based hypermedia storage service. Then, we used the CSC to develop an implementation of a file-based hypermedia storage service with the same set of services. This allows us to compare the two implementations and development methods in a number of ways: the amount of code that the developer needs to write in both cases; the percentage of the code in the service implementation that is auto-generated by the CSC; the different development styles; etc.

The standalone service development used a prototyping approach and went through five iterations in which the set of services where refined. Each development cycle started with a generation of a class diagram (like the simplified example shown in Figure 3) followed by an implementation of the classes in Java.

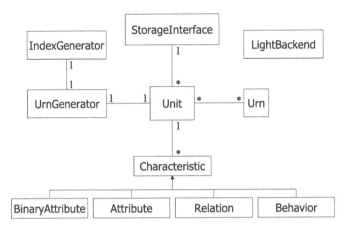

Fig. 3. A simplified class diagram for the fifth (final) iteration in the standalone implementation of the file-based hypermedia storage service.

4.2 Experiment

The first step in the experiment was to transform the class structure diagram into an IDL specification. In the future, when the U2I tools becomes operational, this task can also be automated. The next step was to run the CSC with the generated IDL specification as input. The final step was to write the semantic parts of the generated services. This process was repeated several times in a prototyping manner. Each iteration refined the IDL specification typically by simplifying it. A few iterations were performed before the IDL specification in Figure 4 was developed.

If one compares this IDL interface description in Figure 4 to the class diagram in Figure 3, it can be seen that some of the classes have been removed from the interface. There are typically two different reasons for simplifying a service definition interface:

- *Implementation details should not appear in the interface.* The IDL specification should specify a service, but not provide any notion of how it should be implemented. The above IDL specification (for which we have made a file-based implementation) could also be implemented using other storage techniques such as a database.
- *General-purpose services should not appear in the interface.* A service that is general and can be used by more than one interface should be defined in its own IDL specification. An implementation of the general service can then be reused by other services. An example of this is the Urn service, which has now become part of the "foundation services" of the CSC.

```
module store
{
   interface Characteristic
   {
      void addValue(in java::lang::Object value);
      void deleteValue(in java::lang::Object value);
      void getValues(out java::util::LinkedList values);
      void setValues(in java::util::LinkedList values);
      void deleteValues();
   };

   interface BinaryAttribute : Characteristic { };
   interface Attribute : Characteristic { };
   interface Relation : Characteristic { };
   interface Behavior : Characteristic { };

   interface Unit
   {
      void getPrimaryName(out string name);
      void setPrimaryName(in string name);
      void getPrimaryType(out string type);
      void setPrimaryType(in string type);
      void addSecondaryName(in string name);
      void deleteSecondaryName(in string name);
      void addSecondaryType(in string type);
      void deleteSecondaryType(in string type);
      typedef sequence<char> charArray;
      void getContent(out charArray content);
      void setContent(in charArray content);
      void addCharacteristic(in string characName, in Characteristic charac);
      void getCharacteristic(in string characName, out Characteristic charac);
      void deleteCharacteristic(in string characName);
   };

   interface StorageInterface
   {
      void createStorageUnit(in org::ohswg::construct::core::svc::Urn urn, in string name, in string type, out Unit unit);
      void readStorageUnit(in org::ohswg::construct::core::svc::Urn urn, out Unit unit);
      void writeStorageUnit(in org::ohswg::construct::core::svc::Urn urn, in Unit unit);
      void deleteStorageUnit(in org::ohswg::construct::core::svc::Urn urn, in boolean deleteContentUrn);
   };
};
```

Fig. 4. IDL specification for the hypermedia storage service

So what does the CSC generate for me? The CSC generates a large number of Java classes and interfaces when the above IDL specification is used as input. The following code hierarchy is generated in the directory where the input file (store.idl) is located:

```
store.idl
store/
store/iec/
store/iec/hooks/
```

The CSC generates the following types of output:

A) A Java class named Store.java is generated in "store/". This class contains module specific declarations (if any). In this particular case, none exist (as can be seen in the IDL specification). The developer may subclass (extend) this class to add implementation specific details.

B) A Java class for each of the specified interfaces in the IDL specification (e.g., StorageInterface.java) is generated in "store/". In this particular case, 7 Java classes were generated (StorageInterface, Unit, Characteristic, BinaryAttribute, Attribute, Relation, and Behavior). These Java classes contain the definition of the methods specified in the IDL specification (e.g., createStorageUnit is defined in StorageInterface.java). Each method is invoked with an object as input parameters and returns another object with its output parameters. The following code fragment is taken from StorageInterface.java:

```
public CreateStorageUnitResponseMessageBody createStorageUnit(
  CreateStorageUnitRequestMessageBody requestBody) {
  return dispatcher.createStorageUnitDispatch(requestBody);
}
```

The developer will typically extend these Java classes in subclasses to add implementation specific details such as private attributes and helper methods.

C) 2 Java classes for each method in the IDL specification are generated in "store/iec/". A total of 44 Java classes were generated for the 22 methods in the IDL specification. These Java classes define the input and output parameters for the methods. The file CreateStorageUnitRequestMessageBody.java implements the input parameters (with accessor methods) and the file CreateStorageUnitResponseMessageBody.java implements the output parameters (with accessor methods) for the method createStorageUnit defined in StorageInterface.java. The developer will (import and) use these Java classes to declare and manipulate objects that can hold input and ouput parameters.

D) 4 Java interfaces for each method in the IDL specification are generated in "store/iec/". A total of 88 Java interfaces were generated for the 22 methods in the store IDL interface. Each Java interface defines a different type of hook (with abstract methods). The following 4 types of hooks exist for each method: before, semantic, after and notify. The before hook processes the input parameters of the method (pre process), the semantic hook implements the method body (process), the after hook processes the output parameters (post process), and the notify hook is used to generate event notifications. The developer can decide to implement as many of these abstract methods (hooks) as desirable. At a minimum, the developer should implement a semantic hook for every method.

E) 1 "dispatcher" Java class for each interface in the IDL specification is generated in "store/iec/" (7 Java classes in total). These Java classes define how the hooks are processed in the generated service component. The developer does not need to know anything about these classes.

F) 1 Java class with a set of standard hooks for every method defined in the IDL specification is generated in "store/iec/hooks". A total of 22 Java classes are generated for the 22 methods in the IDL specification. Each of these Java classes provides simple implementations of all four types of hooks. The implementations simply write out the input parameters to standard output. The developer can use the standard hooks to test the generated service skeleton (as mentioned in Section 3).

To sum up, the CSC generates a total of 180 Java classes and interfaces based on the IDL specification (Figure 4). The following equation describes the relation between the IDL specification and what gets generated:

$$J = 2M + 2I + 7O \tag{1}$$

"J" is the number of classes and interfaces that gets generated. "M" is the number of modules, "I" is the number of interfaces, and "O" is the number of operations (methods) in the IDL specification.

And what do I need to generate? A separate code hierarchy (a directory called "lightbackend") was added to develop the file-based implementation of the hypermedia storage interface. The full code hierarchy is now as follows:

```
store.idl
lightbackend/
store/
store/iec/
store/iec/hooks/
```

The term "lightbackend" is used to describe the fact that it is a hypermedia storage component that will run on any machine. It does not require a particular database or anything else to be installed. At the same time, it indicates that it is a lightweight implementation that only provides a core set of storage services. The implementation of the lightbackend involved the following additions to the CSC-generated Java code skeleton (the letters correspond to the letters in the previous section):

A) A LightBackend class that extends the Store class that was generated. This class includes implementation specific details that are meant to be accessible throughout the service component such as global constants.
B) 6 of the generated Java classes were subclassed: StorageInterface, Unit, BinaryAttribute, Attribute, Relation, and Behavior. The subclasses (prefixed with "Lb") extend the generated classes with implementation specific details such as names and types of private variables, accessor methods for variables, and local helper methods. For instance, the LbUnit class declares the following in addition to the methods declared in the IDL specification:
   – Private data structures (String, LinkedList, and HashMap) in order to store names, types and characteristics.
   – Accessor methods to retrieve and update the private variables.
   – A constructor to create new LbUnits.

– A few specific helper methods local to the LbUnit class.

C) Nothing added in relation to this generated code. All 44 Java classes were (imported and) used as is to declare methods in the semantic hooks code described under D.

D) 6 Java classes were generated as container classes to hold the implementation of semantic hooks. The current lightbackend implementation does not use any of the other types of hooks. For instance, the LbUnitHooks class implements the semantic hooks for the methods described under the Unit interface in the IDL specification. A total of 22 semantic hooks (declared as abstract methods in the generated Java interfaces described under D. in the previous section) were implemented in the following 6 classes: LbStorageInterface-Hooks, LbUnitHooks, LbBinaryAttributeHooks, LbAttributeHooks, LbRelationHooks, and LbBehaviorHooks. The implementation of the semantic hooks provides the bodies of the methods described in the IDL specification.

E) Nothing added in relation to this generated code.

F) Nothing added in relation to this generated code. The standard hooks were not used.

To sum up, a total of 13 Java classes were hand coded: 1 corresponding to the module level in the IDL specification; 6 corresponding to the interface level in the IDL specification (one for each interface); and, 6 corresponding to the method level in the IDL specification (one for each interface that implements all the semantic hooks for methods defined in that interface).

4.3 Software Metrics

Some important facts about the two implementations are briefly listed in the following — starting with the handcoded implementation.

– **Handcoded implementation.** A person with good knowledge of Java and hypermedia storage services developed this service in about a week. The development involved the coding of 12 Java classes with a total of approximately 1000 lines of code. This includes the test software.

– **CSC-generated implementation.** The development of this service also took about a week (same person as above). This time included a one-time effort to get to know the CSC. The handcoded part of the service amounts to 20 Java classes with a total of approximately 1500 lines of code. The CSC generated approximately 10500 lines of code. This also includes the test software.

The two implementations are functional identical. They were tested using similar test cases. In fact, more than 90% of the test code was identical for the two implementations.

4.4   Lessons Learned

The present experiment constitutes the first real development with the Construct development environment. In this section, we will capture some of the preliminary lessons learned from the development of the file-based hypermedia storage service.

We have evaluated the CSC by comparing the two examples: standalone development versus CSC-based development and by examining the CSC development process and results. We came up with the following results:

- The amount of substantive code (substantive lines of code or SLOC) is similar in the two examples. In fact, the code from the standalone example was broken into pieces and reused in full in the CSC example. No new SLOC were added in the CSC example. The CSC requires its code to be organized in a certain way. This adds some overhead. However, the code is organized in very regular patterns and much non-substantive code can be reused.
- The CSC generates a lot of code. Not all of this code may actually be used in the continued development. The CSC generated more than 85% of the code in this example.
- The CSC enforces a certain structured way to work. It is very simple: the services must be specified in IDL (or in a UML diagram in future versions) before development can start. The development can be done all at once (in one development cycle) or in a number of iterations. The latter supports a rapid prototyping approach to hypermedia service development, where the service specification in IDL is refined in a number of steps.
- The generated code is overwritten every time the CSC translates an IDL specification. Thus, the hand-generated code should be stored in a separate code hierarchy. Changes to the IDL specification may of course migrate to the hand-generated code. The regular patterns that are enforced on the hand-generated code makes it very easy to identify the piece(s) of code that must be updated or added based on revisions to the IDL specification.
- Using the CSC requires knowledge about Java and the structure of the generated code. Some general guidelines about what code to generate and where to put it are also essential. Thus, the CSC user (the service developer) needs good documentation and helpful examples to look at.

Overall the CSC is not very difficult to use. The example in Section 4.2 gives a high level overview of what needs to be generated. Once the developer has a good overview of the coding patterns, there is little effort involved in expanding or updating a service component with extra functionality.

5   Conclusions

In the Introduction we put out the hypothesis that the Construct development environment reduces the development effort with respect to time and complexity. Is this really true? The example with the file-based storage implementation shows that the coding effort is similar in a standalone component and in a CSC component that provides the same services. So where is the gain? The advantages of the Construct development environment are the following:

- **Complexity**. All developed service components automatically become part of the Construct environment, which can operate in a massively distributed environment. The developer only needs to write the code for a standalone non-distributed version of the service and gets the rest for free.
- **Time**. As the number of services in the Construct environment grows, it will be much easier to develop new services that build on top of or use existing services. The present experiment added a file-based hypermedia storage component to the environment. This component is now available to other Construct developers.

Thus, there is certainly a huge benefit in using the Construct development environment to develop new CB-OHS components compared to developing the same components from scratch.

In Section 2, we argued that a development environment would reduce the effort involved in developing and maintaining OHSWG standards and the effort for system developers to comply with these standards. We believe that this is true for the following reason. The Construct development environment supports a prototyping approach to service definition and development. In fact, the OHSWG OHP-Nav interface was defined and refined in several iterations. OHP-Nav was developed as an XML DTD. The consequence was that we ended up spending much time discussion unnecessary details about the XML DTD itself. The CSC also generates an XML DTD as output based on the IDL specification (as mentioned in Section 3). Thus, the Construct development environment has the tools to keep the standards work at a high level (discussing an IDL interface specification instead of an XML DTD) and the tools to assist the developer in generating implementations of the interface specification.

Acknowledgments. Comments from Kenneth M. Anderson helped improve the presentation of this paper. The Construct development environment is currently being developed at the Department of Computer Science, Aalborg University Esbjerg, Denmark and at the Department of Information Systems, University of Linz, Austria. The development team consists of Peter J. Nürnberg, David L. Hicks, Uffe K. Wiil, and Siegfried Reich.

References

1. Hugh C. Davis, David E. Millard, Siegfried Reich, Niels Olof Bouvin, Kaj Grønbæk, Peter J. Nürnberg, Lennert Sloth, Uffe Kock Wiil, and Kenneth M. Anderson. Interoperability between hypermedia systems: The standardisation work of the OHSWG (technical briefing). In *Proceedings of the '99 ACM Conference on Hypertext, February 21-25, 1999, Darmstadt, Germany*, pages 201–202, February 1999.

2. Siegfried Reich, Uffe K. Wiil, Peter J. Nürnberg, Hugh C. Davis, Kaj Grønbæk, Kenneth M. Anderson, David E. Millard, and Jörg M. Haake. Addressing interoperability in open hypermedia: The design of the open hypermedia protocol. *New Review of Hypermedia and Multimedia*, 5:207–248, 1999.
3. Uffe Kock Wiil. Open hypermedia: Systems, interoperability and standards. *Journal of Digital Information (JoDI). Special Issue on Open Hypermedia*, 1(2), 1997.
4. Peter J. Nürnberg, John J. Leggett, Erich R. Schneider, and John L. Schnase. Hypermedia operating systems: A new paradigm for computing. In *Proceedings of the '96 ACM Conference on Hypertext, March 16-20, 1996, Washington, D.C.*, pages 194–202, 1996.
5. Uffe Kock Wiil and John J. Leggett. Hyperform: A hypermedia system development environment. *ACM Transactions on Office Information Systems*, 15(1):1–31, 1997.
6. OHSWG. Technical report, The web site for the Open Hypermedia Systems Working Group (OHSWG), Available as `http://www.ohswg.org/`, 2000.
7. Uffe Kock Wiil and Peter J. Nürnberg. Evolving hypermedia middleware services: Lessons and observations. In *Proceedings of the 1999 ACM Symposium on Applied Computing (SAC '99), San Antonio, TX*, pages 427–436, February 1999.
8. Kaj Grønbæk and Randall H. Trigg. Design issues for a Dexter-based hypermedia system. *Communications of the ACM*, 37(3):40–49, February 1994.
9. Uffe Kock Wiil and John J. Leggett. Workspaces: the HyperDisco approach to Internet distribution. In *Proceedings of the '97 ACM Conference on Hypertext, April 6-11, 1997, Southampton, UK*, pages 13–23, 1997.
10. Uffe Kock Wiil Towards a Proposal for a Standard Component-Based Open Hypermedia System Storage Service. In *Lecture Notes in Computer Science, this volume, Springer Verlag (2000)*, 2000.

Towards Structure Specification for Open Hypermedia Systems

Michalis Vaitis[1,2], Athanasios Papadopoulos[1,2], Manolis Tzagarakis[1,2], and
Dimitris Christodoulakis[1,2]

[1] Department of Computer Engineering and Informatics
University of Patras
GR-265 00 Patras, Greece
[2] Computer Technology Institute
Riga Ferraiou 61
GR-262 21 Patras, Greece
{vaitis, papadopa, tzagara, dxri}@cti.gr

Abstract. Driven by the philosophy of the "primacy of structure over data", CB-OHS present an open set of structure servers providing structural abstractions of different hypermedia domains. To address the emerged requirements and to facilitate the development of structure servers, structure should be handled as a first class entity. We propose patterns for structure, called *templates*, that define the structural model upon which structure servers operate.

1   Introduction

The transition from monolithic to Open Hypermedia Systems (OHS) envisioned the provision of hypermedia functionality to third-party applications as well as interoperability among different hypertext systems, in a distributed, heterogeneous environment. Much research and development work resulted in the realization that various hypertext domains impose different requirements and need different services. This led to the common agreement that special protocols should be developed for each hypertext domain.

The specification and implementation of the Open Hypertext Protocol (OHP) [2] was the first effective approach to support the well-known navigational domain. New systems and protocols supporting structural abstractions of other domains, such as taxonomic [12] or spatial [6], had to be built from scratch. It is obvious that it would be useful if an OHS could be tailored or extended in order to support more than one hypertext domains. Inspired by the general trend in computing towards component-based, distributed and interoperable systems, Component-Based Open Hypermedia Systems (CB-OHS) emerged [8]. Driven by the philosophy of the "primacy of structure over data", CB-OHS provide an open set of components, called *structure servers*, each one supporting the structural abstractions of a single hypermedia domain in a convenient and efficient way [9]. Functionality that is common among all domains is regarded part of the infrastructure (fig. 1).

S. Reich and K.M. Anderson (Eds.): OHS/SC 2000, LNCS 1903, pp. 160–169, 2000.
© Springer-Verlag Berlin Heidelberg 2000

Besides serving the main hypermedia domains, we claim that the CB-OHS approach may be useful in other situations as well. Sub-domains, subsets of the main domains, impose special requirements. As an example, the *typed* (or *structured*) *navigational* domain can be considered as a sub-domain of the navigational domain. In addition, combinations of domains could be useful in complex applications, such as the *linguistic* and the *digital libraries* domains that could be viewed as combinations of the taxonomic and the navigational domain [7, 10]. Furthermore, a wide number of applications need specific hypertext functionality, not only generic link services. For example, a *lexicographic* application requires specific associative mechanisms to express relations among lemmata in a lexicon (hyponyms, hyperonyms, homonyms, synonyms, etc.)

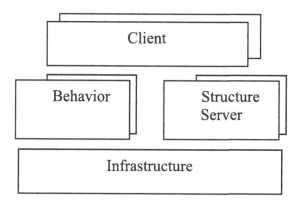

Fig. 1. Component-Based Open Hypermedia Systems Architecture

The research area of *structural computing* is engaged in all aspects of CB-OHS. Structural computing systems may be viewed as part of multiple open service systems [15], i.e. systems supporting arbitrary middleware services that can be divided into infrastructure and application (client) services. We base our view of structural computing on the following observations:

- Hypermedia and structural computing are mainly about relationships among objects in arbitrary ways. The well-known and very important hypermedia domains (navigational, taxonomic, spatial, etc.) are just instances of an unrestricted space of relationship types.
- There is a long way from domain-oriented services to sub-domain and application specific services. Extensibility and tailorability are top priority aims. Generic services are important as well as application specific services, but we have to find a balance among them.
- Structural computing deals with structure. We must be able to understand, specify and manipulate structure in order to profit from it.

The main position of the paper is that in order to enable structural computing, we should be able to specify structure in a precise and formal way. We propose the use of structure patterns, called *templates*, that define the structural model upon which structure servers operate. We perceive the structural model (e.g., navigational, taxonomic) as a first class entity that can be formally defined through templates. This is in contrast to contemporary OHS, in which the structure model is closely coupled to the infrastructure. The interoperability level is thus raised from the infrastructure level (the storage) to the template level. The perception of templates is part of a larger effort towards the creation of software engineering tools for the development of CB-OHS.

In the following paragraphs we aim to:

- Describe the issues that arise in structural computing regarding the management of structure.
- Present the outline of a model for hypermedia structure specification and discuss the problems inherent to this task.
- Portray how the proposed system can be used to assist the development of CB-OHS, giving developers the ability to create patterns of structure, i.e. templates. The main issue here is to provide the necessary tools that will help to bridge the gap between hypermedia system and domain research.

2   The Primacy of Structure

Development and utilization of structure impose several problems and requirements [1,3,13]:

- *Reusability*: How can we reuse abstractions that are common in several structure servers? Is it useful to construct a structure server that extends the functionality of an existing server?
- *Maintainability*: What documentation mechanisms or configurations could help maintenance of a structure server?
- *Scalability*: Can the infrastructure support any number of structure servers? How easily can such a requirement be achieved?
- *Interoperability*: How can clients use services from different structure servers? Should it understand all the protocols or is a mapping between protocols sufficient? How can such a mapping be defined?
- *Flexibility*: Should the specification of the structure-model expressed in a formal model? In this case, how can the notions of arbitrary granularity, extensibility, composability, scope, valence and directionality be expressed [13]? On the other hand, if no formal model is employed, how can the structure abstractions of a domain be defined?

In the recent years, HOSS [11] is among the first paradigms that realize the philosophy of structural computing. The conceptual design of HOSS includes the concepts of structure and structural computation models. The structure model supports sideness, direction, depth, status (n-sided composable structure with direction) as well as the guarantees of resolvability, nonrecursivity and accessibility. The structural computation model provides optional permanence, constancy and temporal invariance guarantees (definitions of these notions can be found in [11]).

The basic element of HOSS is the *generic structure object* that may have content, arbitrary attribute/multi-value pairs and arbitrary named and partitioned endsets. Various structural elements can be specified by customizing the structure object and masking away unneeded functionality.

Although operating system services that support arbitrary structures could cover many of the aspects of the structural computing area, further research is required from a software engineering point of view. The construction of a structure server is a complicated project to be repeated from scratch every time a new domain, sub-domain or application appears. Thus, software development tools should be introduced to facilitate such a task. These tools should have structure specification capabilities, providing the fundamental elements upon which behavioral operations can be defined or programmed, such as traversal semantics, structure constraints and even presentation and transition effects.

3   Structure Specification

Devising a structure specification formalism is a difficult task since it should be convenient to use it without compromising expressibility. The formalism should be open to extensions, model-neutral and provide a common ground for cooperation. Our proposal for such a formalism is described in section 4.

Given the aforementioned issues, we propose the inclusion of structure templates in CB-OHS. Structure templates are used to maintain the structure model specifications of hypermedia domains, sub-domains or applications. Figure 2 outlines the proposed architecture of the CB-OHS.

In the following paragraphs we briefly illustrate the various parts of the architecture:

- *Structure server*: It consists of a structure model (template) and a set of behaviors that are used to deliver domain, sub-domain and application specific abstractions and services to clients.
- *Structure template*: The formal specification of the abstractions that define a hypermedia domain, sub-domain or application.
- *Behavior*: Behavior models the computational aspects of a domain, sub-domain or application. Behavior can be divided—depending on its purpose—into two main categories: Services that are available to clients through the use of a specific protocol (e.g., openNode, traverseLink, etc.). Internal operations that are used by the structure server mainly for consistency reasons (e.g., to affirm conditions and constraints or to interpret abstractions in a specific manner).
- *Infrastructure*: Includes the fundamental hypermedia functionality that is available to all other entities. Services such as naming [14], persistent storage (hyperbase service) and notification constitute an essential part of the infrastructure.

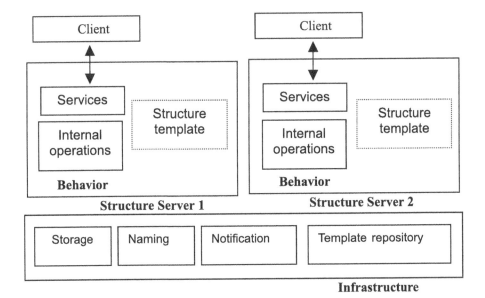

Fig. 2. The role of structure templates in CB-OHS

- *Template repository:* Provides storage services for structure templates. Its main purpose is to support reusability and extensibility among structure servers.
- *Client:* Any program that requests hypermedia functionality. Clients may request hypermedia operations from one or more structure servers, using the appropriate protocols.

There are various benefits from having a model and methodology to specify structure:

- Better understanding of the domain. So far domains are hard coded into services and are informally described.
- The structure model could be the framework of a structure server. In an extreme case, it may be possible to configure a structure server by modifying the structure model specification.
- Exploitation of common structures among different domains, thus enhancing reusability and interoperability.
- Narrowing the gap between hypermedia domain and system research [8] by providing a common framework to express structural abstractions.

4   Structure Elements

Our methodology for defining the structure model of a domain, sub-domain or application consists of the specification and inter-relation of *structural types*. A structural type is either an instantiation of a basic abstract class, the *Abstract Structural Element* (*ASE*), or a specialization of another structural type. The notion of ASE is inspired by the *structure object*, proposed by Nürnberg [11] and is similar to the *Object* abstract class in the majority of the object-oriented programming languages. The set of structural types and the relationships among them, defined by the model-designer at the same context, establish the template of the domain, sub-domain or application. During the definition of a new structure model, already existing templates may be reused or extended.

In the following subsections we describe the elementary constructs of the methodology, as well as the structure model definition process.

4.1 Elementary Constructs

The Abstract Structural Element (ASE) is a meta-class that consists of two attributes: an identifier and a name. The instances of the ASE are structural types that are identified by a system-defined unique *identifier* (*sid*) and a unique *name* assigned by the designer. A structure type may have an arbitrary number of *properties* and *endsets*. The instances of a structural type are *structural objects* in the sense described in Nürnberg [11] but they are constrained by their structure type specification, regarding the endsets and properties. Each structural object is identified by a system-defined unique *structural object identification* (*oid*).

The structure type properties are specified by a name, a data type and they may be *single-valued* or *multi-valued*. A special property, named *content*, may be defined in the context of a structural type. At the instantiation level, the value of this property is an address specification of an arbitrary amount of data. Since our purpose is to specify structure, not data, we do not define other semantics for that property (like within-component layer in the Dexter hypertext reference model [5]).

The *endset* of a structural object is a set of oids of other structural objects. It is the most significant construct, since it enables associations, i.e. offers hypertext functionality. An endset of a structure type has the following attributes:

- *Name*: unique among the endsets of the structural type,
- *Order number*: an integer that designates the sequence of the endsets in the context of the structural type,
- *Total participation indication*: a [min, max] notation that indicates the minimum and maximum number of oids that can participate in the endset
- *Multiplicity*: a [min, max] notation that indicates the minimum and maximum number of endset instances that can be created in a single structural object.

To enforce the nonrecurcivity notion [11], the oid of a structural object is not allowed to participate to any of its endsets. Also, since an endset is a set, no oid can appear to it more than once.

Along an endset is defined a set of the structural types (sids), called *s-set*, which configures the structure types whose instances may be end-points of the endset. An s-set may be *inclusive* or *exclusive*; an inclusive s-set specifies the allowed structure types, while an exclusive one specifies the forbidden structure types. A *partial participation indication* may be defined for each structure type in an inclusive s-set, indicating the minimum and maximum number of objects of this type that can participate in the endset.

A *cardinality indication* for each structural type in the s-set (also a [min, max] notation) specifies the number of structural objects of that type that are allowed to be included in a single endset instance. This is similar to the cardinality ratio ([4]) in the E-R diagrams that specifies the number of relationship instances that an entity instance can participate in.

As a last notation, an endset with more that one structural types in its s-set, may be characterized as *homogeneous* or *heterogeneous*. At the instantiation level, a homogeneous endset can include structural objects of one type only, while a heterogeneous endset may point to structural objects of different types at the same time.

4.2   Customizing Structure Types

Structure types capture the semantics of domains, sub-domains or applications. It would be useful to be able to customize structure types of a domain in order to support the structure requirements of a sub-domain or an application. One important point is the relation of the customized to the original structure type and the ability to compare them. We claim that instances of customized types are in fact a subset of the instances of the original type. In this way, compatibility is established between the two types, and instances of customized types can be used in places where instances of the original type are expected.

We define the *extent* of a structure type as the set of the possible instances of it. The extent of a customized structure type is always a subset of the extent of its parent type.

Customization also means different behavior. Customized types should support original behavior and extend it in order to accommodate additional functionality.

We model customization of structure types using the *is-a* abstraction, which may connect two structural types to express that the one is a specialization of the other. The customized type inherits all the properties and endsets of the parent type. In addition, new properties may be defined and the various constraints of the endsets (participation indication, s-sets, cardinality indication, homogeneity-heterogeneity, multiplicity) may be restricted. It is not allowed to add or eliminate endsets, since this will change the physiognomy of the structural type.

4.3   Templates

As a template we define the container of the structure types modeling a domain, sub-domain or application. A template is modeled itself as a structural object.

More specifically, a *template-class* is a system-defined structure type that consists of a single endset, with the purpose to group together the sid(s) of one or more designer-specified structure types. When the designer specifies the structure types to define a structure model, in fact he creates an instance of the template-class (a template) and assigns a *name* to it. Templates are stored in a special part of the storage infrastructure, called *template repository*.

A template may be created from scratch or by utilizing existing templates, stored in the repository. Each template may have a set of templates that inherits from. This set can be considered as an endset, the *uses* endset. A template inherits all structure types defined in the templates in its *uses* endset.

A question that arises is how useful is such a *multiple inheritance* functionality? We identify the following situations:

- A new structure model may be constructed that requires abstractions of two or more other structure models. The inherited structure types may be customized to express special needs (as long as the rules of the customization hold).
- A new structure type may be defined that *combines* structure types from different templates, i.e. enabling its endsets to point to the inherited structure types.

Templates could better be represented in a formal specification language, since they include various attributes and complex relationships. A visual representation would be easier to use, but it is not easy to visually express all the details of the specifications. We considered that XML is well suited for such a task, as it enables composition and arbitrary details. Furthermore, it is a well-known language and can be easily manipulated.

5   Case Study

In this section we are taking the argumentation-support domain as an example to examine how templates can be used to specify the domain and sub-domain structural abstractions. We outline a simple example focusing on the process of customization.

In the general case, the argumentation-support domain requires n-sided links, optional direction, composition of at least two levels, resolvability and nonrecursivity guarantees [11]. The generality of these requirements allows the structure server to support a large number of applications, even belonging to different domains.

On the other hand, sub-domains or applications are more concrete. Although they can be accommodated by a general structural server, such an approach would lack two important criteria: convenience and efficiency. Suppose we have a sub-domain of argumentation-support where there are two types of objects: "questions" and "answers" linked by two-sided links driving from a question to the respective answers. In this case, it would be useful to have a server that supports this sub-domain, by restricting the sideness and the participating objects of the links. In fig. 3 we present a description of the aforementioned domains in XML.

```
<template name="Argumentation" id="1" nonrecursivity="yes"
         resolva ility="yes" accessi ility="yes">
<structure_type name="Argumentation link" id="2">
         <endset name="general" multiplicity="2..n">
                <s-set><mem er type="any" /></s-set>
         </endset>
</structure_type>
</template>


<template name="Simple Argumentation" id="3" nonrecursivity="yes"
         resolva ility="yes" accessi ility="yes">
<uses>
         <template_id> 1 </template_id>
</uses>
<structure_type name="question" sidedness="0" id="4" />
<structure_type name="answer" sidedness="0" id="5" />
<structure_type name="link" sidedness="n" is-a="2">
         <endset name="the question">
                <s-set><mem er type="4" min="1" max="1"/></s-set>
         </endset>
         <endset name="the answers">
                <s-set><mem er type="5" min="0" max="n"/></s-set>
         </endset>
</structure_type>
</template>
```

Fig. 3. Templates for argumentation-support in XML

6   Conclusions

OHS in their move from domain-specific frameworks to cross-domain CB-OHS, should clearly expose the *primacy of structure* and thus need the proper foundations and tools to handle structure as a first class entity. Towards such an evolution path, we outlined a method for the specification of structural models. OHS would benefit from such structure specification, mainly in the areas of reusability, interoperability and tool development. In such a context, applications have to couple structural services with structured data and require custom services, thus there should be a way to extend and combine general services in multiple levels.

The rough design presented in this paper must be further investigated in order to demonstrate the feasibility and benefits of structure specification. A more detailed model is clearly necessary and various questions should be addressed. A basic issue is whether the specification is powerful enough to model a sufficient set of structures and whether specifications could be used to automatically configure structure servers. Behavior of structure servers should be included in the specification, as it is the main way of providing and extending services. Finally, the coupling of structural services and structured data deserves special attention, as application specific structural services must be aware of the data structures involved.

References

1. K. M. Anderson. Software Engineering Requirements for Structural Computing, Proceedings of the 1st Workshop on Structural Computing, Technical Report AUE-CS-99-04, Aalborg University Esbjerg (1999) 22-26.
2. H. Davis, S. Reich, A. Rizk. OHP-Open Hypermedia Protocol, Working Draft 2.0, 20th June 1997.
3. S. Demeyer. Structural Computing: The case for reengineering tools, Proceedings of the 1st Workshop on Structural Computing, Technical Report AUE-CS-99-04, Aalborg University Esbjerg (1999) 27-29.
4. R. Elmasri, S. B. Navathe. Fundamentals of Database Systems, 2nd edition, Benjamin/Cummings (1994).
5. F. G. Halasz, M. Schwartz. The Dexter Hypertext Reference Model, Hypertext Standardization Workshop, NIST (1990).
6. C. C. Marshall, F. M. Shipman, J. H. Coombs. VIKI: Spatial Hypertext Supporting Emergent Structure, Proceedings of the European Conference on Hypermedia Technologies, Edinburgh, Scotland (September 1994) 13-23.
7. A. Ntoulas, S. Stamou, I. Tsakou, Ch. Tsalidis, M. Tzagarakis, A. Vagelatos. Use of a Morphosyntactic Lexicon as the Basis for the Implementation of the Greek Wordnet, Proceedings of the 2nd International Conference on Natural Language Processing, Patras, Greece, Springer-Verlag LNAI 1835 (2000) 49-56.
8. P. J. Nürnberg, J. J. Legget, U. K. Wiil. An Agenda for Open Hypermedia Research, Proceedings of the 9th ACM Conference on Hypertext and Hypermedia (1998) 198-206.
9. P. J. Nürnberg, J. J. Legget. A Vision for Open Hypermedia Systems, Journal of Digital Information (JoDI), Special issue on Open Hypermedia Systems, 1, 2 (1997).
10. P. J. Nürnberg, U. K. Wiil, J. J. Leggett. Structuring Facilities in Digital Libraries, Proceedings of the 2nd European Conference on Digital Libraries (ECDL '98), Crete, Greece (1998).
11. P. J. Nürnberg. HOSS: An Environment to Support Structural Computing, Ph.D. dissertation, Dept. of Computer Science, Texas A&M University, College Station, TX (1997).
12. H. Parunak. Don't link me in: Set based hypermedia for taxonomic reasoning, Proceedings of the 3rd ACM Conference on Hypertext, San Antonio, TX (December 1991) 233-242.
13. J. Rosenberg. A Hypertextuality of Arbitrary Structure: A Writer's Point of View, Proceedings of the 1st Workshop on Structural Computing, Technical Report AUE-CS-99-04, Aalborg University Esbjerg (1999) 3-10.
14. M. Tzagarakis, S. Reich, N. Karousos, D. Christodoulakis. Naming as a Fundamental Concept of Open Hypermedia Systems, Proceedings of the 11th ACM Conference on Hypertext and Hypermedia, San Antonio, TX (2000) 103-112.
15. U. K. Wiil. Multiple Open Services in a Structural Computing Environment, Proceedings of the 1st Workshop on Structural Computing, Technical Report AUE-CS-99-04, Aalborg University Esbjerg (1999) 34-39.

Structural Computing: Evolutionary or Revolutionary?

David L. Hicks

Department of Computer Science
Aalborg University Esbjerg
Niels Bohrs Vej 8, 6700 Esbjerg, Denmark
hicks@cs.aue.auc.dk

Abstract. The structural computing paradigm has been described as one which holds significant promise and potential for the developers of both applications and infrastructure services. So far, however, structural computing can be viewed mainly as an evolutionary step along the developing line of computing infrastructures for supporting hypermedia. The field is still a new one though. The fundamental ideas that define structural computing appear to be sufficiently different to have the potential for a revolutionary effect. However, for this to occur, it is necessary for the field to advance beyond its present stage and for researchers to start focusing on the essential features that define this new paradigm and the implications they will have.

1 Introduction

Structural computing has been described as a new paradigm for computing, one in which the fundamental ideas inherent in hypermedia are generalized and built upon to create a new type of computing environment [2]. The fundamental feature of this new computing paradigm is that structure is elevated in status to assume primacy over data. The creation of a paradigm in which structure becomes the primary building block is perceived to hold significant promise and potential for the developers of applications and middleware services. The hope is that a structural computing environment will provide a more natural setting for the implementation of many types of applications and services that have proven awkward to develop within existing paradigms. In addition, structural computing might even enable the development of completely new kinds of capabilities and services which have been impossible or at least very difficult to implement in existing conventional computing environments.

This definition of structural computing predicts that its effect on computing will be a revolutionary one. In any good revolution, a natural desire exists to examine the fundamental ideas that drive the revolution within the context of existing, more conventional ones. This process is insightful and helps to highlight and allow closer inspection of the revolutionary forces at play. This in turn helps to determine how revolutionary the ideas actually are, and in what direction the revolution might be leading. This paper seeks to examine structural computing

S. Reich and K.M. Anderson (Eds.): OHS/SC 2000, LNCS 1903, pp. 170–178, 2000.
© Springer-Verlag Berlin Heidelberg 2000

in this way. It will make the case that to date, structural computing can largely be considered an evolutionary step in the development of hypermedia computing paradigms. The paper then raises a series of questions regarding the essential differences between a structural computing environment and a more conventional one in order to explore whether these differences will be sufficient to spark a revolution as research in the structural computing area continues.

2   Structural Computing as an Evolutionary Step

Structural computing environments already have been described in a number of places [1], [5], [6]. Figure 1 illustrates one possible view of a structural computing environment. Applications reside at the top level of the environment. These are the tools such as word processors, browsers, spread sheets, editors, etc., that have been created to help users perform their tasks. When applications are created in a structural computing environment, their designers and implementers are able to utilize a variety of structure servers during the design and implementation process, as illustrated by the middle level of Figure 1. A structure server is an entity that provides a specialized structural abstraction to client applications. Example structure services include those that provide abstractions to support navigational hypermedia, structured argumentation, spatial hypermedia, or taxanomic hypermedia [3]. In practice, a wide variety of structure servers is possible in a structural computing environment. When appropriate, structure servers can utilize the services of other structure servers to create the structural abstractions they offer to applications (or to each other). The bottom level of Figure 1 contains the structure store. The structure store provides for the persistent storage of basic structural entities. Its capabilities are built upon by structure servers to construct the abstractions they provide to applications.

In general, the lower levels within the arrangement depicted in Figure 1 provide structural building blocks for the levels above, and each level offers an extended or more elaborate structural abstraction than the one below. The proper level of structural abstraction to offer at any particular level in the arrangement can be determined by factoring out the set of common aspects of the structural abstractions from the level above it. This greatest common denominator of structure can then be offered as a set of building blocks for the level above. This arrangement has the benefit of offering programmers who are building applications (as well as those building structure servers) a higher base of structural abstraction from which to begin their efforts.

Encouraging a consideration and analysis of structure such as the discussion above is one of the tangible influences that structural computing can already claim. This was evident in many of the position papers from the first workshop on structural computing held at the Hypertext '99 Conference [4]. Useful though this paradigm may be for promoting the examination of structure, however, a structural computing environment such as the one depicted in Figure 1 is in many ways a natural evolutionary step in the development of computing paradigms designed to support hypermedia. This is not really surprising since

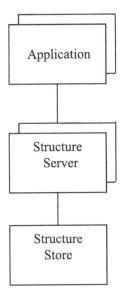

Fig. 1. A Structural Computing Environment

many of the fundamental ideas of structural computing grew directly out of early research on Open Hypermedia Systems (OHSs) [6]. For comparison purposes, Figure 2 illustrates a multiple open service system environment. Multiple open service systems represent one of the latest stages in the continuing evolution of OHSs. Notice that the basic arrangement of levels within Figure 2 is quite similar to that of Figure 1. The factorization of common functionality from one level in order for it to be provided at the level below (and thereby supply a higher level of abstraction from which programmers can start their work) is a common characteristic between structural computing and multiple open service environments.

Structural computing, when viewed in this way, can be considered to be not so dramatically different than the latest open hypermedia systems research results—i.e., it can be viewed as more of an evolutionary step than a revolutionary one. Indeed, some who have considered structural computing from this perspective have even questioned whether it should exist at all as a field that is separate and distinct from open hypermedia system research [6].

3   Structural Computing as a Revolution

Although structural computing can be seen as having evolved from existing computing paradigms (as noted in Section 2), important differences exist between a structural computing environment and a more conventional one. For example, at the lowest level of the multiple open service system environment illustrated in Figure 2, a hyperbase provides persistent storage. In the structural computing

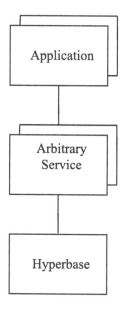

Fig. 2. A Multiple Open Service System Environment

environment of Figure 1, a structure store resides at the lowest level. Similarly, the middle level of Figure 2 contains general servers providing arbitrary middleware services to applications. In Figure 1 the middle level contains structure servers providing structural abstractions to applications. These differences between the two environments are very important ones. Studying and understanding these differences will be instrumental in helping to determine whether structural computing will eventually become more than an evolutionary step in the development of computing paradigms, and will instead have a revolutionary effect.

To date, few comprehensive structural computing environments such as the one depicted in Figure 1 have been completely specified and designed, much less implemented. This reflects that the field is still a new one. However, it also makes it difficult to study the differences between a structural computing environment and a conventional one. Even though there are presently not yet many implementations of structural computing environments available with which to experiment, there are many questions and issues that it is useful to examine in trying to assess what the ultimate impact of a shift to a structural paradigm might be. In the remainder of this Section a number of these questions are discussed. The paper does not attempt to supply the answers for all of the questions. Indeed, it is probably too early to know the answers for most of them. However, it is important to start considering the questions and the issues they raise. Note also that the list in this Section is only a starting point. Undoubtedly there are many additional issues and questions that will be important to consider in addition to these.

What Exactly Is Structural Computing (and What Is Not Structural Computing)?

Though they have been described in several places, a consensus has not yet emerged as to what exactly constitutes a structural computing environment. When does an environment have enough structure to qualify? Some have described the structural computing paradigm as a comprehensive one in which "... structure is regarded as the ubiquitous, atomic building block available to all systems at all times and from which all other abstractions are derived" [5]. This definition would seem to correspond to an environment such as that depicted in Figure 1. Notice that in the arrangement depicted in Figure 1, a structure store provides for the persistence of structure at the lowest level. A central characteristic of this type of environment is that all of the abstractions within it, either directly or indirectly, are built upon the structural atoms that the structure store provides.

Another type of structural computing environment that has been described in the literature is illustrated in Figure 3 [6], [3]. This environment is similar to that of Figure 1, but is built upon a foundation of a general store (possibly a hyperbase) rather than a structure store. Is the environment illustrated in Figure 3 also to be considered a structural computing one? Is it disqualified because it does not have a structure server at the lowest level? How ubiquitous must structure be within an environment for it to qualify as a structural computing one?

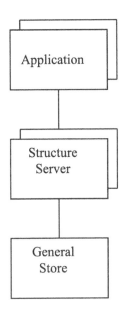

Fig. 3. A Structural Computing Environment Built Upon a General Store

What Are the Essential Differences between a Structural Computing Environment and a Conventional One?

A basic question that can be asked of structural computing concerns how different it really is from existing systems and paradigms. Consider a conventional environment in which data rather than structure has primacy. Many if not most/all standard computing environments of today have this characteristic. Examples include those built upon a filesystem or some type of object server. Is it possible to transform such a conventional computing environment into a structural computing environment?

For example, suppose that the basic units within a computing environment, e.g. the files in a filesystem or the objects in an object system, were augmented to include metadata fields (or possibly a set of metadata fields) to contain structural information. In addition, suppose that well enforced rules were established concerning these fields, e.g. that the new structure metadata field is required to be present for all of the basic units (files or objects) within the environment, that the field can only be assigned valid structural values, etc. Finally, suppose that an appropriate set of commands were added to the environment for manipulation of the structural metadata fields. In this type of environment, all of the basic units are clearly structure aware. Would such an arrangement be sufficient to transform a conventional environment into a structural computing one? If so, would the newly transformed environment be a "real" structural computing environment, or just a functionally equivalent one, much like a Turing Machine is computationally equivalent to a personal computer? If a conventional environment transformed in this way is not a structural computing one, what are the essential characteristics that are missing?

What Form Should the Structure Take in a Structural Computing Environment?

In a computing environment in which structure takes precedence over everything, like the one illustrated in Figure 1, clearly it is important for the structure to have the right form. This is especially true for the structural components defined at the lowest level of the environment. They are the fundamental building blocks upon which everything else in the environment is based. What should the structural atoms served by the structure store in a structural computing environment look like? Should they simply be capable of referencing some number of other structural atoms? What level of granularity is appropriate for the references of a structural atom? Should structural atoms only be capable of referencing at the structural atom level, or should it be possible to define references to locations within a structural atom? Is it even meaningful to reference locations within structural atoms? What set of basic operations should be supported by a structure store for structure manipulation purposes?

The form of structure at other levels of the environment must also be considered. For example, how many structure servers are needed at the middle level of an environment such as the one illustrated in Figure 1? What structural abstractions should they serve? Of course, the most appropriate answers to many of the questions concerning structure at the middle levels of such an environment are largely determined by the needs of applications. If a given structural abstraction is general enough to be useful to a number of different applications, it should probably be provided by a structure server. Research experiences from the OHS area will be a useful place to start in examining issues concerning structure at the middle levels of a structural computing environment [7].

In What Direction Will Structural Computing Evolve? How Can Existing Experiences Be Used to Help Guide Its Course?

Fundamental to structural computing is the notion that structure is more important than data. In fact, data in a structural computing environment is modeled as a degenerate case of structure. This suggests that it is not possible in a structural computing environment for data to exist independently of structure. Is such an arrangement necessarily a step in the right direction? The separation of data and structure is well accepted to be a desirable characteristic in the hypermedia field. Will structural computing create a situation where data and structure become inextricably coupled?

It will likely be the case that the degree to which data and structure are actually coupled in a structural computing environment will depend largely on how designers and developers use the structural atoms/building blocks available to them. It may be possible for the two to be separated, much like designers within a more conventional computing environment in which data has primacy can, through the appropriate modeling and design decisions, effectively separate data from structure. However, what characteristics should a structural building block have to facilitate and encourage this separation? What lessons have already been learned about this issue in the hypermedia field that apply to structural computing? In a broader sense, what general hypermedia modeling principles can and should be considered by designers of structural computing environments to help avoid undesirable characteristics?

What Does It Really Mean to "Get Structural"?

This is, perhaps, the most important of all the questions raised in this Section. As described earlier (Section 2), structural computing environments promote the consideration and analysis of structure, and provide a useful framework within which to do so. However, if structural computing is to ever have a revolutionary influence, at some point the field must move beyond this initial analysis phase and really "get structural". An environment in which a structural atom is the basic building block upon which all other abstractions are modeled is quite different from existing conventional ones. In this type of paradigm, all of the rules are changed.

Designers and developers must explore the impact of structural computing on the design and development process. What does it mean to think, model, and design in this type of environment? What things are easier, more natural, or even harder to model and design in a structural world? What is the impact of structural computing for programmers implementing systems? Many of these questions are ones that can only be addressed once structural computing environments become available. The answers to these questions, though, will largely determine if the structural computing paradigm ultimately has a revolutionary effect on computing.

4   Conclusion

Structural computing offers a useful framework within which to analyze and examine the role structure plays in modeling and application development. In this role structural computing can be viewed largely as a natural evolutionary step following from the open hypermedia systems line of research. The fundamental basis of structural computing, however - that structure takes complete precedence over data, does make it quite different from conventional computing paradigms. It is precisely these differences that may one day spark a structural computing revolution. However, since structural computing is still a new field, very few structural computing environments have so far been designed and implemented. This makes it impossible to know yet if the new ideas that structural computing promotes will eventually reach critical mass and have a revolutionary effect. There simply are not yet enough environments for designers and developers to experience and experiment with.

What does seem to be clear at this point, though, is that for the field to move forward it is critical for researchers to move beyond the view of structural computing as being only an analysis tool, and to focus on and examine more closely the essential differences between this new paradigm and conventional ones - they need to "get structural". In this paper a preliminary list of questions were offered as a starting point from which this process can begin. These questions along with others need to be discussed and debated in order to help guide this evolving field and to determine if its ultimate effect will indeed be a revolutionary one.

References

1. Kenneth M. Anderson. Software Engineering Requirements for Structural Computing. In Proceedings of the 1st Workshop on Structural Computing held in conjunction with Hypertext 99, Darmstadt, Germany (1999), pp. 22-25.
2. Peter J. Nürnberg, John J. Leggett, and Erich R. Schneider. As we Should Have Thought. In Proceedings of Hypertext '97: The Eight ACM Conference on Hypertext and Hypermedia, (1997), pp. 96-101.
3. Peter J. Nürnberg, Uffe K. Wiil, and John J. Leggett. Structuring Facilities in Digital Libraries. In Proceedings of the Second European Conference on Digital Libraries (ECDL '98). (Crete, Greece, September) (1998), pp. 295-313.

4. Peter J. Nürnberg, (ed.): Proceedings of the 1st Workshop on Structural Computing. Technical Report AUE-CS-99-04, Aalborg University Esbjerg (1999).
5. O. Reinert, D. Bucka-Lassen, C. A. Pedersen, and P. J. Nürnberg. A Collaborative
   and Open Spatial Structure Service Component Based on Structural Computing.
   In Proceedings of the 1st Workshop on Structural Computing held in conjunction
   with Hypertext 99, Darmstadt, Germany (1999), pp. 18-20.
6. Uffe K. Wiil. Multiple Open Services in a Structural Computing Environment. In
   Proceedings of the 1st Workshop on Structural Computing held in conjunction
   with Hypertext 99, Darmstadt, Germany (1999), pp. 34-39.
7. Uffe K. Wiil, and Peter J. Nürnberg. Evolving hypermedia middleware services:
   lessons and observations. In Proceedings of SAC' '99, (San Antonio, TX, USA,
   Feb), ACM Press (1999), pp. 427-436.

Repositioning Structural Computing

Peter J. Nürnberg

Department of Computer Science
Aalborg University Esbjerg
Niels Bohrs Vej 8
DK-6700 Esbjerg, Denmark
pnuern@cs.aue.auc.dk

Abstract. Structural computing was first proposed within computer science as a largely technological solution to a set of system design and implementation issues. However, we believe that structural computing as proposed is actually only one expression of a more general philosophical view that stresses the importance of structure in human problem solving and communication. Seen from this perspective, we can identify a host of related schools of thought from such seemingly distant fields as anthropology, linguistics, sociology, and critical theory, the most pronounced of which is the structuralist movement. We examine this connection and posit that instead of the traditional connection made between hypermedia and traditional deconstructionist postmodernism, hypermedia (and its generalization, structural computing) are in fact more closely related to a "neo-structuralist" philosophical viewpoint.

1 Introduction

Structural computing was originally billed as a kind of "generalized" hypermedia. Hypermedia is usually thought of as a technology, either in the form of a computer system or sometimes more generally as a work practice. The implication is that structural computing, too, is a technology. Most of the work presented at the First Workshop on Structural Computing [4] very much treated structural computing as a technology—*as something in need of implementation.*

Is this really so? Or is it perhaps true that structural computing is not a technology as much as it is a philosophy? When approached from this angle, we can look in new directions for inspiration, guidance, and lessons. Structural computing as technology has taught us to look at computer science, especially hypermedia, as our intellectual cousin. Structural computing as philosophy may inspire us to look much farther afield.

Is there much to be gained from such an exercise? As of yet, this is unclear. But initial thinking in this direction is exciting and intriguing. In this paper, we present a very brief review of the basic building blocks of structural computing. We follow this with a brief introduction to the philosophical movement called structuralism, popular in a number of fields in the earlier part of the 20th century. We then ask the question of how closely these two schools of thought are. We hope that this provides a useful starting point for the discussion of repositioning structural computing from technology to technological exponent of philosophy.

S. Reich and K.M. Anderson (Eds.): OHS/SC 2000, LNCS 1903, pp. 179–183, 2000.
© Springer-Verlag Berlin Heidelberg 2000

2   Structural Computing

Hypermedia concerns structure. Hypermedia interfaces present structure to knowledge workers. Hypermedia middleware builds services from structural primitives. Hypermedia-based computation processes and generates structure and structural behavior.

However, Nürnberg et al. [3] claimed that the hypermedia research field had only partially bought into its own claims of the importance of structure in intellectual work by building systems that portrayed structure from infrastructure that was essentially data-oriented, with poor or no explicit support for structure. Why tolerate this state of affairs if structure is so important for knowledge work? Should not the computing environment itself be modified to reflect the belief in the centrality of structure?

Structural computing was originally presented as a call to change the way our infrastructure works, from the traditional data-oriented models currently pervasive to a structure-oriented model, in which every atom, every primitive (both object and computation) is in essence structural. The implications of such a shift are not yet fully laid out, but it is clear that a number of well-understood or "solved" problems in the data-oriented world, such as versioning, access control, and notification control have added layers of complexity in the structural case, which in general remain unsolved (or even undiscussed).

3   Structuralism

This position statement is far too limited in scope for any serious discussion of structuralism, the subject of thousands of books and academic articles. However, we present here a short introduction to the history of structuralism as well as a description of the major essential characteristics of this school of thought.

Structuralism is a movement of thought that swept through many fields in the early and middle parts of the 20th century. Its intellectual ancestors most probably include formalist schools of thought of the late 19th century, although it seems to have gained widespread acceptance first in linguistics, where, in many ways, it still forms the basis for much work. Most people from the hypermedia research community will be most familiar with structuralism in literary critical theory, where it took hold relatively late (compared to its rise in other disciplines), was relatively short-lived, and has inspired a particularly violent counter-movement known as deconstructionism.

Structuralism is an integrative philosophy in that it attempts to tie together diverse fields through a common methodology [5]. The structuralist method was boiled down to four characteristics by Nikolai Troubetzkoy, who was a prominent proponent of structuralism in linguistics. This method:

1. shifts the focus of study from conscious phenomena to their unconscious infrastructure;
2. does not treat independent terms as the object of study, but rather the relations between these terms;

3. introduces the concept of system by explicitly elucidating the system of relations and terms described above; and
4. aims at discovering general laws. (N. Troubetzkoy, quoted in [2])

In many ways, linguistics is the textbook example of a field that benefited greatly from the structuralist movement. Pre-structuralist linguistics was a field characterized by disjointed observations, empirical work without a coherent analysis to tie observations together. It was essentially "language ethnography". Structuralist linguistics rigorously pursued the notion of system, introducing notions like distinctive features and phonemes which were abstractions that allowed a formal representation of aspects of language that stood in relation to one another. As we noted earlier, these abstractions still from the basis of linguistic work today. Linguistics, at least at levels below discourse analysis, is still essentially structuralist.

The worst failures of structuralism seem to have come in literary critical theory. Structuralism is in such great disfavor today, that there is a nearly religious zeal on the part of modern critics in its repudiation. The literary critical world is a decidedly post-structuralist one. And, with the 20/20 vision of hindsight, its not hard to see that critical structuralism was often extremely simplistic - a sort of cartoon-like formalism which, at its worst, was responsible for such follies as generating grammars to describe the structure of novels or the positing of ultra high-level analogs to linguistic phonemes to describe genres. This was structuralism for the sake of structuralism. Techniques were crudely borrowed from linguistics, where structuralism seemed so effective, often without reference to the actual problems facing critics.

4   Structuralist Computing?

Aside from the obvious naming similarities between structural computing and structuralism, are there other similarities? One approach to finding an answer to this question is to examine the four pillars of the structuralist method described above.

Shifts the focus of study from conscious phenomena to their unconscious infrastructure. Of all the pillars of the structuralist method, it may be most difficult to find an obvious analog to this one. What is the "object of study" of structural computing? It may be that this question makes no sense. If we allow ourselves to reach a bit here, though, we can talk about hypermedia interfaces as empowering users to express unconscious infrastructure of conscious phenomenon. What are the rules that govern placement of objects in a spatial hypermedia system? The incremental formalization that is spoken of in this domain and in this context may be a way of expressing exactly this shift from the conscious data (note cards, "phenomena") to their organization (spatial layout, "infrastructure").

Does not treat independent terms as the object of study, but rather the relations between these terms. This seems clear enough. Structural computing "asserts the primacy of structure over data" [3]. There seems to be a clear match in intention on this point.

Introduces the concept of system by explicitly elucidating the system of relations and terms described above. From the structural computing perspective, it may be difficult to differentiate this point from the previous. A "system" seems to be the analog of a "context" of structures in most hypermedia systems, and at least in some systems, the notion of context (linkbase, hyperspace, etc.) is in fact a central one for users of the system.

Aims at discovering general laws. This seems to be mirrored in the structural computing notion of moving functionality down through the various layers of the system as far as it can be moved. The notion of providing structurally-oriented storage services, version control, computation, and even operating system services may be restated as a search for general laws of system construction.

So, should we change the name of our work to structuralist computing? Probably not just yet, but there does seem to be some amount of overlap between the structuralist method and the structural computing approach to system construction. This suggests that there may be valuable lessons to be learned by searching harder for analogs between these ideas. We may be able to co-opt ideas, learn from failures, and become inspired by the unwitting, different formulations of our ideas by others.

Those with literary critical backgrounds may feel anathema at this idea. Why examine a patently dead philosophy for inspiration? Firstly, as has been pointed out above, structuralism is in fact not dead, but alive and well (often under new names) in a number of fields. We should not be dissuaded by the failure of structuralism in critical theory. It may very well be that structuralism was simply never applied correctly in critical theory. Secondly, we should treat with caution the anathema of our literary colleagues. There are powerful political forces at work in that field (as there are in all fields) that sometimes make objective discussions of certain topics difficult or impossible. Finally, we are not carrying out literary criticism! It may be that structuralism is a fruitful field for computer science.

5   Conclusions

One difficulty we as computer scientists face is that we have never been trained to reflect upon our own field or the methodologies we use. We do not think in terms of fashionable philosophies, schools of thought, or the like when we talk about computer science as a discipline. This is, after all, a science, right? What is there to discuss? Hypothesize, test, repeat until you retire.

Of course, we know that things are not quite that simple. Computer science is only partly science, and there are of course school of thought in our discipline, just as we've known for a long time that there are schools of thought in areas within computer science. Hypertext is certainly more than just a technology. It makes implicit epistemological assumptions about what is knowable and how it is knowable in its discussions of knowledge workers' use of structure. Vannevar Bush spoke as much about philosophy as he did about technology in his seminal article "As We May Think" [1], but the philosophy is all subtext, as it has largely remained in the intervening years. It may be that one contribution of structural computing to the hypermedia field will be to lift the level of these philosophical claims to that of explicit discourse, repositioning both itself and the larger community closer to the humanities than to engineering and the sciences.

References

1. Vannevar Bush. As We May Think. Atlantic Monthly 176, 1 (July 1945) 101–108.
2. Claude Lévi-Strauss. Structural Anthropology. Basic Books (1963).
3. Peter J. Nürnberg, John J. Leggett, and Erich R. Schneider. As We Should Have Thought. Proceedings of the Eighth ACM Conference on Hypertext and Hypermedia (HT '97), Southampton, UK, Apr. ACM Press: New York (1997) 96–101.
4. Peter J. Nürnberg (ed). Proceedings of the First Workshop on Structural Computing. Technical Report AUE-CS 99-04, Department of Computer Science, Aalborg University Esbjerg, Denmark (1999) (see <http://www.cs.aue.auc.dk/pu lications/>).
5. Robert Scholes. Structuralism in Literature: An Introduction. Yale University Press: New Haven, CT (1974).

List of Participants

Kenneth M. Anderson, University of Colorado, Boulder, USA (SC2)

Steven Blackburn, University of Southampton, UK (OHS6)

Niels Olof Bouvin, University of Aarhus, Denmark (OHS6)

Simon Buckingham Shum, The Open University, UK (SC2)

Michel Crampes, Ecole des Mines d'Alès, France (SC2)

Hugh Davis, University of Southampton, UK (OHS6)

David De Roure, University of Southampton, UK (OHS6)

Joachim Feise, University of California, Irvine, USA (OHS6)

Kaj Grønbæk, University of Aarhus, Denmark (OHS6)

Jörg Haake, GMD-IPSI, Germany (SC2)

David Hicks, Aalborg University Esbjerg, Denmark (SC2)

Gu Lin, New Software Technology Lab of Guangxi, China (OHS6)

Ahmed Mahfouz, Texas A&M University, USA (OHS6)

Danius Michaelides, University of Southampton, UK (OHS6)

Dave Millard, University of Southampton, UK (OHS6, SC2)

Luc Moreau, University of Southampton, UK (OHS6)

Moritz Neumüller, Vienna University of Economics and
Business Administration, Austria (OHS6)

Peter Nürnberg, Aalborg University Esbjerg, Denmark (SC2)

Siegfried Reich, University of Linz, Austria (OHS6, SC2)

Yoon-Jung Rhee, Korea University, Seoul, Korea (OHS6)

Jim Rosenberg, Grindstone, PA, USA (SC2)

Michael Shepherd, Dalhousie University, Canada (SC2)

Mark Thompson, University of Southampton, UK (OHS6)

Manolis Tzagarakis, University of Patras, Greece (OHS6, SC2)

Uffe Kock Wiil, Aalborg University Esbjerg, Denmark (OHS6, SC2)

Author Index

Lecture Notes in Computer Science

For information about Vols. 1–1844
please contact your bookseller or Springer-Verlag

Vol. 1882: D. Kotz, F. Mattern (Eds.), Agent Systems, Mobile Agents, and Applications. Proceedings, 2000. XII, 275 pages. 2000.

Vol. 1883: B. Triggs, A. Zisserman, R. Szeliski (Eds.), Vision Algorithms: Theory and Practice. Proceedings, 1999. X, 383 pages. 2000.

Vol. 1884: J. Štuller, J. Pokorný, B. Thalheim, Y. Masunaga (Eds.), Current Issues in Databases and Information Systems. Proceedings, 2000. XIII, 396 pages. 2000.

Vol. 1885: K. Havelund, J. Penix, W. Visser (Eds.), SPIN Model Checking and Software Verification. Proceedings, 2000. X, 343 pages. 2000.

Vol. 1886: R. Mizoguchi, J. Slaney /Eds.), PRICAI 2000: Topics in Artificial Intelligence. Proceedings, 2000. XX, 835 pages. 2000. (Subseries LNAI).

Vol. 1888: G. Sommer, Y.Y. Zeevi (Eds.), Algebraic Frames for the Perception-Action Cycle. Proceedings, 2000. X, 349 pages. 2000.

Vol. 1889: M. Anderson, P. Cheng, V. Haarslev (Eds.), Theory and Application of Diagrams. Proceedings, 2000. XII, 504 pages. 2000. (Subseries LNAI).

Vol. 1890: C Linnhoff-Popien, H.-G. Hegering (Eds.), Trends in Distributed Systems: Towards a Universal Service Market. Proceedings, 2000. XI, 341 pages. 2000.

Vol. 1891: A.L. Oliveira (Ed.), Grammatical Inference: Algorithms and Applications. Proceedings, 2000. VIII, 313 pages. 2000. (Subseries LNAI).

Vol. 1892: P. Brusilovsky, O. Stock, C. Strapparava (Eds.), Adaptive Hypermedia and Adaptive Web-Based Systems. Proceedings, 2000. XIII, 422 pages. 2000.

Vol. 1893: M. Nielsen, B. Rovan (Eds.), Mathematical Foundations of Computer Science 2000. Proceedings, 2000. XIII, 710 pages. 2000.

Vol. 1894: R. Dechter (Ed.), Principles and Practice of Constraint Programming – CP 2000. Proceedings, 2000. XII, 556 pages. 2000.

Vol. 1895: F. Cuppens, Y. Deswarte, D. Gollmann, M. Waidner (Eds.), Computer Security – ESORICS 2000. Proceedings, 2000. X, 325 pages. 2000.

Vol. 1896: R. W. Hartenstein, H. Grünbacher (Eds.), Field-Programmable Logic and Applications. Proceedings, 2000. XVII, 856 pages. 2000.

Vol. 1897: J. Gutknecht, W. Weck (Eds.), Modular Programming Languages. Proceedings, 2000. XII, 299 pages. 2000.

Vol. 1898: E. Blanzieri, L. Portinale (Eds.), Advances in Case-Based Reasoning. Proceedings, 2000. XII, 530 pages. 2000. (Subseries LNAI).

Vol. 1899: H.-H. Nagel, F.J. Perales López (Eds.), Articulated Motion and Deformable Objects. Proceedings, 2000. X, 183 pages. 2000.

Vol. 1900: A. Bode, T. Ludwig, W. Karl, R. Wismüller (Eds.), Euro-Par 2000 Parallel Processing. Proceedings, 2000. XXXV, 1368 pages. 2000.

Vol. 1901: O. Etzion, P. Scheuermann (Eds.), Cooperative Information Systems. Proceedings, 2000. XI, 336 pages. 2000.

Vol. 1902: P. Sojka, I. Kopeček, K. Pala (Eds.), Text, Speech and Dialogue. Proceedings, 2000. XIII, 463 pages. 2000. (Subseries LNAI).

Vol. 1903: S. Reich, K.M. Anderson (Eds.), Open Hypermedia Systems and Structural Computing. Proceedings, 2000. VIII, 187 pages. 2000.

Vol. 1904: S.A. Cerri, D. Dochev (Eds.), Artificial Intelligence: Methodology, Systems, and Applications. Proceedings, 2000. XII, 366 pages. 2000. (Subseries LNAI).

Vol. 1906: A. Porto, G.-C. Roman (Eds.), Coordination Languages and Models. Proceedings, 2000. IX, 353 pages. 2000.

Vol. 1908: J. Dongarra, P. Kacsuk, N. Podhorszki (Eds.), Recent Advances in Parallel Virtual Machine and Message Passing Interface. Proceedings, 2000. XV, 364 pages. 2000.

Vol. 1910: D.A. Zighed, J. Komorowski, J. Żytkow (Eds.), Principles of Data Mining and Knowledge Discovery. Proceedings, 2000. XV, 701 pages. 2000. (Subseries LNAI).

Vol. 1912: Y. Gurevich, P.W. Kutter, M. Odersky, L. Thiele (Eds.), Abstract State Machines. Proceedings, 2000. X, 381 pages. 2000.

Vol. 1913: K. Jansen, S. Khuller (Eds.), Approximation Algorithms for Combinatorial Optimization. Proceedings, 2000. IX, 275 pages. 2000.

Vol. 1917: M. Schoenauer, K. Deb, G. Rudolph, X. Yao, E. Lutton, J.J. Merelò, H.-P. Schwefel (Eds.), Parallel Problem Solving from Nature – PPSN VI. Proceedings, 2000. XXI, 914 pages. 2000.

Vol. 1918: D. Soudris, P. Pirsch, E. Barke (Eds.), Integrated Circuit Design. Proceedings, 2000. XII, 338 pages. 2000.

Vol. 1920: A.H.F. Laender, S.W. Liddle, V.C. Storey (Eds.), Conceptual Modeling – ER 2000. Proceedings, 2000. XV, 588 pages. 2000.

Vol. 1921: S.W. Liddle, H.C. Mayr, B. Thalheim (Eds.), Conceptual Modeling for E-Business and the Web. Proceedings, 2000. X, 179 pages. 2000.

Vol. 1922: J. Crowcroft, J. Roberts, M.I. Smirnov (Eds.), Quality of Future Internet Services. Proceedings, 2000. XI, 368 pages. 2000.

Vol. 1923: J. Borbinha, T. Baker (Eds.), Research and Advanced Technology for Digital Libraries. Proceedings, 2000. XVII, 513 pages. 2000.

Vol. 1924: W. Taha (Ed.), Semantics, Applications, and Implementation of Program Generation. Proceedings, 2000. VIII, 231 pages. 2000.

Vol. 1926: M. Joseph (Ed.), Formal Techniques in Real-Time and Fault-Tolerant Systems. Proceedings, 2000. X, 305 pages. 2000.

Vol. 1927: P. Thomas, H.W. Gellersen, (Eds.), Handheld and Ubiquitous Computing. Proceedings, 2000. X, 249 pages. 2000.

Vol. 1931: E. Horlait (Ed.), Mobile Agents for Telecommunication Applications. Proceedings, 2000. IX, 271 pages. 2000.

Vol. 1766: M. Jazayeri, R.G.K. Loos, D.R. Musser (Eds.), Generic Programming. Proceedings, 1998. X, 269 pages. 2000.

Vol. 1933: R.W. Brause, E. Hanisch (Eds.), Medical Data Analysis. Proceedings, 2000. XI, 316 pages. 2000.